Rethinking Public Relations

Rethinking Public Relations second edition builds on the first edition with new thoughts, data and evidence presented in an accessible style. It develops thinking on the most important question facing PR today – its relationship with democracy – and finds a balance of advantages and disadvantages which leaves a residue of concern. The text sustains the view that PR is weak propaganda and argues that the most effective way to counter its negative effects is for all organisations and groups to have an effective PR 'voice', so that all can be heard and then supported or rejected by the public. Moreover, these 'voices' have to be scrutinised in a PR-saturated society by a more independent and competitive media, and by PR-wary citizens and consumers.

This exciting new edition challenges the conventional thinking about public relations and expands and updates the arguments put forward in the previous edition. It is designed to appeal to final-year undergraduates, postgraduates and all those with an interest in public relations.

Kevin Moloney has spent one half of his career working in PR, and the other half teaching and researching it. He teaches at Bournemouth University, and researches into how PR intersects with politics, economics and the media.

Rethinking Public Relations
PR Propaganda and Democracy

Second edition

Kevin Moloney

Routledge
Taylor & Francis Group

LONDON AND NEW YORK

First published 2000
Reprinted 2002

Second edition published 2006
by Routledge
2 Park Square, Milton Park, Abingdon, Oxon OX14 4RN

Simultaneously published in the USA and Canada
by Routledge
270 Madison Ave, New York, NY 10016

Routledge is an imprint of the Taylor & Francis Group, an informa business

© 2000, 2006 Kevin Moloney

Typeset in Sabon by
Taylor & Francis Books
Printed and bound in Great Britain by
Antony Rowe Ltd, Chippenham, Wiltshire

British Library Cataloguing in Publication Data
A catalogue record for this book is available from the British Library

Library of Congress Cataloging in Publication Data
A catalog record for this book has been requested

ISBN10: 0-415-37061-2 ISBN13: 978-0-415-37061-5 (hbk)
ISBN10: 0-415-37062-0 ISBN13: 978-0-415-37062-2 (pbk)
ISBN10: 0-203-03059-1 ISBN13: 978-0-203-03059-2 (ebk)

To Muriel, Rachael and Paul

Contents

Foreword

Public relations pours a Niagara of persuasive attitudes, words, visuals and events over liberal democracies such as the UK. This great flood of promotional messaging attracts many critics, and a low reputation for PR itself. But it is futile to lament the pervasiveness of public relations, for it is not going to disappear from the political economy or civil society. Rather, it will increase because it is an expression of the powerful, promotional culture of these societies.

Rethinking PR 2: PR Propaganda and Democracy (2006) is the sequel to *Rethinking PR: The Spin and the Substance* (2000), building on it with new thoughts, data and evidence. It develops thinking on the most important question facing PR – its relationship with democracy – and finds a balance of advantages and disadvantages that leaves a residue of concern. The text sustains the view that PR is weak propaganda and argues that the most effective way to counter its negative effects is for all organisations and groups to have an effective PR 'voice' when they want to speak publicly. But these 'voices' have to be scrutinised in a PR-saturated society by a more independent and competitive media, and by PR-wary citizens and consumers.

Breaking out from the current Grunigian paradigm of PR thinking, *Rethinking PR 2* argues that, empirically, public relations is not the search for communicative symmetries, but instead the search for communicative advantages that strengthens the interests of those it services. In the light of this, the book develops a normative theory of PR practice, namely that it should happen in a state of communicative equality. It argues for public and private subsidies to resource-poor, marginalised groups, and to technical and social innovators in order to give them the equality of a threshold level of PR 'voice'.

The effects of today's PR practice are analysed in markets, politics and the media. Positive effects are citizens and consumers put in contact with politics and markets by attention-getting, persuasive, popular messages in words, visuals and events, often delivered via the media. PR 'voice' also helps put new issues, which might otherwise never be heard, on to the public agenda. These benefits, however, are matched by the negative effects of one-sided, persuasive messages of selected facts and emotional appeals;

and by the fear that powerful interests have too much influence with government through lobbying PR. The first reaction to PR in a democracy must always be the vigilance of *caveat emptor* (buyer beware), a vigilance that is the first act of civic resistance to promotional culture.

Watchfulness is particularly needed towards PR in markets where it can hinder competition by price and instead substitute competition via emotion created by brands. More wariness is needed from both individual journalists who have been too passive before the PR-isation of their copy; and also from more competitive media institutions publishing a wider range of opinions. In politics, it is now harder to distinguish between the work and style of politics and PR, and thus easier to see the beginning of a 'public relations state'.

This controversial text is for teachers and researchers inside and outside the PR academy, seeking to develop their critique (positive or negative) of an emblematic activity that has been called the 'profession of the decade'. These academics will note the global spread of PR as market economics and democracy appear in countries where they did not exist before 1989. This book is for third-year undergraduates and masters students on communications, media studies, popular culture, politics and sociology courses who want, after reading the standard PR textbooks, a more evaluative view about this most pervasive and persuasive component of promotional culture.

Rethinking PR 2 is also a building block for MPhil/PhD students at the cutting edge of PR, communications and media studies.

Preface

This book is a continuation and development of the arguments about public relations set out in *Rethinking PR: The Spin and the Substance* in 2000. PR is such a pervasive form of promotional culture in modern liberal democracies with active markets, and has such a large impact on their media and politics, that it is important to keep it under close watch. Indeed, if the PR academic has any claim on the role of public intellectual, it is to speak out about the impact of their subject on democracy, demonstrating benefits and costs to our most foundational institution. *Rethinking PR 2: PR Propaganda and Democracy* attempts to continue that watch; staying with the description of PR as weak propaganda, and exploring the positive and negative effects of PR propaganda on the democratic political economy and its civil society.

PR always has consequences for democracy but most literature by its academy keeps the subject comfortably embedded in a technical environment where traditional and grounding assumptions are not questioned. Because of the democracy connection, this methodology of efficiency and effectiveness needs to be diluted with a look at PR fundamentals. I take such a stance and it often leads to a critical tone but this should not be interpreted as root objection to public relations by the author. I did the work – more or less happily – for some twenty years, and was involved in some worthwhile social and commercial outcomes. Overall, though, the evidence finds strongly that PR suffers from a poor reputation for partial truthfulness, excessive promise of performance, and for use by powerful interests to sustain their positions. PR, however, is not going to disappear from liberal democracy, or from market economies. All this creates an agenda for scrutiny, and if the outcomes are critical of PR, so be it. Democracy is more important than PR.

There is a secondary reason for keeping a PR watch. It is a narrower one than the democracy connection. It is that the academic study of PR has got stuck, I believe, in a conceptual paradigm (the Grunigian one) that needs to be challenged. The way that the thinking of this school has taken hold in many universities and colleges has been to over-emphasise PR as a practice of virtuous messaging, known as two-way communications between equal, listening, negotiating, mutually respectful message senders and receivers. Ironically, this emphasis on a practice of communicative virtue is not supported by much evidence from the field, and so takes teaching and writing by the PR academy into a neverland of perfection. Thus the second task of this book is to describe (without enthusiasm) another conceptualisation of PR, one of it as weak propaganda that can co-exist theoretically with democracy; to assess evidence on the positive and negative effects of actual co-existence, and to present mechanisms for a state of communicative equality that will attenuate negative effects. If the Grunigian school seeks to frame the study of PR in terms of communicative equity, this work privileges a focus on the equity of power distribution in liberal democracy.

Kevin Moloney
Bournemouth University
May 2005

Acknowledgements

Thinking and writing about this book has been made much easier by help in many of its parts from colleagues at Bournemouth, elsewhere in the UK, and wider afield. They include David Alder, John Brissenden, David Gray, Matt Holland, Nigel Jackson, Conor McGrath, Rachael Moloney, Simon Moore, Barry Richards, Peter Simmons and Ian Somerville. Students doing undergraduate, postgraduate and doctoral studies have also helped by sharing ideas and experiences, and by asking the simple but penetrating questions which remind teachers that they always ought to have Occam's razor close to hand. Error of fact and lapses of style are, of course, mine alone, as are all opinions.

Note on the text

Several styles are used throughout the text to refer to its subject. Some PR people avoid writing or saying 'PR' because of the negative connotations associated with it. Instead they use 'public relations'. 'PR' is favoured here because that is the most common term used in academic, professional, lay conservations and writing; and because a debate should be in the language of the majority of the participants. To avoid repetition and to ease reading, 'public relations' will be used periodically.

PR is also presented as a communicative exchange function where messages are 'produced' by PR professionals for their principals and are 'consumed' by those who receive them. This means that the formal function of public relations people is 'to message'. The verb is used transitively in the sense defined by the *Oxford Dictionary of English* (2003, 2nd edn, p. 1102) as 'send a message to (someone)'. This messaging produces what is called here 'PR effects', which are benign or negative.

This messaging is done by 'organisations' and 'groups'. These terms are used throughout for two reasons. First, to indicate that the greatest volume of PR is done on behalf of those entities, rather than for individuals; and second, that PR is done across the range of collective entities, from highly structured and regulated businesses and public bodies, to less organised and coherent interest and cause groups in civil society.

1 A great Niagara of PR

There is a strange consequence to using PR for communication in societies like ours. It is widely and freely used yet most people do not like it.

Some 48,000[1] people do PR in the UK, and they pour over us millions of citizens, media users and consumers a Niagara of spin: lifestyle features; ideological messages; soundbites; kiss-and-tell tales;[2] press conferences; news leaks; special events; stunts; staged photos; consumer leaflets; corporate brands, brochures and apologia; competitions, exhibitions and incentives; road shows; conferences; policy briefings; lobbying campaigns; demonstrations; community support; sponsorships; managed issues; reassuring communications in crisis, and messages about their social responsibility. This Niagara rises as more businesses, interests, causes and individuals pour more money and effort into PR. This great swirl of communications catches millions of voters, media audiences and consumers in its sweep; and is read, believed and acted on. It sweeps by millions of others, unread, unbelieved and unnoticed. Some of Niagara's most powerful currents are pointed at ministers, MPs and civil servants so that public policy is carried off in the right direction. Often these currents are hidden from us and therefore dangerous to our democratic safety. The rising flood also sweeps up nonentities and lands them on small islands of uncertain fame known as celebrity, as well as buoying up aggrieved individuals, waving their protests at us.

Yet despite the volume and variety of this flood, PR has a low reputation and is dismissed by most of us as just 'spin', or is disdained as a 'PR job'.[3] This asymmetry of usage to reputation is an extraordinary irony, for PR has to endure the fate that it seeks to avoid for those in whose name it works. Not only an extraordinary irony, but a longstanding one also noted by Tunstall (p. 183) in 1964. And one with a classical dimension for Baistow (1985, p. 72) who calls the multiplicity of PR forms Protean in their scale. Say 'PR' then and now and not far away from mind and mouth are concerns about manipulation of opinion, promotion of the rich and powerful, puffery, slick presentation, hidden persuasion, the one-sided presentation of fact and figure and changing form.

Rethinking PR: The Spin and the Substance (2000b), the accompanying critique to this, explored this blighted reputation and concluded that historically public relations in the UK and USA has been weak propaganda produced by government, business and other dominant interests to maintain their positions. It is unknowable, unquantifiable, how many millions of audiences, consumers and voters have been swept along by the great Niagara, have believed and acted on PR propaganda; but our witness of life in a liberal democracy tells us that our fellow electors, consumers, and citizens have believed and acted on it some, much or most of the time. Indeed we ourselves probably have felt and still feel the experience of being propagandised. It is these observations about others and our own experience that produce a culture of suspicion and mistrust about PR, and so generate its low reputation.

But a Niagara of PR propaganda – or any other sort – is conventionally thought to be bad for democracy, and for its politics, media and markets. It is noisome, dirty water, thought not clean enough to mix with the sweeter and purer waters of democracy. It is this mixture of PR propaganda and democracy, and the consequences of the mixing, which is a principal theme here.

This work is critical of many PR practices and consequences (e.g. impact on democracy; unequal spread of resources, invisibility in the media) but it does not deny the right of others to do PR in societies such as the UK and USA. It is futile to 'lament' the presence of PR, because public relations is expressive of foundational features of liberal democracy in its representative variety – its pluralism and promotional culture. It is still surprising who finds PR useful: note an ornithologist curator of the Wildfowl and Wetlands Trust saying 'you also had a public relations duty to sell conservation'.[4] One cannot legislate to abolish PR: the task rather is to assess its effects, good and bad, and examine arguments that make it at least a neutral influence on democracy. This book, therefore, is not an apologia for, nor an indictment against, its subject. It seeks to be an even-handed critique of PR practices and consequences. It even ventures – beyond balance – to argue that in a liberal egalitarian society, ready to redistribute communication resources inside a strong civil society, PR makes public debate more equal, more vigorous, more appealing, more likely to conclude with some truth. This venture rests on two beliefs. The first is that communicative equality is a realisable goal in liberal democracy. The second is that communicative equality neutralises some of the dangers in PR propaganda for democracy.

The Niagara of PR needs dams and weirs in place to make the waters safer.

Context

It is arguable that conceiving of PR propaganda as compatible with democracy is a foolhardy project. It may be that the triad of ideas 'PR–propaganda–democracy' cannot bear the compatibility conclusion. If the middle term 'propaganda' were cut out, the task would be easier. Some US textbooks do make that reduction to the diadic. But this work cannot, after reading the historical and contemporary record and after thought, accept a divorce between PR and propaganda, in practice or in theory. There are no texts known to this author that argue for the compatible triad, and the author takes this as both a warning about the untenability of his argument, and an encouragement to explore. It would be too much to expect PR textbooks to present the case for the compatible triad, for they invariably rest on the contemporary paradigm of ruling ideas about a subject. That paradigm can be called the Grunigian one, and has its foundation text in *Managing Public Relations* (1984) by J. Grunig and T. Hunt. This set up a four-part typology of PR, which has a first category of propagandistic PR called press agentry, and a fourth category of two-way symmetrical PR that is balanced, negotiating, respectful dialogue. Whether intended by the authors or not, this typology became in the teaching of PR academics, certainly in the UK, a Whig history of public relations: PR is on a progressive journey towards betterment, if not perfection.[5] James Grunig is owed an intellectual debt for being the major progenitor of the typology, and for defending and amending it over time. He drew an intellectual route map that in its stages distanced PR from propaganda, and made public relations intellectually respectable, decently practisable, and legitimately teachable at public expense in the ideological and geopolitical circumstances of the 1980s. These years were the time of the Cold War between capitalism and communism in economics, and between liberal democracy and dictatorship in politics. The intellectual task here is to take away the Grunigian fourth category and to integrate the other three into the triad 'PR–propaganda–democracy' in a way that does not damage the last.

This author believes that UK academic literature in sociology, communications, media and political studies does not pay enough attention to public relations as a subject worth critical attention in its own right. It is due this attention because of its impact on the political economy, civil society and the media. These older disciplines appear not to see a Niagara; more a smallish waterway, a tributary off the wider media river, a stream disappearing into the political caves. It may be that there is a strain of cultural snobbery here, with academia touched by popular perceptions of PR as 'froth', 'workaday deceit',[6] 'a victory of presentation over content', just 'spin'. Rather than causing the scholarly back to turn away, this poor reputation of public relations should be a trigger for investigating why a promotional mode used by both powerful and subordinate interests is so commonly dismissed. Contemporary PR raises enough substantial questions about its relationship with liberal democracy to warrant its own critical space. Those of us teaching and researching PR have to ask ourselves whether we have played our part in marking out that space.

Whatever the criticism of PR made in these pages, there is no assumption that it had a 'golden past' or that it will have a 'golden future'. Golden ages are suggestive of a romantic and idealised approach to communicative relations in the public domain.[7] Such times do not fit with another position developed here: there is little evidence that public relations produces 'goodwill and mutual understanding' as the definition of the Chartered Institute of Public Relations says;[8] instead PR provides the 'voices' for competing interests as they struggle for advantage with regard to ideas, values, behaviour, policy or *material*.[9] Much of the professional and textbook literature has strong traces of the idealised approach (communication for goodwill and understanding in the UK; for more democracy in the USA). That literature pays little regard to a social phenomenon much in evidence in this thesis, namely power where this is defined as the transformative capacity of individuals, organisations and groups to make their preferences prevail.[10] Goodwill and understanding from other organisations and groups are always welcome, but they are by-products, secondary benefits of the search for advantage by PR users. It is, however, hard to sustain a reformist thesis about a public activity without any hope of improvement in practice. This text, therefore, will allow itself a little idealism, here and there, by holding to the hope that its argument will lead to more equal distribution of PR resources and skills between powerful and marginal interests.

Would such a redistribution include advertising resources? Yes, but the inclusion is omitted (mostly) here as the focus is on PR. Public relations does not now make imperialist claims to be all forms of promotional communication. It is self-presentation-for-attention-and-advantage in the forms listed at the start of this chapter, but excluding paid advertising for goods and services (though including paid advertising for corporate bodies and causes). It does not shriek from the page like the paid advertisement. It sees itself as saying 'true' or 'real' things and as representing 'important' activity. Many times an outside observer would agree. Sometimes, it says that it is 'educational'.[11] It claims – even insists – that it should be displayed, noticed and given advantage because of these qualities. It often wraps up self-interest in the terms of a wider interest. PR's self-presentation-for-attention-and-advantage is a particular expression of a larger cultural environment, for it is clear that PR self-presentation has the same purpose as advertising's and marketing's. Indeed, what links these technically different displays together is the concept of promotion – self-interested exchange through exhortation and compliance.

By volume of production, public relations is mostly media relations; by level of concern about policy making, it is lobbying. It is therefore promotional communication, minus most advertising, done by organisations (corporate bodies) and by groups (voluntary associations and causes). Increasingly, it is done by individuals with a grievance (outraged foxhunters in the UK) and individuals seeking fame. Individuals either develop their own PR skills or hire professionals to do them. Its constant purpose is the advancement of the interests of its source, but it is flexible in its forms. Perhaps this flexibility explains why there are famously 472-plus definitions of it.[12] Such prolixity is a warning not to attempt definitions based on technique. A more productive approach is, instead, to identify PR productions by way of their goal of self-advancement for their principals, rather than by their multiple forms of display.

PR takes many organisational forms as well. It is a highly organised service industry, but it also finds more localised, individual expression. This is PR as a 'cottage industry' done by the amateurs, say, in the local tennis club. It is PR as the 'personal kit' of the fame-addicted celebrity or of the aggrieved individual fighting for a cause. The individual may be facing trial and PR aid is given, as when Max Clifford was employed by the legal team defending a householder who shot dead a burglar.[13] This organisational flexibility suggests answers to questions about in which social networks is PR produced and consumed. A principal social location is civil society, that area of public life bounded by individuals and the family on one side and by government and markets on the other, and characterised by all manner of voluntary associations. The communicative relations amongst these associations in civil society, between civil society and politics, between politics and the market economy (together forming the political economy), and the presentational activities of government itself are the four social sites of PR.

PR is mostly public behaviour of self-presentation-for-attention-and-advantage from the significant other(s). Sometimes, however, this display is private, when the significant other is a private person or private body, or when it is hidden behind official secrecy. PR in its lobbying form is often a private activity done with government, and this privacy linked with the power of the interest doing the lobbying is a matter of concern in the light of the principles of access and transparency into elected governments.

Media relations PR and lobbying PR raise the question of whether PR constitutes neutral techniques for promotion, or value-laden ones. Is the stick blameless for the hurt? Does the bandage cause the healing? Answers involve three considerations: that human intention activates technique; that intention transmits via technique both benefits and costs to others; and also that poor technique stymies good intention. For example, writing a press release is an imitation of journalistic form in order to serve an interest. Wanting the message to be reproduced in papers without stating sources raises questions of access and transparency. Writing the release badly means that its benign message will be lost when it is thrown in the wastepaper bin. The neutral technique is put to work in the service of better or worse intention, and its effect is marred by bad technique.

Overview

The most important question about modern public relations in the UK, and in the growing number of other countries where it flourishes, is how it relates to democracy. The question is particularly pressing if PR is defined as weak propaganda. The answer offered is that PR is sourced in the pluralism of representative democracy. It brings democracy benefits but also endows it with costs. The balance between the two leaves a residue of serious concern. The workings of these benefits and costs are enacted out in democracy's three foundational institutions – politics, markets and media. To push the balance decisively towards a beneficial relationship that strengthens democracy, two reforming developments are needed. First, all organisations and groups wanting to use PR should have a threshold minimum of PR capacity so that there exists the technical condition of communicative equality in public debate. Second, citizens and consumers, organisations and groups should develop more vigilant 'radar' in order to detect PR messages.

This analysis borrows from neo-pluralist and neo-Marxist perspectives about the political economy and civil society, while its reforming hope for communicative equality rests on a classical pluralist one.[14] The argument starts by noting that PR is legal, well funded, noticeable and widespread activity in contemporary UK society but, despite these qualities, it still attracts a poor reputation. Why? It could be that this asymmetry of prominence to reputation is small change in the currency of our daily, social relations in the public domain, and not worth enquiring into. This would not be the case, however, if the low esteem were the consequence of substantial concerns about PR effects on important public institutions such as democracy, civil society, the political economy, and markets.

Chapter 2 looks at the inverse pervasiveness and reputation relationship. PR is now an industry, when it was once an adjunct to advertising and marketing. It was once done by a group of people called 'the gin and tonic brigade', recruited from the louche end of the metropolitan middle classes. Today school-leavers want a degree in it, and many campuses oblige when twenty years ago they would have left what they considered training to employers. All divisions of The Establishment do it – Monarchy, the Church, the Armed Forces, the City, the elite universities, the higher professions. Even trade unions do it. It has ennobled practitioners in the House of Lords. It is an instinctive reaction of all modern governments and, very publicly, the instinctive behaviour of New Labour. There is hardly an organised group of people in the land, from the local tennis club to Virgin, which does not seek 'effective communications', does not issue 'press releases', 'lobby' or have amongst its members a 'public relations officer', an 'information officer', or a 'campaigns co-ordinator' – all in order to improve their 'image', 'reputation' and 'corporate social responsibility'.

PR in the UK employs some 48,000-plus people and has a £3 billion budget. For those who pay the bills, PR is a worthwhile activity that delivers value for money. It delivers desired results for BP and Greenpeace, for parish councils and Whitehall, and for local charities and model railway enthusiasts. Viewed as management, PR has developed from an optional extra to a mainstream function that enhances corporate reputation. Viewed as campaigning, PR provides the techniques for pressure and

cause groups to influence public policy. Viewed as entertainment, it generates enough television, radio and books[15] to entertain for a long weekend.

Yet this prominence does not bring PR social prestige, high status or good
opinion. PR people often speak and write in two alternating ways about
their work, but never at the same time: 'PR is coming of age' and 'It still has
some way to go'.[16] PR does not attract the acclaim of, say, computing or
marketing, other activities that have grown mightily over the last forty years
and whose status has prospered. Comparisons are made with advertising,
and the role of journalism as a denigrator of PR will be explored. PR has a
drag anchor; it is summed up in the colloquial phrase 'It's a PR job'. The
implication is of something not being what it appears, a victory of presentation over content, 'the substitution of words for performance'.[17]

PR pervasiveness suggests connections with wider and deeper trends in
the host society. PR flourishes so fruitfully today in the UK that it has been
called the 'profession of the decade'. Some commentators, employing
medieval descriptors of power and influence, have called it the Fifth
Estate.[18] Could it be the iconic 'profession of the twenty-first century'?
Chapter 3 notes that public relations has become more noticeable in the
last forty years in the UK and is set to be the most pervasive communication mode of this century. It will flourish as a structured industry serving
other industries, as a 'cottage industry' done by voluntary bodies and
social activists, and 'personal kit' for celebrities and aggrieved individuals.
It is embedded in liberal democracies with market economies and is much
of the public conversation of these societies. It has grown out of the accelerated civic (values and groups) pluralism and commercial (markets and
business) pluralism evident in Britain since the liberalising 1960s. It is the
'voice' of this pluralism.

PR is a low-cost distribution of information, done before large or small
audiences, using multiple techniques of self-display. PR's most influential
client has been – and still is – business, which has used it as a specialist
management function to defend and advance capitalist interests in public
policy-making, and in markets to increase the sale of goods and services.
There is no organic link between PR and business, just a highly successful
instrumental one.

PR is part of the UK's promotional culture in which the majority of
communications are self-interested: PR always serves the interests of those
who deploy it. When dealing with serious opportunities and threats,
organisations and groups employ 'issues management', which usually has a
strong communications, and therefore, PR element. Because PR serves
interests and causes seeking their own ends, its messages may or may not
have full, partial (or any) truth statements in them. It is only after public
wrangling amongst competing PR messages that truths in them are most
easily identified.

Chapter 4 looks at the nature of PR messages, and argues that they are
propagandistic. This conclusion is reached after reviewing the US academic

literature (and, in the next chapter, the UK experience of PR). Examination of the US experience is appropriate because modern PR originated there in the last quarter of the nineteenth century. The literature demonstrates that PR has been manipulative communications to promote business interests generally and certain federal government policies.

US PR grew up in an intellectual climate pessimistic about a mass democracy's influence on public affairs. Its first use was to defend the 'robber barons' of US capitalism before the First World War. Then it promoted federal governments' policies in support of war, and later in support of the New Deal in the 1930s. Its US pioneers (Bernays and Lee) were supportive of these uses and saw PR's linkage with propaganda positively. However, after experience of the fascist regimes between 1919 and 1941, and of the Cold War with communism after 1945, PR in the USA had a bleak future as a publicly acceptable activity, unless the link with propaganda was fractured. That break was achieved conceptually by Grunig and Hunt in 1984. Turning to the consumers of PR propaganda (citizens, and buyers of goods and services), the question of measuring their compliance with PR goals is highly problematical. No clear answer is available but the safest conclusion is that PR was, and is, a major, conditioning factor in compliance.

Chapter 5 continues to look at PR propaganda by business and government, this time in the UK. Modern PR has been established in Britain for some eighty years and its early founders shared the same fear of social change as their more established US colleagues, and had the same resort to PR as social guidance, if not control, by elites over the masses. Propaganda still carried positive connotations in the 1920s and 1930s but these were turning negative throughout the period in the face of its use by fascist and communist states. PR is shaped by the political economy in which it is found and early UK PR was influenced by specifically British circumstances. It was a public communications system able to tell the population about new state welfare services. It often took the form of filmic, visual and graphic work that is still appreciated today. *Night Mail*, the promotional documentary done for the General Post Office in 1936, is a minor classic popular today. It was produced by John Grierson (see p. 71). It was market support for large, prestigious businesses, official bodies and Empire countries. It was used to promote trade and diplomatic policies overseas by projecting a positive identity of the UK. It was very much official and establishment communications.

PR in the UK has been, and still is, public communication designed to manipulate or persuade. It is weak propaganda – more 'ordering' and 'telling' than 'listening' and 'talking'; with a selection of supportive facts and some appeals to emotion in the message,[19] presented many times, often without the source being identified. Three sources of evidence confirm this general conclusion: the academic literature (Chs 4 and 5); the current PR paradigm that classifies much PR as propaganda; and PR's low reputation in public opinion as self-interested, untrustworthy communications (Chapter 2).

Previous chapters argued that public relations is weak propaganda 'voicing' interests competing over policy, material, ideological and reputational advantage in a market, capitalist, liberal democracy. This thesis raises the question of how PR relates to democracy, and it is examined in *Chapter 6*. The relationship is first viewed as both a neutral and a beneficial co-existence. Both views theorise democracy as representative democracy that places interests in competitive and co-operative relationships with each other. PR is the communicative element in the reciprocal negotiations for advantage amongst organisations and groups representing interests. PR is their 'voice' in the wrangling for these advantages. The media are full of these competitions and many contemporary ones focus on the power of the state to regulate industry and individual behaviour, alongside the historic contest for advantage between labour and capital. Empirical support for neutral co-existence comes from the observation that in the last century PR has flourished (especially in the UK and USA) as democratic apparatus (spread of the franchise) and liberal expression (pluralism of views) has grown.

PR has a beneficial co-existence with democracy from the perspective of liberal equalitarianism, which argues for a diminution of discrimination between individuals through a redistribution of resources in the name of social justice. The chapter applies such a redistribution specifically to PR resources in order to move towards communicative equality in public debates. The aim is equal 'voicing' among interests in a representative democracy; the means is monitoring differences of PR resources amongst interests, and then subsidy (public or private) to transfer more resources towards the resource-poor. A conception of civil society can also create a beneficial relationship. It argues that serious inequalities amongst groups of individuals who come together in voluntary association to represent their interests threatens civil society as a democratic enterprise. This view also argues for a redistribution of PR resources, but differs from liberal egalitarianism in that it accepts civil society's expression in varied, often conflicting associations.

But PR as weak propaganda 'voicing' rival interests has social disadvantages, even if there is communicative equality amongst them. It 'sours' pluralism through endless public argument, and tends towards a culture where 'having arguments' takes precedence over 'making arguments'. PR also expresses the negative sides of civil society where special pleading and structural inequalities are reinforced.

Chapter 7 examines the negative effects thesis of PR on democracy, namely that dominant PR 'voices' are heard more than those of subordinate interests, and that this asymmetrical communication expresses and reinforces unequal power relationships in a democracy. The anti-capitalist form of the thesis takes a determinist view that no reform of PR will change the power inequalities, on the grounds that changing the communicative agent will not change its principal.[20] Less determinist critiques see some halting progress towards more symmetry over recent times; while neo-pluralists argue that business as the dominant interest bloc in liberal democracies is privileged over other interests but in a challenged and fractured way.

The Lukes (1974) typology of power can be usefully applied to PR: competitive messaging in public conflicts amongst interests fits his first dimension of power as the expression of visible conflict; lobbying (usually private) to mobilise bias amongst elites in order to control political agendas is evidence of his second, less visible, but still behavioural, dimension of power; while PR that conditions people's thinking to accept asymmetrical power distributions as normal is supportive of his third dimension – sociological, structural power which reproduces the culture of compliance.

Vigilance towards PR's presence is a neutralising agent against its negative effects on democracy, a vigilance leading to scrutiny and then avoidance behaviour if needs be. This vigilance is an initial act of citizen and consumer resistance to promotional culture. Vigilance is exercised by individuals as media users, as citizens and as consumers through the rule of *caveat emptor* (buyer beware). Media literacy reproduces this vigilance in individuals. Vigilance, however, is also institutional. The media has a professional and constitutional role here, although its effectiveness is hampered by its growing PR-isation, or dependency on PR material. Government is vigilant as well in its role as legislator and executive, for lobbying by special interests dilutes the broader public interest. Vigilance towards the most visible expression of PR power (its messaging in pluralist competitions for advantage) is the easiest to operationalise. There is much more concern, however, about effective vigilance over the more private form of lobbying PR, and over the intangible consequences of PR as a cultural reproducer (PR for agenda shaping and for entrenching dominant groups). Thus the examination of the consequences of PR on democracy ends on an uncertain and worrying note.

Concern continues in *Chapter 8* when the focus turns towards PR and ethics. PR people in the UK are now more aware of their ethics since business and political scandals in the 1990s. Those trying to be ethical have to confront the relationship of PR and propaganda; and then their personal relationship with the client or the employer for whom they produce messages. If they judge that the organisation or group they represent is a good, right or true interest, they have taken the first step to communicating in good conscience. The next is to follow professional rules of conduct so that they produce PR messages in a moral way. There is, however, another consideration. PR propaganda is always self-advantaging communication, making PR people 'hemispheric communicators' (Jensen 1997), who draw attention to the positive values and behaviours of the interest they represent and not the negative ones. Even if PRs adopt a case-by-case ethical evaluation, they have to decide whether they are morally comfortable with this imbalance. If not, they should leave public relations work.

Communicating about corporate social responsibility (CSR) is work that links corporate values and the ethics of individual PRs very directly. CSR came on to the PR agenda because of concern about the social, environmental and political impacts of big business.[21] It is a focus on corporate citizenship, placing businesses in 'society' as well as in the 'economy'. CSR programmes provoke the same question as asked about PR: are they 'window dressing'? If they are, the PR person is confronted with ethical questions about verbal deception. If ethics and social responsibilities are believed to be grounded in individuals rather than in corporate entities, the PR producer cannot avoid them. Increasingly, questions of responsibility are asked of cause and pressure groups as well. A more political question is whether CSR programmes allow government to privatise welfare provision.

CSR programmes by business are a subsidy paid out of shareholder funds to outside interests. Most PR textbooks take an instrumental position that such programmes represent enlightened self-interest. They are usually directed at the stakeholders of an organisation, defined as others who do or can affect an organisation, and who are or can be affected by it. Stakeholder theory obliges PR people to consider on whom they are dependent in their search for communicative advantage. It is the precautionary principle applied to the sustainability of effective public relations. Its main advantage for doing PR is that it identifies to whom messages should be sent. Otherwise, it is under-developed theory with considerable disadvantages. But the concept still has a strong attraction for PR producers: it requires them to consider 'significant others' in their communications.

Chapter 9 starts an examination of three public institutions (politics, markets and journalism) that deliver important public goods to citizens and consumers, and which are scanned by them to see if they deliver what they proclaim that they do. In doing this, active citizens and consumers seek evidence of 'fair play', and avoidance of 'flannel' or 'bullshit' or propaganda. In politics, citizens see a merging of style and content between PR and politics, especially so on the boundary between policy-making and presentation. A half of special advisers to UK ministers now do media relations work to some extent, and New Labour has developed spin (aggressive political news management) to such an extent that it is seen as its governing style. UK governments' relationships with journalists can be conceptualised either as a market exchange of information given for publicity granted, or as a militaristic contest for control of both. The universal usage of the 'spin' word is, moreover, a sign of how prevalent the PR mindset and wariness about it are.

Corporate PR is also about news management, and about lobbying by (mostly) business and large public sector organisations (NHS and education). Lobbying by powerful 'insiders' is always a concern in a democracy because most of it is in private, and policy can then be influenced without the constraints of the public's opinion, and that of elected representatives. More marginal, resource-poor groups are lobbying now than forty years ago, and their access to policy-makers would increase with more measures (private and public subsidy) to produce PR communicative equality. Until this happens, lobbying remains a concern for democrats because it mostly mobilises bias in favour of powerful or dominant organisations and groups. Campaigns (intense bursts of PR activity) are often brought on as 'megaphones' alongside lobbying, especially by voluntary organisations and cause groups. They are used so much that their frequency may have blunted their ability to change attitudes and behaviour. They often, however, draw upon popular culture for eye-catching effects, and so bring the creativity of the carnivalesque into public relations.

Chapter 10 looks at markets, corporate branding and corporate reputation, and notes that PR is well established in these three areas. By volume of production, there is more marketing PR (MPR) than any other type of public relations. It plays a valuable role when markets are categorised as systems for information distribution. That role serves mature and new markets that are national, offer a wide range of goods and services, and have frequent product launches. Consumers benefit from this PR flow when they operate the *caveat emptor* role. As PR is principally a word-based promotional skill, it sells 'lifestyle' effectively because it expresses the complexity of the product offered in luxuriant language. Indeed, it does it so well that modern PR people would recognise Mr Puff from Sheridan's *The Rivals*. Apart from MPR (and advertisements), market PR also flows into markets, being messages from non-profit seeking sources (government, regulators, watchdog bodies, consumer activists) about market offerings to avoid (e.g. pyramid selling) and products to recall. Both these types of marketplace communications are still persuasive in intention, and that status illustrates an important argument of this book: all PR is persuasive communication.

Another link with marketing is the construction of corporate brands (corporate identities). The skills of branding products are now transferred to branding organisations and groups. It is marketing at the corporate level done by PR people and involves the anthropomorphic attribution of human characteristics to businesses and cause groups. Banks become 'caring', train operators are 'friendly', and environmental groups 'save' the planet. As human characteristics attract criticism so do personalised institutions, and cultural jammers[22] such as *Adbusters* have turned corporate features into ironic and mocking parodies that encourage campaigners against multinational corporations. Indeed these cultural jammers have promoted the most heretical idea known to marketing – 'Buy Nothing Day'.

Markets in a capitalist liberal economy are an important source of reputation, and to this important social asset British public relations has paid much more attention since 1990. Now reputation management is probably the most commonly stated professional goal of PR in the UK and has relegated to second place the achievement of 'goodwill' and 'mutual under-standing'. The clearest way to see reputation is to regard it as a 'credit' or 'debit' in the 'bank' of public and stakeholder opinion. It is, however, a professional deformation of PR to see it as a manageable quantity, for it is the gift of others to give. It is not bestowed on the business, university or pressure group by their own dominant coalitions, i.e. their policy-making group of most powerful people (Toth 1992, p. 9). It is a consequence of being perceived to do other tasks well. The primacy of good reputation as a PR goal has, however, its own costs for the PR professional. His or her principals will often follow goals of growth, acquisition, innovation and policy change that damage organisational reputation. Profits are increased, but redundancies are as well. By making one goal the master, PR is setting up a competition with other goals it is asked to communicate about. It shoots itself in the professional foot by elevating reputation.

The media provide much of the distribution system by which PR messages are sent from their producers to their consumers in markets, in politics and in civil society. Of the three lines of defence against the negative effects of PR (the others being *caveat emptor* and communicative equality for all PR 'voices'), the media in a democracy should provide an institutional bulwark of scrutiny. With the growth of UK media outlets since the 1980s, there has been an accompanying doubt about whether this watchdog role has been weakened by a PR-isation process. This is the way by which PR characteristics of one-way messaging, news creation, selective argument and invisible sourcing have colonised journalism. In the UK, this is noticeable in coverage of celebrities, lifestyle sections, and business and financial news. *Chapter 11* argues that this is happening for several reasons: the media as a business and so regarding readers and audiences as consumers; the weakening of the labour market power of journalists through over-supply of new entrants and lower salaries; and the use of the information subsidy offered by PR people to cut news room expenses and supply pre-packaged news free. These developments undermine the optimum role of a media that calls itself free and independent in a liberal democracy – the role of investigation into public matters. The way back from this entanglement of public relations and journalism is to regard PR as a media system in its own right, with separate news creation and distribution systems, and with specific stakeholder publics. Seeing PR as separate from journalism will encourage different working practices in them, and create a working environment of wariness and polite hostility between them. This is the critical distance between the two media systems that strengthens public debate in a PR-saturated liberal democracy.

Chapter 12 explores the consequences of PR as weak propaganda, and of it remaining a permanent feature of market, capitalist, liberal democracies that are sites for civic and commercial pluralism, and which generate a promotional culture of self-advantaging messaging. In such an environment, PR messaging cannot generate trust, the social consequence often claimed for it, because PR reflects and generates social competition, not harmony. It is in other circumstances that consumers and citizens give trust: they give it in response to repeated acts towards them of benign behaviour, and any link between PR and trust only comes when its messaging reflects such behaviour. These general conclusions will not be welcome to practising PR professionals who recoil from any association with the word 'propaganda'. They would also recoil from any project that attempted to salvage the word from its deeply negative connotations. Nor will PR academics welcome the conclusions, for they are in tension with the ideal of two-way symmetrical communication, the fourth element in the ruling Grunigian paradigm. The PR-as-weak-propaganda thesis will not be welcome by anti-capitalist and Marxist academics either, for they coalesce around a false notion that 'information' dissemination and 'campaigning' by non-big-business interests is acceptable communication activity. For them, such activity is not PR by virtue of it being promotion done by non-capitalist, non-global and non-exploitive interests. These distinctions cannot be sustained for all three categories are self-advantaging and constructed to gain compliance.

Even if PR is accepted as the single category for all such communication, the case for its reform remains, especially so as it is likely to continue growing in the promotional culture of accelerating pluralism. The PR literacy of individuals as consumers in markets and as citizens is the first line of defence against all types and intensities of propaganda. At the level of organisations and groups, the production of a state of communicative equality, where all interests that want a PR 'voice' have the resources to produce it, will be achieved by a system of private and public subsidies for the resource poor.

Through this equalisation, the public, stakeholders and government will be able to listen to the full set of values, interests, behaviours, goods and services vying for advantage. The third line of defence against PR propaganda is a media less beholden to 'PR-isation', and more ready to recognise the damage done to journalism by reliance on PR attitudes, resources and sources. In these three ways, the dangers to a market, capitalist, liberal democracy from PR propaganda will be marginally outweighed by the advantages it brings.

2   PR from top to bottom

Public relations is such a pervasive activity in our society today that it is impossible for a citizen or consumer to avoid. The establishment and the political class have taken to it with enthusiasm. The Queen has had a Communications Secretary since 1998 and the brief for the job was one that puts PR right at the centre of the establishment: 'to devise a PR strategy for the Queen and the other Royals'.[1] The world's richest man, Bill Gates, gives PR a glowing testimonial: 'If I was down to my last dollar, I would spend it on PR.' The Church of England has a media office, as does the Roman Catholic Church, and other faiths.[2] British schools are told that they 'need to be savvy about PR'.[3] Vigilante groups seeking out paedophiles on a housing estate have press officers.[4] The media has feasted on PR's ubiquity and confected up popular sitcoms to laugh it out of respectability – *Absolutely Fabulous* and *Spin City* on television and *Absolute Power*[5] on BBC national radio. Even the more obscure edges of the media have nodded towards PR's existence: there was a 'king of spin' in the University of the M25 satire in *The Times Higher Education Supplement*.[6] Indeed, this weekly house journal for academics urges them to 'work with press officers to ensure their peer-reviewed work is reflected accurately in publicity'.[7] It also tells them how being insulted as 'third rate' can be turned to institutional advantage.[8]

One of the most noticeable features of New Labour governments has been their presentational skills and media management, so much so that in popular language 'New Labour' and 'spin' are synonymous. They have been persistently criticised for 'spinning' policies, for representing them serially in different versions, and condemned for spending between two and three times the amount their predecessor had on special advisers, many of them public relations experts. Peter Mandelson and Alastair Campbell are held to have promoted Tony Blair up to Downing Street through handing out exclusive new stories, favouring some journalists, controlling timing and briefing unattributably – classic PR media relations. The management continued in government; the Prime Minister presented 'state of the nation' reports and held 'big conversations' with the public – classic PR event management. Indeed, to stop digging deeper into the hole of PR's most embarrassing fate, Alastair Campbell resigned from the post of the Prime Minister's Press Secretary in 2003 because he had become the news, not the messenger.

The tabloid and broadsheet newspapers are not far behind in their use of PR. They report and photograph for their front pages the lifestyles of celebrities, those who are famous for being famous, through deals struck with their PR agents. The industry has firms and individuals specialising in 'celebrity PR': Freud Communications for example. But first in this field for over a decade has been the ubiquitous, plainspeaking personage of Max Clifford, famous for engineering the human and animal circumstances in 1986 that led to the *Sun* headline 'Freddie Starr ate my hamster'.[9] Fun and frothy their work may be, but these promoters and protectors of the glitterati carry negotiating clout. It is Max Clifford, as well as libel lawyers, who gets £100,000 plus outcomes for his 'kiss-and-tell' clients.

Well entrenched in royalty, politics, the media and entertainment, PR is now edging towards the domain of individual self-development. It has been personalised and customised as part of the self-improvement culture – *Mastering Public Relations*,[10] *Be Your Own Spin Doctor*[11] and *Public Relations for Dummies*[12] are in the bookshops. Rein *et al.* (1997) see it as the means to high social and public profile for the professional middle classes. Its jargon has spread into everyday language and flourished. The verb 'to spin' is used without flicking apostrophe marks. The verb to 'unspin' has been heard on BBC Radio 4, as has 'spin nurse'. 'Spin dodger' has been uttered.

Indeed, so pervasive is public relations that we can write of the saturation of UK society with PR activity. Ewen (1996) found that state already existing in the USA when he started tracing the intellectual history of corporate PR there: 'Living in a society in which nearly every moment of human attention is exposed to the game plan of spin doctors, image managers, pitchmen, communications consultants, public information officers and public relations specialists, the boundaries of my inquiry appeared seamless' (p. 19). Now there are no boundaries to PR in the UK.

PR as personal behaviour, as organised activity, as attitude, and as language is part of Britain's cultural weather. A forecast in *The Times* has come true:[13]

> Criticise Sophie Wessex for being a poor PR, but not for being a PR. Tony Blair marching through the countryside in a silly yellow plastic suit, the Queen buying the Big Issue, Prince Charles giving to farmers, everyone is in the PR game now.

With this sort of social and political endorsement, the *Spectator*[14] was right in 1989 to proclaim that 'PR is the profession of the decade'. The magazine will be writing the same for decades to come.

If public relations is widely manifest in the UK today, it is also highly organised. Thirty years ago, we would not have talked of it as an 'industry':

that word connoted high physical production volumes in mineral extraction and manufacturing. Then, it was still a novelty to hear of services described as industries. Now, the Department of Trade and Industry commissions reports on PR. In 1994 they commissioned one from management consultants BDO Stoy Hayward who found that 'the UK PR sector is one of the most highly developed in Europe'. A decade later, the Department, along with the Chartered Institute of Public Relations, published another entitled *Unlocking the Potential of Public Relations*. It 'highlights that the already significant contribution of the public relations industry to the UK economy can be greatly increased through better understanding by business leaders of what the best of public relations can achieve'.[15]

In the early 1960s, West (1963, pp. 8–9) estimated for the UK that there were some 4,000 PRs (four-fifths of them in London), 300 PR companies and a £50 million expenditure. Kisch (1964, p. 22) also put turnover at £50 million in 1961/2. In 1967, there were 766 PR companies and in-house departments in the UK, and 9,200 in 1997.[16] In the early 1990s, turnover was estimated at £1 billion. The 1998 figure was £2.3 billion and for 2004 was in excess of £3 billion,[17] with an estimated 40,000 people employed. The figures are from the Chartered Institute of Public Relation (CIPR), the professional development and representative body for PR individuals. By 2005, the CIPR put turnover at £6.5bn and employees at 48,000. A former president of the Institute (2003–4) estimated that the industry was growing at 17 per cent a year and that it employed more people than advertising.[18] The Public Relations Consultants' Association (PRCA) represents the interests of larger PR consultancies. Their fee income grew from £33 million to £220 million between 1984 and 1996, and in 2004 was £400 million. In the same year, these 120 consultancies earned an estimated 70 per cent of the industry's fee income and employed 4,600 people. *PRWeek* (May 2004)[19] reports that the industry is supported by twenty-nine service sectors ranging from fireworks to translators. Moreover, PR producers and their suppliers are comforted by the knowledge that their industry is a good place in which to invest. According to Plimsoll's Industry Investment Index, PR ranks 25th out of 1,000 UK business sectors for investment attractiveness: every £100 invested brings in a profit of £14, compared with an average of £5.[20]

But employment figures underestimate the actual number of people doing PR for they appear to measure only explicit job titles, and persons who self-declare. For example, government PR people never publicly use the term, calling themselves instead information officers. There is also, as detailed below, a flight from the term 'public relations' by many businesses and by some PR agencies because of the negative connotations. Moreover, the methodologies for counting are not clear. A better sense of the saturation of PR is got by looking at it as persuasive communications (excluding advertising) done by people in honorary, voluntary and paid posts in the public, private and voluntary sectors. This would push the total number of people doing PR higher than the 48,000 above.

Young people like PR. *The Times Higher Education Supplement* reports[21] that 'Advertising, public relations and media jobs were the most coveted careers – about one in four students aspire to jobs in these fields'. These aspirants want qualifications to help them get their first job paying between £18,000 and £23,000 in London.[22] The education system has noticed their interest. Since the late 1980s, the subject has been taught at higher education (HE) level in colleges and universities. There are few, if any, estimates of what proportion of business studies courses in further education colleges have an identifiable and separate PR curriculum, but in higher education the subject is taught at diploma, bachelor and masters degree level at, mostly, 'new' universities. PhD students research aspects of PR.[23] An increasingly marketised HE sector wants those extra student numbers and the fee income they bring in. In 2004, there were over 200 PR-related courses on the universities' and colleges' application service website. Twenty universities or colleges offered courses approved by the CIPR, compared with three at the end of the 1980s and before the Chartered Institute offered validation. A PR degree has been offered at Bournemouth University since 1989, once with applications running at ten for every place but dropping since the introduction of tuition fees and more competition from thirteen CIPR approved undergraduate degrees.[24]

The natural response by the British PR industry to these many indicators of expansion is more confidence. The CIPR has developed many of the features of a professional body. It runs a diploma and advanced certificate taught at fifteen centres in the UK and three abroad. It has an 'accredited practitioner' category. It has a training programme. It has 'excellence awards' which acknowledge that work accorded that mark are 'judged the best in Britain, home of the most thriving public relations business in the world'.[25] It gained 'chartered' status in 2005 and said that this 'marks the "coming of age" of the PR profession and is official recognition of the important and influential role that public relations plays in business, government and democratic society'.[26] It has opinions about public policy, e.g. lobbying to stop ministerial special advisers instructing government information officers; and giving evidence to the Phillis committee on how government media relations should be organised after the departure of Alastair Campbell.[27] As the CIPR puts it 'public relations is a flourishing management function'. There is, undoubtedly, a spring in the modern PR person's step.

The public relations of public relations

Yet while it thrives, PR does not enjoy a high reputation with the general public or with some professional groups. Reputation is the social prestige or dislike that a person, job or institution attracts. High reputation can be seen as large amounts of 'credit' in the 'bank' of public opinion. For example, many student readers would give different 'credit ratings' to the reputations of Balliol College Oxford, Bath, Birmingham, Bournemouth, Bradford, Brighton, and Bristol universities. They base their ratings on a combination of experience, surveys, league tables and gossip. When they do this, they are comparing reputations.

There is, however, an irony here. Despite the expansion of PR, the public relations of public relations remains in a poor state: PR generates low opinion about itself. Compare this state of affairs with other activities. The parallel would be if observers of an activity criticised it for not bringing about the outcome it existed to make come about. It would be as if medicine did not increase health, teaching reduced knowledge, or gardening meant fewer flowers. This point is sharper when we remember that the CIPR's double-head definition of public relations focuses on reputation and its management as well as goodwill and mutual understanding. The CIPR president for 2000/1 wrote[28] that 'PR is about reputation and being transparent and open, not about deviousness or manipulation'. The CIPR website states[29] that

> Public Relations is the discipline which looks after reputation, with the aim of earning understanding and support and influencing opinion and behaviour. It is the planned and sustained effort to establish and maintain goodwill and mutual understanding between an organisation and its publics.

That more PR should lead to less of the benefit it promotes for others being available to itself is a rich irony, an irony that was enriched by the infamous 'false sheik' meeting with the Countess of Wessex.[30] This debacle inflicted serious damage to the reputation of PR in a precise way: it revealed how important personal contacts are to many of its operations; how much PR is more about who you know than what you know, or what you do.

The abbreviation 'PR' has entered everyday language, as has some of its jargon (campaign, press release, image, spin doctor, soundbite, on message, off message, prebuttal, rapid rebuttal, minder, positioning, relaunch) – but rarely with positive connotations. It is a fairly safe bet that the proverbial Martian would see that government, business, charities, pressure groups and celebrities 'do PR', and yet be amazed that the public and many non-PR professionals use the term as a mocking colloquial reference. For example, the jibe 'It's a PR job' describes words or actions about which there is a perceived or actual gap between presentation and reality, a gap that is either actively disguised or not owned up to. That is the gap connoted by other commonplace phrases such as 'It's a PR disaster'[31] or 'It's just spin'. For nearly all the media and public, the term 'PR' generally carries a negative charge.

'PR' is what 'spin doctors' do, and people are wary. Max Clifford, who is the *bête noire* of the UK public relations establishment, was in tune with popular perceptions when he talked about his Favourite Hypocrisy:[32] 'I stand up and say that an important part of public relations is lies and deceit. We all know that but they won't ever admit it. It gives me tremendous pleasure to hear PRs say they don't lie.' Max Clifford is right about PR people not admitting to lying; but they are aware of their low reputation. A former editor of *PRWeek*,[33] the industry's trade magazine, wrote at the fiftieth anniversary of the then IPR:[34]

> Part of the problem is that public relations which is all about the 'management of reputation', according to the IPR definition, itself has a reputation which is right off the end of the Ratner scale. In fact, you would be hard pushed to find an industry which is as gleefully vilified as the noble profession of public relations – otherwise known as 'the latrine of parasitic misinformation' as it was dubbed by *The Guardian*.

The more socially sensitive PR people have doubts about reduced status through association with 'PR' and there is evidence of a flight from the term towards substitutes, which usually include 'communications'. Some graduates hesitate to admit that they have a BA Public Relations. It is embarrassing to find a book titled *Public Relations for Dummies* when you have spent three years studying the subject. English, history, architecture and medical students do not face that public scepticism about their subjects' worth. The large agency Burson Marstellar dropped the term in favour of 'perception management'.[35] Even *PRWeek* noted[36] that 'the term "PR" is giving public relations a bad name' and it wrote of 'anecdotal experience of consultants and in-house practitioners in the UK . . . [that] communications is on the up but "public relations" is consistently undervalued as a management asset, and seen instead as a downstream "packaging" function'.[37] When Peter Hehir, a leading PR entrepreneur, said[38] that the term 'has lost its way as a description of what people are doing in the business', he was voicing a common view among senior business people.

Lord McAlpine updated Machiavelli's *The Prince*[39] as a handbook for success in business. He sees the value of PR, but calls those who practise it 'twitchers of image' who use half-truths and convenient words. His advice to employers is never tell PR people more than they need to know. Indeed, the term 'Machiavellian marketing' has been coined[40] to describe what PR people call public affairs and government relations. Some lobbyists publicly distance themselves from 'PR', and most prefer in their literature descriptors such as 'public affairs' and 'government relations'.[41] This bias away from the words 'public relations' is summed up in the titling priorities of two UK textbooks: *Strategic Communications Management: Making Public Relations Work* and *Handbook of Corporate Communication and Public Relations*.[42]

The lecturers who teach PR know about the low status of their subject: when asked if it had a low reputation with the general public, 78 per cent of the academics in a survey of the PR Educators' Forum[43] answered 'yes'. There was a small majority in the same survey who thought PR had a poor reputation with managers and employers. Respondents also felt looked down upon by their peers in traditional disciplines outside of business studies. L'Etang (2004a, p. 346) observes that 'Media academics to varying degrees reflect the prejudices of journalists and may therefore regard PR academics as either nefarious or unthinking functionaries operating in an atheoretical and thus inferior environment.' These academics, therefore, largely dismiss PR as worthy of study but when they do take notice of it, they are heavily critical – which is acceptable – and very dismissive of its significance – which is shortsighted. Typical is Webster[44] who, in his review of 'the information society', sees PR as a pollutant of disinterested, rational and transparent debate in society.

Olasky (1987) is also concerned. A PR man turned academic, he wrote for public relations people 'who want to understand why corporate public relations is sinking deeper into ethical and political quicksand' (preface). He wrote for the conservative, libertarian right; from the neo-Marxist left, Gandy (1982) argued that public relations people used an 'information subsidy' to reduce the cost to politicians, public officials and journalists of access to information favourable to their employers, the large corporations.

The low status of PR is not a new phenomenon. It was noticed by Pimlott (1951) in the USA of the 1940s, the land that Chomsky declares invented public relations.[45] Pimlott was a British observer of the US scene in the early post-war period up to 1950 and he remarked that 'the fact is public relations practitioners have never enjoyed good public relations' (p. 201). He notes that the US 'father' of PR, Ivy Lee, who was an adviser to the Rockefeller business empire, was known as 'Poison Ivy' (p. 202). More generally, public opinion saw PR as a technique favouring the rich. The PR man is a 'plutogogue' (p. 206) used by business to counter attacks on capitalism (p. 207); who identifies with 'unworthy' causes, who is thought to use dishonest techniques, and who makes claims that are 'eyewash' (p. 205).

Advantages for funders and producers

A rebalancing of the argument, however, is needed at this stage. Whatever the strength of the case against, PR in the UK is a growing activity and a prosperous business with at least 48,000 people turning over £6.5 billion a year, and with plenty of openings for young people. It is a major component of the UK's promotional culture, a pervasive activity done by business, non-business and anti-business groups, by all points of the political compass, and by all classes of material and ideological interests. They use it – as an organisational activity and as a state of mind – because they judge that it will advance their interests. How is that? These are questions for the production supply side of PR. So what value does it return to its paymasters, employers and clients? (See Chs 9–11 for benefits of PR in politics, markets and media). Here is what those who pay for public relations say in advertisements about the needs PR fulfils for them.

A global software company describes the role of its communications manager: 'What we need you to do is to focus on managing our public reputation.' A tobacco company wants a corporate affairs manager for 'close monitoring and guidance of competitive market environment' and 'management of UK legal activity relating to compliance, regulation and commerce' (both from *PRWeek*, 11.6.04, pp. 42, 44). A local authority looks for a principal press officer who will 'proactively shape our reputation with opinion formers locally and nationally' while a university wants a senior press officer 'passionate about delivery of quality communications for a global brand leader' (both in the *Guardian* jobs section, 22.05.04, pp. 50–63). The CIPR wants internal communicators at a conference (June 2004) because they play 'a crucial role in managing change, and motivating and informing the workforce to help organisations to achieve corporate goals and deliver results'. The pressure group Age Concern wants a media relations officer (the *Guardian* jobs section, 31.5.04, p. 7) to join a team that 'creates national headlines that help improve life for older people now'. A headmaster says that 'we do need to drip-feed positive messages all the time' (the *Guardian* education section, 1.6.04, p. 8). A 'fast-moving council' wants a communications manager who will be . . . spearheading the strategic direction of our e-government and customer services' (the *Guardian* media section, 7.6.04, p. 43). A skills council for the chemical industry wants 'an advocate for the needs of employers in our sector to stakeholders, including Government' (the *Guardian* jobs section, 12.6.04, p. 8) while a police authority wants a communication director 'to develop an innovative communication and marketing strategy, and lead the marketing and publicity team to deliver a media service that gets heard' (the *Sunday Times* appointments section, 13.6.04, p. 9). Those who fund it believe that PR pays back.

Comparisons with advertising and journalism

If these outcomes and advantages are real, why does PR provoke more criticism than advertising? Peter Mandelson is known to his critics as 'Prince of Darkness', but no such soubriquet attaches to Philip Gould, the Labour Party's former advertising specialist and current pollster. Gould has been associated with the advertising side of Labour since 1985, when Mandelson was appointed the party's director of campaigns and communications. He set up the Shadow Communications Agency, an informal agency ready to run election ad campaigns for the party. He advised the 1992 Clinton election campaign on how to avoid the sort of presentational mistakes made by Labour earlier that year in the UK general election. He was as much a party apparatchik as Mandelson, but not as much decried. Advertising has been established longer than PR as an industry and was critiqued by Vance Packard in 1957 in *The Hidden Persuaders*[46] – a title more fitting to PR people than to those who persuade off the page in an eye-catching mixture of visuals and words. Yet high visibility and critical attention have not brought advertising into such low regard.

One explanation is that advertising has been the more established industry and has in the past been subject to obloquy – witness *The Hidden Persuaders*. Grant notes (1994, pp. 28, 31–4) in her review of inter-war UK domestic propaganda that its reputation was low and worse than that of the press. She writes (p. 32):

> If the First World War gave propaganda a bad name, advertising already had one. Long regarded as the purview of quacks and swindlers, it was becoming respectable only slowly, as the industry's attempts to curb abuses, set standards, and organise itself in a profession began to take effect.

If there is a maturation process for the status of new types of work and it matches the cycle of diffusion for an innovation, growing acceptance and reputation awaits PR. But it is taking a long time to arrive; in 1948 Goldman was writing (p. 23) that it 'has so far failed of complete acceptance as a profession'. He noted that because of 'cultural lag', surgeons took more than a century to avoid 'the barber's tag'. On that timetable, PR is coming up to its century.

Another argument is that advertising does not attract low regard precisely because it is so visible. It is very obviously display, where the display is a 'shriek' from the page.[47] It is easy to imagine a PR person smiling at the compliment that their work was subtle: PR often seeks to 'whisper' from the deep background. To an advertising person, the compliment is dubious. More generally, in terms of work prospects and budgets, PR saw itself in the UK as the junior partner to advertising until the later 1980s. It was advertising agencies that had PR sections and not the other way around: these advertising agencies were called 'full service'. Advertising budgets were often in £millions, while PR mostly worked for less than £100,000. Further back in the 1960s, Kisch (1964, pp. 24–5) estimates that PR fees ranged between £1,500 and £8,000. Now, with the spread of integrated marketing communications, it is more difficult to measure separate contributions to total promotional spend but the judgement is that PR is gaining ground because of its lower cost, multiple forms, and because of more editorial space to fill. One estimate is that £400,000 is a medium-sized fee for a large London agency.[48] PR imperialists and loyalists will read with pleasure *The Fall of Advertising and the Rise of PR* (Ries and Ries 2002) and their judgement that 'we see a dramatic shift from advertising-orientated marketing to public relations-orientated marketing' (p. xi).

The role of the media in the creation of the parlous public reputation of PR needs evaluation. Some PR people believe that it is the determining factor, for journalists seem to have an instinct to label any public presentation malfunction as PR. The *Guardian* reported in summer 2000[49] that the Prime Minister was slow handclapped by the Women's Institute when he addressed their annual conference in the Queen Elizabeth Conference Centre, London. The headline was 'PR disaster as No 10 fails to get the message'. Why not political disaster, speech disaster? Media dislike is not new, for West (1963) reported the existence of a Society for the Discouragement of Public Relations, and Tunstall (1964) noted both journalistic resentment towards PR and dependence on it. Today, the bad feeling happens at a time when journalists need PR more than ever: they have so much more space to fill. Satellite, cable and digital television have at the same time finished off the BBC and ITV duopoly. The BBC has eight national TV channels and ITV sixteen national and regional ones.[50] Over 200 local and three national commercial radio stations compete with the BBC's forty local and five national.[51] Many, if not most, PR people blame journalists as their most dangerous bad-mouthers because of their control over the content and tone of public debate. A columnist on *The Times* comment page[52] can write of 'the pseudo-profession that calls itself public relations' and hundreds of thousands of readers will note the put down. PR people also note that, like traffic wardens, journalists are everywhere; moreover that journalists do not deal with advertising agents. Stand back, however, from these inter-professional hostilities and the relationship can be seen as attempts by both sides to gain the most from the supply and demand of information.[53] One survey showed that, on average, editors believed that a quarter of all media coverage is based on PR-sourced material, while PRs believe that the sourcing is 40 per cent. The relationship has been summed up as a choice between 'a partnership or a marriage of convenience?'.[54] 'Relationship in permanent crisis' is another option.

PRs and journalists inside the relationships often find them aggressive and painful. There is a 'love–hate' dimension with strong potential to become 'hate–hate' (see Ch. 11 for a full analysis of PR/media relations).[55] Though they have to deal with them, journalists professionally do not like PR people because they see them as a block, a barrier to facts, figures and people to which the media want access for a 'good' story. The story is usually showing up the fact, figure or person involved in a sensational, critical or false light. PR people tend to offer the less critical fact, figure or person to the journalist for write-up or interview. Journalists complain that this behaviour leads to a blander story than the one that they could get if the PR person was not guarding the gateway to information.

On the other side, the PR person feels that the journalist is usually seeking a critical view of the organisation, cause or person the PR person is representing. It is irritating to be always asked negative questions of an organisation or person one likes or believes in, or which pays one's wages and/or which one fears. The constant stress on the negative grates on the soul of the PR person after a while, but the balance of power in the PR/media relationship does not normally allow this to be shown – another source of negative feeling for the PR person. The supply and demand for information and publicity determines the balance of advantage to both sides, and it is usually the case, given the growth of PR, that there are fewer journalists 'buying' than sources 'selling in' to them. Against that, journalists may weaken their bargaining hand by being pressed for time; under news desk instruction to get a story; or over-worked in an under-resourced newsroom. The outcome on both sides is at best formal politeness: minimum information given away by both sides, and a search for more amenable sources or journalists.

Other structural, less personal factors also work their way in to make the relationship tense. There is the journalist's perception that their paper or station carries too many 'puffs'[56] on behalf of advertisers, powerful interests or the editor's cronies. Some journalists go so far as to talk about the 'courtier media'. Second, there is the perception of a dumbing down of content and journalistic standards in the broadsheet press and terrestrial TV. Third, it is believed that PR people are better paid and have an easier professional life than journalists. To these perceptions can be added cuts in journalists' staffing levels occurring at the same time as the growth in media outlets over the last twenty years, culminating in a feeling among journalists that they are being colonised by PR values and behaviour. As Davis (2003, p. 32) puts it: 'Clearly, as British journalism is repeatedly cut and squeezed, so standards drop and the need to cut corners becomes crucial. Journalists must do more with less resources and are becoming out-numbered and out-resourced by their PR counterparts.'

In these circumstances, journalists are likely to be critical of PR and they are in the better position to voice their feelings: they control the words read and heard by their audiences – audiences that PRs want to influence.

It is the (usually private) contention of PR people that journalists continuously bad mouth them out of spite, fear or envy, and that they are the prime builders of their low reputation. The bad mouthing is either mildly derogatory, or acidly insulting. For the latter category, note this: the *Financial Times* carried the headline[57] 'The pioneer of today's spin-doctors' and stated that 'Goebbels was a master manipulator' who 'pioneered the techniques of "news management" and public relations'.

Summary

This chapter has argued that PR is an activity that is noticeable and widespread in our society today – so much so that it is a major pillar of our promotional culture. By volume of activity, it is an industry spread throughout the UK; by social reach, it is done by the establishment and by immigrant groups; by diversity of source, it is done by government, big business, social campaigners, charities, celebrities of all lists, and aggrieved individuals. Its funders and producers spend £6.5 billion on it and employ at least 48,000 people. For them, there are beneficial outcomes and operational advantages for all this money. But despite this pervasiveness, the PR of PR is bad, and through tense relationships with journalists, the low reputation is reported widely. All these factors combine into an unusual asymmetry – a voluntary, legal, universally practised activity, devoted to raising the reputation of what it represents, generating disquiet about itself. This is the starting point for the next chapter. Is this pervasive activity with low reputation linked to other trends in UK society?

3 A future with PR

We can look back to 1900 in the USA and see the beginnings of the public relations that we recognise today. We can look to the 1920s in the UK for that point of recognition, and if Dr Who, the scarfed time traveller, was a PR man, he would find the work then similar to now.[1] With this history, perhaps the *Spectator* magazine was too cautious when it heralded PR as the 'profession of the decade' in 1998, and Michie too narrow when he declared the UK 'in the midst of a PR explosion' in the same year. Indeed, so well fitted to Britain was PR in the last century that three authors gave it the title of 'fifth estate', adding it after the fourth estate of a free press to the traditional sites of power in the realm.[2] In this vein, Miller and Dinan (2000) were right to argue that PR people played an important, identifiable role in the political and economic changes in the UK of the 1980s.[3] But these references look back to the twentieth century, and if the case made in the last chapter for PR pervasiveness is accepted, PR will flourish in the twenty-first. It is a theme of this book that the last and current decades show PR to be an emblem of liberal, market democracies in conversation with themselves.

The sense that citizens of such polities are embedded in a PR environment has been captured by Ewen (1996). He described the USA as a PR-'saturated' society and it is a description that transfers easily to the UK. Its sense of excess mirrors Moore's (1996, p. 7) image of PR producing 'walls of sound' in society. He notes the similarity between Jonathan Swift's description of straining to be heard in eighteenth-century England and modern communications: 'Whoever hath an ambition to be heard in a crowd must press, and squeeze, and thrust, and climb with indefatigable pains, till he has exalted himself to a certain degree of altitude above them.'

Michie (1998, pp. 314–15) developed the saturation theme when he wrote that 'individuals, companies and organisations of all kinds have become acutely aware of the need to raise their profile in the news media if they are to exist in the minds of their target audiences' at a time when 'we are also caught up in an equally spectacular multiplication of available media channels'. He adds that 'PR-consciousness is dramatically rising', as are the business opportunities created for market-making by such 'consciousness'. No PR person shows this contemporary 'consciousness' more exquisitely than Max Clifford. In 2004, Faria Alam, a secretary at the Football Association, became his client after her affairs with two employees, leading to 'kiss and tell' media deals of £500,000.[4] Imagine those deals happening in 1954 – one cannot, for there was not the media space to be filled. In 1998, the journalist Lynn Barber, who interviews allegedly well-known personalities, observed the increasing power of celebrity over the decade. There is little doubt that this power still grows; six years later Katya Hoffman, a *Financial Times* journalist, was asked to submit her interview with actress Claudia Schiffer for text and headline approval.[5]

This sensation of PR saturating our society, of PR being embedded in it, of PR being the style for our civic conservations, is symptomatic of the sociological and political condition known as pluralism. Before examining that condition in the contemporary UK, however, it is necessary to first explore the opposite thesis, namely that PR is a free-floating, spontaneous activity – one that is noticeable, pervasive *and unconnected* to underlying social phenomena. It is worthwhile doing this for PR is often dismissed – especially by academics – with two charges against it: it is trivial, frothy promotion not worth analysis; and that it is secret influence peddling that undermines democracy. It is also worth noting that there is a contradiction between the two dismissals: if it is undermining politics, it cannot be trivial.

It is hard to argue that PR is just promotional excrescence if it is an industry. To put it into the category 'industry' (as does the DTI and the CIPR) implies that it is the outcome of supply and demand from substantial market and productive elements in society. For example, the media/PR trade in 'kiss and tell' stories happens because editors believe that it draws in readers and audiences. The lobbying sector of the PR industry grew in the UK from the mid-1980s onwards because government changed its relationship with business (e.g. deregulated markets, supply-side reforms, privatisation) and big business bought PR services to influence outcomes. Dibden Bay Residents' Association on Southampton Water might have been charged with frivolity when they flew barrage balloons along two kilometres of sensitive, unspoilt shoreline to indicate the impact of putting a dock there, but they were building favourable public opinion ahead of a planning inquiry.

This reference to a residents' association is an example of PR as a 'cottage industry' (the work of volunteers) as opposed to a professional service supplied by an industry. Another example is the PR of divorced fathers seeking attention, through stunts, to grievances about access to their children. They are connecting to an alleged bias in the courts against their interests and to family social policy. An earlier example is protesting against by-pass roads. Bryant (1996), a former Conservative councillor turned roads activist, describes the attempt to stop the bulldozing of Twyford Down to clear the way for the Winchester by-pass. As well as these campaigns by non-professionals, PR can also be conceptualised as a set of portable attitudes and techniques available to individuals. This is PR as 'personal kit', as a set of techniques and attitudes that the individual or small group can deploy in the media, via lobbying or event management to secure advantage. An example is the grandchildren of British soldiers shot for cowardice in the First World War seeking public pardons. Another is the media relations, televised appeals and leafleting in Baghdad[6] during September 2004 by the Bigley family in unsuccessful attempts to save their brother from murder by hostage takers in Iraq.

This typology of PR into the three categories of professional industrial, cause group 'cottage industry' and individual 'personal kit' allows its instrumental nature to be identified. PR is a promotional type serving the interests of its users. Without connection to interests, causes and grievances expressed by organisations, groups and individuals, PR is just promotional form without meaning. You do not do PR for its own sake. It is instrumental activity, display-for-attention-and-advantage; done to influence favourably the significant 'other'. It is done by large companies; by national interest and cause groups; by local charity and protest groups; and by individuals. The eighteenth-century political philosopher Edmund Burke would recognise in these latter micro-grouplets the contemporary equivalent of his 'small platoons' and 'sub-divisions' of society, in which feelings of commitment and of service are generated between members; in which 'public affections' are nurtured and in which today's community feeling – and its predecessor 'public spiritedness' – are expressed in shared effort.[7] These groups connect PR with civil society, and thus located it in the voluntary associational life of a society (see Ch. 6).

If PR cannot be described as free-floating promotional activity in a society, but instead connects to foundational social structures (markets, politics, voluntary groups in civil society), how can these connections be characterised?

PR and civic pluralism

PR is the communicative expression of the competition between the plural values, behaviours and interests in a market, capitalist, liberal democracy. Berger (1998) argues that this pluralism is the most important consequence of modernity.[8] Edwards (2004, pp. 21–2), in his review of civil society, estimates that the numbers of registered non-profit organisations 'have increased at rates not seen before in history, especially in developing countries'. In Northern Europe and the USA, he notes the decline of some older associations (e.g. trade unions and parent–teacher associations), but at the same time the increase of non-governmental organisations (NGOs) and advocacy groups. The UK has seen this increased pluralism over the last four decades. A precise count is difficult but Grant (2000, p. 18) reckons that 'A count of primary and secondary pressure groups in Britain that included locally based groups would almost certainly run into the tens of thousands'. There are 7,000 entries in the Directory of British Associations for 2005.[9] This pluralism is of two kinds – civic and commercial.

Since the 1960s, the UK has witnessed great, observable changes in personal behaviour by its citizens and in collective behaviour by voluntary groups. Jackall and Hirota (2000, p. 155) note that the greater and lesser tendency of people to come together 'into "intellectual" and "moral" associations for purposes of advocacy . . .' occurs in cycles and they too identify the 1960s as a 'flowering'. The personal behavioural changes derive principally from altered values regarding sex, gender, lifestyle, the environment, race, consumption and religion. The collective behavioural changes derive from the need to establish enough social acceptance and tolerance for these changed personal behaviours to be practised by individuals, free from the harassment of prevailing, hostile social forces. These two kinds of changes have given individuals a choice of personal behaviours, and of collective action in pressure groups[10] to promote and defend those choices. These groups have come to stand alongside the two centuries-old clash of values and behaviours between capital and labour.[11] This increased pluralism of values and groups has been associated with social movements (e.g. feminism, environmentalism, consumerism, multi-ethnicity, sexual equality, secularism) and it is open to question which of the two changes described above (the individual's values and behaviour or individuals' desires to promote and protect their choices) is the more influential in the growth of modern social movements. These latter desires are, however, distinguished by 'contentious collective action' that, argues Tarrow (1994, p. 2), is created by judging opportunistically the political circumstances to successfully sustain 'contention by convention' (p. 17, e.g. sit-ins, media events, petitions, demonstrations, networking). Stonier (1989, p. 31) argues that 'Social movements are of prime importance to the PR practitioner.'[12]

Since the 1960s,[13] the trend to more pluralism of publicly expressed values and behaviours, and to more voluntary associations for their promotion has accelerated.[14] An indicator of this is that general charities (e.g. helping the homeless, visiting prisoners, patient support groups) have increased from 100,000 to 160,000 from 1991 to 2001.[15] But specifically what is the connection of this accelerated pluralism with PR? The key link lies in the need of individuals for new personal values and behaviours to be accepted or at least tolerated by society. One cannot be comfortably transsexual if one's legal status is unclear; one cannot be a sovereign consumer without the labelling of food ingredients; one cannot be a fully informed citizen if advice to ministers is secret; one cannot be secular if religion obtrudes into civic life; one cannot worship if one's religion is harassed. PR is a set of flexible techniques for the promotion of values by interest and cause groups, by voluntary associations, and by an individual alone. It can be used by them in paid professional form, or in 'cottage industry' and 'personal kit' forms. This shift in UK society to more expression by individuals of different personal values via voluntary, often local, groups is identified here as value pluralism and group pluralism of a civic kind. Brought together they will be called civic pluralism. Grant (2000, p. 33) expressed the point as follows: 'Today, there is a far greater number and wider range of pressure groups, reflecting a more fragmented society. . . . Supporting a particular pressure group can almost be a lifestyle choice.'

PR and commercial pluralism

In addition to this kind of pluralism, a commercial variant has come to the fore in the UK in approximately the same period. From the middle of the 1970s, it was noticeable that the climate of ideas about markets and business was shifting away from the collective and the planned towards the singular and the autonomous. This altered paradigm for the UK political economy has resulted in business and pro-market interests predominating over their ideological and material competitors. Collectivism and corporatism have faded, whether temporarily or not. Now, mainstream political parties vie to be more business-friendly. They do so because of a broader shift in ruling ideas in favour of many business values. In this shift, competition is proclaimed over monopoly; consumers are flattered rather than producers cared for; markets have grown up where the plan once regulated; private wealth is privileged over public goods. As a result, there is now in the UK a pronounced commercial pluralism. This is the condition where market and business values, ideas and practices in the pursuit of monetary advantage prevail, despite substantial challenge from non-business or anti-business groups. Without it, pluralism would not affect the lives of the whole population of the UK. Tens of millions are affected by personal and civic value changes: all are affected by market and business changes.

Overall, the increased emphases on different values and differing personal behaviours, on voluntary associations for their promotion and defence, and on the marketable and the profitable have combined to create a sustained pressure for change in private and public life. Taken together this civic and commercial pluralism in the UK since the 1960s can be described as accelerated pluralism. Its communicative expression is very largely via the attitudes, behaviours and techniques of PR. Other expressions are advertising, marketing, journalism (often too much sourced by PR material: see Ch. 11), and what remains of a Habermasian public sphere.[16]

PR is principally concerned with actors, ideas and events in the political economy and civil society. The former term is used throughout following Mosca's definition (1996, p. 26) that it is about control and survival in public life, where control is politics and economics is survival. The argument is that pressure for change in these public domains can be described as more obvious, numerous and varied than in the period between the Second World War and the 1960s. The outcome since then is a more competitive, argumentative and commercialised public domain: one reached through the dual agencies of increased individual expression and group representation, and of more powerful businesses and markets. It is an outcome that encourages promotional activity generally, and which encourages PR in particular as an appropriate means to secure advantage for individuals, interest and cause groups in civil society; and advantage also for the suppliers of goods and services, both publicly and privately owned in the political economy.

PR, neo-liberalism and promotional culture

Benefiting from this generalised acceptance of the promotional mind-set, PR has prospered and become a set of attitudes and techniques acceptable for work and non-work behaviour. It is clear that the increased resort to PR involves both the business and public sectors, which were early, major users of PR (L'Etang 2004b), and newer users in non-business and anti-business groups. In addition, late adopters, such as aggrieved and ambitious individuals, have taken to PR, noting its perceived efficiency in the struggle for advantage and its low cost. In terms of political philosophy, increased PR activity is at root connected with the communicative aspects of the rise of the political economy paradigm known as neo-liberalism. This is characterised by unregulated markets, serviced by unfettered, capitalist enterprise in societies that encourage possessive individualism. Yet neo-liberalism has also been an incubating environment for a more civic pluralism, where the latter is a competitive condition (in and outside markets) in which the 'one' has to compete for advantage or survival amongst the 'many', and where PR is an accessible, low-cost set of promotional attitudes and techniques for existing and thriving in this competition.

The argument so far embeds PR in the pluralism of values and behaviours associated with a neo-liberal political economy and civil society. It is beyond the scope and competence of this book to analyse the direction of causality between pluralism and neo-liberalism, but Wernick (1991, pp. 181–2) has identified a societal condition associated with them. It is promotional culture where self-advantaging communicative acts are 'virtually co-extensive with our produced symbolic world'. A society has such a culture when the majority of messages circulating in it are self-interested. Greater choice of lifestyles for individuals since the 1960s, more personal consumption, deregulation of markets and the rise of marketing as a major business discipline since the 1980s are the demand and supply factors that encourage individuals to seek out the fulfilment of their personal needs, and to support businesses and groups that satisfy and promote their interests. To say this is to restate the pluralist phenomenon as a marketplace for ideas[17] as well as goods, and to pave the way for linking individuals' cognitive preferences to supportive organisations and groups, via the signals of self-interested promotional communications. The value, therefore, of the promotional culture concept to an analysis of PR is that it focuses on the self-interested nature of public relations. If PR can be segmented into the tripartite entity of display-for-attention-and-advantage, the concept allows us to note that the prior activities of display and attention-getting serve the end of self-advancement. The *Encyclopedia of Public Relations* (Heath 2005, p. 477) makes the point: 'The current socio-economic culture in the United States drives the need for a favourable image since image often determines whether an organisation will or will not be successful at achieving its goals.'

If PR happens inside a promotional culture, another major contextual feature is that it is principally a communicative mode for organisations and groups for they produce most PR. Celebrity PR is a growing exception to this corporate, collective nature of PR and is treated here as a supportive activity for it (see p. 171). The concentration is on organisations (businesses and public bodies) and groups (professional, interest and cause ones) doing PR, not individuals. It is common to attach 'corporate' to the PR done by businesses but it would be inadequately descriptive to narrow the term just to them. Friends of the Earth, the Trades Union Congress, and Help the Aged are as organisationally corporate (rational-legal, hierarchical and stable) as McDonalds, Tesco and British Airways. Indeed, Jordan and Maloney (1997, p. 24) believe that Friends of the Earth and Greenpeace in the UK, with their corporate structures, marketing and fundraising, are closer to being *protest businesses* rather than protest groups. Moreover, churches, mosques, synagogues and temples are frequent communicators of the collective views of their faith groups. Think of the Board of Deputies of British Jews and the Catholic Media Office. The professional associations for teachers, nurses and police speak to the media and lobby government more often than most businesses. The definition here of 'corporate' and 'collective', however, does not include anti-globalisation, anti-capitalist groupings.[18] They come from another important tradition in liberal, democratic societies: anti-establishment thinking and street protests by marginalised, anarchic groups. Their PR is very public in that it reflects values in important social movements; it is very effective for identifying tensions in the political economy and civil society, but it is not corporate and is only collective in a weak, chaotic sense.

This PR of public protest is a reminder of another context. PR does not operate in the private domain of individuals where intimacies are found, even though analogous processes of display, attention and advantage exist there. PR is *public* relations aimed at the distinct public 'other'. These relations are observable, at least, to the subjects and objects of the display, and to third parties, whether in small numbers or in masses. In the private domain, the distinction between subject and object is blurred by the intensity and proximity of relationships. This is the difference between influencing a life partner, a parent or a child as opposed to a legislator, a trade association or an employer. PR, therefore, deals indirectly with private matters and only in a public way. It is involved with private domain matters (e.g. families, religion, human rights) when they are in the public domain for one or more of three reasons: commercialisation (e.g. sex as an industry), conceptual and ideological dispute (e.g. marriage versus same-sex partnerships), or regulation (e.g. access to children by parents).

Finally, it is important to restate the pervasive nature of PR to see that it is done by the very greatest diversity of organisations and groups: otherwise UK society would not be saturated by it. Businesses, charities, professional bodies, trade and industry associations, cause and protest groups are PR producers. They operate internationally, nationally, regionally, locally and at the micro-neighbourhood level (e.g. residents getting speed restrictions for their road).

PR is produced in very different circumstances by this diversity. National businesses and interest groups (e.g. Help the Aged) have PR departments with press officers;[19] campaign teams; specialists in social responsibility and community relations; issue and event managers, and government liaison officers. These are the resource 'rich', in contradistinction to the 'resource' poor. These latter are, for example, voluntary groups in inner-city neighbourhoods or disadvantaged groups in rich communities. They want safer housing estates, free from drug users and hooligans; they have fixed incomes and want lower council tax, danger-free streets at night or disabled access. They are 'A voice for the Over 50s'.[20] They lobby local councillors, community relations officers, and people on public bodies with regeneration funds. They do not talk about 'doing PR'; rather they 'speak out', 'give information' and 'campaign' by talking to councillors and the local media. Their unconscious PR seeks to promote community change (Homan 2003). This scaling of PR by resources brings attention to another dimension. It is that of Grant (1995, 2000) that measures cause and interest groups on an 'insider' and 'outsider' scale of access to policymakers. A question for both scales is how their dimensions correlate to PR effectiveness. It cannot be assumed, however, that 'resource-poor' PR is ineffective: its high and continuous production suggests otherwise.[21]

PR and its most influential client – business

It was a commonplace amongst PR people that PR was more practised to the west of the UK than to the east. It was held to be true because neo-liberal ideas and behaviour were more entrenched in North America. These were the conditions that encouraged commercial pluralism. Modern public relations developed in the fourth quarter of the nineteenth century as marketing communications in the USA for land-selling companies and for railways as the west was settled. It was also used defensively by business interests when they were defending monopolies, breaking strikes, explaining railway crashes in the 'trust busting' and 'muckraker' era. It was later used by press agents working for the new film studios in Hollywood. The history of PR in the USA was almost exclusively associated with business until 1916, when its techniques were used by the federal government Committee on Public Information (known as the Creel Committee) to gain support for US entry into the First World War. PR developed significantly in the UK from the 1920s with prestigious, large organisations, both public and private. (See Ch. 5.)

The west/east axis of strong/weak PR has, however, been rebalanced. PR people in the UK today still consider their practice to be nearer to the US than to the Western European but they have noted rapid growth of PR in Eastern Europe,[22] the Middle East and in Asia.[23] The collapse of the Soviet Union in the early 1990s and the spread of liberal democracy and market, capitalist economies account for this strengthening in the east. The US author Brady writing in the middle of the Second World War (1943, pp. 287–93) prefigured this navigational rule of thumb when he linked the direction of travel to political forms: 'Broadly speaking the importance of public relations . . . decreases as one moves away from countries with long and deep-seated liberal, democratic, and parliamentary institutions.' It was 'almost non-existent' in the Germany, Italy and Japan of the 1930s.

His argument is that public relations is a technique used by dominant business and social groups in liberal capitalist democracies to ensure their dominance, while the same groups in other forms of society rely on feudalism and totalitarian government. Brady associated PR with liberal societies and with Anglo-American societies in particular. Together with lawyers and the press, PR people are among the 'pliant agents of organised business' (Foreword, p. xv).[24] They 'sell the public' 'the enterprise system' with appeals to 'social harmony' and 'class collaboration', and the 'middle-class' perspective on behalf of the 'big businessman' who 'educates' or 'leads' the general public for the 'community' good (ibid.). This line of argument makes PR a 'manufacturer of consent' in favour of business interests, and is taken up by Carey (1995), Herman and Chomsky (1988), Tedlow (1974) and Ewen (1996).

Historically, PR has been used by big business in the USA and the UK to promote and protect its interests; in the UK today that process continues. Business is the largest user, if not employer, of PR in the UK: the connection between the two is so close that it is wrongly assumed to be organic. The peak organisations for business – big and small – lobby government privately and are heavily reported in the media when they go public. Individual businesses do the same when their interests are affected. Business leaders and spokespeople are in the media with views on a gamut of issues – much more so than trade unionists. PR texts written by UK authors devote more space to PR as a business service than to alternative users in the public and voluntary sectors.

In the 1960s, when government policy towards the political economy was corporatist (the opposite of neo-liberalism), business and trade union representative bodies used PR as communicative support for price and incomes policy, industrial restructuring, investment and productivity increases, national planning,[25] and industrial relations reform. Since the middle of the 1970s, and the successful challenge of the ideas, attitudes and policies known as Thatcherism (the UK version of the neo-liberal paradigm) to corporatism and social democracy, the intellectual and affective climate has become even more nurturing of closer links between PR and business. The pre-Thatcherite ideas and attitudes were collectivist, equalitarian and hesitant or unenthusiastic towards markets and business. It is clear that these ideas have not been reinstated as policy drivers by New Labour governments since 1997: rather New Labour has adapted Thatcherism into their fiscal, industrial and labour policies, and has extended it into the public services (e.g. top-up fees for university students, foundation hospitals, parental choice of secondary school). This ideological continuity means that the intellectual incubator for PR remains fertile.

Onwards, therefore, from the first Thatcher government in 1979, PR as a set of communications techniques and as an industry has been put to effective service in the promotion of business in three distinct but interrelated ways. It has been the 'voice' for a greater commercial pluralism. First, it was used to promote business as an important – if not the most important – interest in the UK political economy (through the media relations PR of business peak organisations and leading company executives). Second, it was used to promote the specific interests of business sectors and individual companies (through the lobbying PR of trade associations and single firms). Third, it promoted the goods and services produced by tens of thousands of businesses for sale in markets (through PR for markets). In the light of this efficient, long-term deployment of PR techniques by business, it is understandable how an organic relationship has been assumed by critics. While noting the business connection, this book, however, argues for its use throughout civil society.

The PR 'voice' and issues management

This chapter has connected the prominence of modern PR with the value and behaviour pluralism of liberal democracies and their market economies. In these polities, PR is a noticeable, major part of the communications of hundreds of thousands of businesses, public institutions, professional bodies, trade and industry associations, charities, interest and cause groups (which make up societies like the UK) as they seek to advance their interests in competition, co-operation and conflict over markets, material resources, policy, ideology and reputation. From this vantage point, PR expresses the diverse conversations of liberal democracy. PR is the 'voice' of pluralism.[26]

PR people today often observe this clamorous wrangling and say it needs 'issues management'. They use the PR 'voice' as the communications component in the response to serious matters that benefit or threaten the organisation or group they represent. Examples are bio-technology companies introducing genetically modified seeds to farmers, or a car manufacturer recalling a model for safety reasons; less dramatically a university pricing courses as higher education becomes a market, or a farmers' union planning for the end of production subsidies. Issues therefore can be defined as matters, usually external to the organisation or group in question, which can positively or negatively affect its prosperity or survival. PR involvement requires 'boundary scanning' of the operating environment, a role that PR has traditionally claimed for itself; and then the communication to internal and external stakeholders of the overall strategy for handling the issue. Strategy here is more than a communications one. It has to be organisation-wide. If PR is to avoid the charge of 'presentation without performance', of 'greenwashing', strategy has to include internal changes to operations and new codes of behaviour. In doing this, PR people work under the dominant coalition running the organisation or group, and alongside other professionals such as scientists, engineers, planners, marketeers and lawyers. Issues management is teamwork where the PR contribution is external research of the operating environment, and communications strategy and tactics. Given the work touches on the fundamental integrity and direction of the PR person's employer or client, it is right to regard issues management as highest-level PR work.[27]

Issues management first developed in the USA in response to anti-business and public interest pressure groups in the 1970s as they developed agendas inspired by environmental and consumerist social movements. These agendas involved government regulation, a policy anathema to neo-liberal capitalism. Heath and Cousino (1990, p. 7) write that because 'many executives assumed that critics of business could be "shouted down", [issues management] started with a communication bias'. In its first US phase, therefore, issues management often expressed itself as one-way communication in the form of advocacy advertising, or issues advertising. Mobil Oil was a famous exponent of this decide–announce–defend approach to issues. Heath and Cousino urge (p. 8), instead, a multi-disciplinary sequence of identifying the issue, evaluating its impact, setting company policy, implementing it and then communicating it. This more dialogic form has been noticeable in the 1990s as policies of stakeholder involvement and social responsibility were taken up by some business sectors (e.g. oil companies, sportswear manufacturers and food retailers). It is a matter of speculation, however, about alternative PR futures whether this dialogic, respectful paradigm will be challenged by a more subject-centred and power-orientated one. The 2004 re-election of a Republican administration in the USA may be a trigger for such a shift.[28]

Several points can be drawn from this short account. The first connects issues management and democracy, and is that issues management can be business lobbying against policies of regulation wanted by an elected government. In this sense, issues management is against the public interest. This critique was stronger when issues management was largely a big-business practice. Today issues management is as likely to be done by an overseas development agency managing the donations and logistics aspects of a famine appeal, or an NHS hospital raising private money, as a big business. This spread of the practice does not solve the difficulty of deciding what is private or public interest, but it dilutes that difficulty in the wider scrutiny brought on by a general public competition of interests in a democracy. For example, anti-business or public interest pressure groups will counter-argue the business case put, and so alert public opinion and government. Moreover, these general circumstances of conflicting powerful interests would have been familiar in 1787 to James Madison, the early US political thinker, for he would have identified them as the 'mischief of faction', i.e. when a dominant interest in an elected public system is likely to overwhelm others. His solution pre-shadowed modern pluralist competition: 'Extend the sphere, and you take in a greater variety of parties and interests; you make it less probable that a majority of the whole will have a common motive to invade the rights of other citizens.'[29]

The second point connects issues management with the status of public relations and its relationship with other work disciplines. Heath and Cousino's article (ibid.) was an implied appeal to US PR people to step outside their traditional communication role and gain new skills in monitoring public policy and developing responsive business strategy. They argue that communication as counter-assertion against critics was inadequate for securing advantage. The work problem for PR people was – and is – that the other skills areas were – and are – already occupied by professionals, such as corporate planners, business strategists and chief executives. Moreover, looked at from the point of view of a managing board, issues management is a large part of their usual agenda. If PR seeks to move into these functional areas, it will invariably have to fight professional 'turf wars'. Professionals may want to 'think outside their box', but to act outside it the necessary conditions of functional free space or occupier tolerance need to obtain. In these ways, issues management raises for PR people questions about what their core skills are. For this author, the answer always lies in communication and closely associated functions such as monitoring and evaluation. Effective issues communication alone is difficult enough for most PR people to master, and it would be professional hubris to colonise further functions before mastery of the core.

Another point connected with issues management will perhaps assuage any professional hurt to PR people caused by concentration rather than expansion. The arrival of stakeholder theory and social responsibility thinking onto business and group agendas means that the PR task is more complex than it was in the 1960s. Pluralism creates many public voices to listen to, and to respond to. PR is the communicative capacity to reply. This messaging and counter-messaging is happening as class and institutional deference declines, as litigation thrives, and as the forensic skills of critics increase. In these quarrelsome circumstances, the case for effective PR strengthens. It is the case for producing the most persuasive voice to defend or promote the interest being represented. It takes considerable skill to enter the marketplace of ideas and data; and to persuade in the face of competing interests, the media, government and the public. Waffle, obfuscation, lies have much less chance of sustained credence than forty years ago. Trust, if it is wanted, comes slowly after a record of truthfulness. In this way, PR today is conducive of at least one public good. The sustained and intense scrutiny by third parties of public wrangling[30] amongst PR voices can produce more accurate fact and truth statements in public life. Heath (1992, p. 20), who writes from a rhetorical perspective about public relations, puts the same point this way: 'Professional communicators have a major voice in the marketplace of ideas – the dialogue in [*sic*] behalf of various self-interests.' He notes that 'voices can lie and appeal to base and unwholesome opinion and motives' (p. 20). How can truth emerge? He writes that 'One answer to this question is that interpretation of facts, soundness of arguments, and accuracy of conclusion can only be hammered out on the anvil of public debate' (p. 20). This faith in wrangling for truth is, however, challenged by Mickey (2003) who brings a critical cultural theory approach to PR texts, asserting that they encode the power relationships to be sustained, rather than messages to be validated.

Note, however, that the subjects of the last few sentences are 'public wrangling amongst PR voices' and '"the anvil of public debate"', and not 'effective PR'. The argument always is that while accurate fact and truth statements may or may not be delivered by PR messages, their accuracy and truth components will invariably only be demonstrated to third parties after competitive public challenges from other messages. Accurate fact and truth statements are a residue of competing PR messages. This idea of truth as a residue connects the competitive PR 'voicing' process with one of J.S. Mill's conditions for truth-through-debate: truth remains after the collision of different opinions.[31] Whether there is a transformative connection of truth statements to power relationships is the sociological question raised by the critical cultural theorists.

Summary

PR in the UK has become more noticeable in the last forty years, and is set to be the most pervasive communication mode in the twenty-first century. It is embedded in liberal democracies with market economies like the UK and is a large part of the public conversation of these societies. It exists both as a professional, management activity and as a portable set of attitudes and techniques for individuals. It is a structured industry serving other industries, a 'cottage industry' done by voluntary bodies and social activists, and 'personal kit' for celebrities and aggrieved individuals. It has grown out of the accelerated civic (values and groups) pluralism and commercial (markets and business) pluralism of the last forty years of twentieth-century Britain. It is the 'voice' of this pluralism.

PR can be (but often is not) a low-cost distribution of information, done before large or small audiences, using specific techniques of display-for-attention-and-advantage. It is done by 'resource-poor' and 'resource-rich' organisations and groups; by local and national voluntary bodies; by interest and cause groups; by public bodies; by businesses of all sizes. PR's most influential client in the UK has been – and still is – business, which has used it as a specialist management function to defend and advance capitalist interests in public policy-making, and in markets to increase the sale of goods and services. There is no organic link between PR and business, just a longstanding and highly successful instrumental one.

PR is part of the UK's promotional culture in which the majority of communications are self-interested: PR always serves the interests of those who deploy it. When dealing with serious opportunities and threats facing them, organisations and groups employ 'issues management', which usually has a strong communications, and therefore, PR element. Because PR serves interests and causes seeking their own ends, its messages may or may not have full, partial (or any) truth statements in them. It is only after public wrangling amongst competing PR messages that any truths in them are most easily identified.

4 PR and propaganda

The previous chapter concluded with the argument that truth in competing PR messages is established through scrutiny by third parties. This process raises many unsettling questions about PR, one of which will be explored in this chapter: the propagandistic nature of its messages. This conclusion is reached after reviewing the academic literature, largely American in the first instance.

The US experience

The argument in *Rethinking PR* (2000b) that PR is weak propaganda is still maintained here. The PR 'voice' speaks propaganda. More precisely, the intention of the PR message producers towards their audiences is to construct messages that are manipulative and propagandistic. They are messages of 'tell' rather than 'say': constructed to get compliance from their audiences. What is more problematic is whether that intention is achieved with the consumers (people as citizens and buyers of goods and services) of those messages.

On balance, the evidence from the academic literature is that the principal[1] use of PR in liberal, market-orientated democracies in the twentieth century has been by big business, in defence of their economic and political interests, and by governments, to maintain power or to promote a social engineering agenda.[2] The major conclusion remains that PR has manipulated public opinion in favour of ideas, values and policies that economic and political elites (some elected) have favoured. The manipulation is a consequence of the following characteristics of historic PR: hidden sourcing of the message at the point of (usually media) publishing; consequent difficulty for PR consumers of knowing intent of message producer; low factual and cognitive content in relation to high emotional content; and one-way communications flow. There has been little scholarly rebuttal of that conclusion.[3] It is indirectly, unscientifically, but powerfully, endorsed by the public's low estimate of PR, which is almost universally sensed to be a device for gaining people's compliance in a way that is less than open or trustworthy. (See Ch. 2.) Overall, therefore, for most of the twentieth century, PR has been an effective, one-way communications resource on behalf of the 'big battalions' in US and UK societies. Lambert noted this over sixty years ago (1938, p. 104): 'The art of public relations is obviously a form of propaganda which flourishes only during a certain stage in the development of liberal capitalist democracy. . . . For the art . . . is essentially part of a method of social leadership by conciliation, manipulation, and diplomacy.'[4]

This conclusion of PR as manipulation and propaganda (terms used interchangeably in this argument) can be aligned with the neo-pluralist perspective of authors such as Dahl (1971, 1982, 1989), Lindblom (1997), Useem (1984) and Vogel (1996) who argue that business in Western democracies is the single most powerful interest facing government, even though businesses are divided on specific issues (Lindblom), and are stronger or weaker over time (Vogel). The business interest in market, capitalist economies is dominant, in the sense of having more power than any other interest, but that dominance is fractured and is under challenge. To maintain its dominance, business uses PR at two levels: via the mass media to maintain support or induce acquiescence for its ideas and values from the general public, and via the private lobbying of government for favourable public policy (Moloney 1996).

The manipulative use of PR has been most identified in the USA, where such usage took hold from the birth of modern PR in the last third of the nineteenth century. Indeed, PR came first into identifiable existence as untruthful exaggeration in press stories and stunts to promote circuses (very successfully that of P.T. Barnum), and when its effectiveness for the ring was recognised, it was taken up as communications to defend US business interests. Harris (1973)[5] provides an account of the 'huckster' period and McElreath (1997) of the business one. The latter records (p. 8) that 'The modern roots of public relations were established in an anti-big-business environment brought on . . . by the "public be damned" attitude of powerful capitalists', an attitude common in the 'robber baron' period at the end of the nineteenth century. Lambert (1938, p. 97) says that PR 'originated in the need felt by "big business" in the USA to overcome its apparently growing unpopularity'. Ellul (1962, p. 225) notes that US PR tended to successfully change the general climate in which people worked, and tended to psychologically integrate with their work. Tedlow (1979) tracks the pioneering use of PR by US business and its peak organisation, the National Association of Manufacturers, for fifty years until 1950. Cutlip (1995, pp. 174–81) dates the first reference to a press agent (for a circus) to 1868, and the first reference to a press clippings agency to 1888. PR was used as propaganda to ward off trade unions, government regulation and to increase sales. Raucher (1968, p. 151) notes, in his history of the US business relationship with PR, that 'The business policy called public relations was primarily initiated as a political device.' Business PR was caused by three factors (pp. 149–57): a defence against Progressive Era politics; a means of promoting economic rationalisation policies via trusts and business alliances; and a managerialist response to a developing mass society that could be reached via PR in the media. Ewen (1996) also sees PR in the service of business interests. He has written a history of US PR as defensive activity by business and conservative interests to control mass public opinion.[6] He notes that before the First World War the major emphasis by public communicators – the political progressives, the muck-rakers, as well as the growing number of PR people – was on facts and reason as the dominant influence on public opinion; after the war, it was on emotion. He stresses (pp. 131–45) the influence of war for this switch of emphasis and how, by 1920, observers had identified the success of the Committee on Public Information (the Creel Committee) in increasing public support for the war. Jackall (1995, p. 392) notes how in eighteen months the Committee organised 75,000 speakers in 5,200 communities to give 755,290 four-minute speeches; issued a daily newspaper with 100,000 circulation; mobilised advertising people, artists, novelists; set up a Bureau of Cartoons as well as censored the press and films for material considered unsupportive of the war effort. Indeed Goldman, for whom PR was 'the most common form of opinion engineering' (1948, Foreword), judged that its PR campaign 'dwarfed anything that American businessmen had ever imagined in its magnitude and its results' (p. 12). Public communicators believed by 1918 that emotion played a more persuasive role in message reception than reason. Ewen quotes Roger Babson, an influential business analyst, as saying in 1921: 'The war taught us the power of propaganda. . . . Now when we have anything to sell to the American people we know how to sell it.'[7]

Many authors (Bernays 1928, Ewen 1996, Goldman 1948, Herman and Chomsky 1988, Jackall 1995, Sproule 1997, Tedlow 1974) have noted the success of the US government, via the Creel Committee, in promoting war through the use of PR and propaganda. US government was later to make PR integral to the dissemination of its policies and to become a major producer. Mattelart and Mattelart (1998, p. 27) note the use of PR people (information officers, photographers, films) by the Roosevelt administrations in the 1930s: 'The Roosevelt administration aimed to mobilise public opinion in favour of the welfare state in order to bring the country out of the Depression. Opinion polls were created as tools for day-to-day management of public affairs.' Pratkanis and Aronson (1992, p. 225) note that in 1936 the Roosevelt administration employed 146 full-time and 124 part-time publicity agents who issued 7 million copies of 48,000 press releases. Pimlott (1951, p. 95) remarks on the federal government's use of PR in the New Deal, calling it 'official publicity or more bluntly, govern-mental propaganda' and judging (p. 100) the mass media as willing partners with official information services. Lee (2005) describes the life of the first permanent public relations agency in the federal government in 1941, the Office of Government Reports. Its functions were twofold – to disseminate information and report to the President (Roosevelt) on public opinion. It was closed down in 1946 and its functions disappeared from public view until 1969 when President Nixon set up an Office of Communications in the White House. Snow (2003) argues that contemporary US governments continue to use PR, advertising and marketing techniques, and to co-opt willing journalists in an 'information war' against terrorism. Richards (2004) argues that this promotional push should be seen in the context of a globalised struggle for symbolic resonance and moral authority in which governmental actors are competing with the communicative campaigns of hostiles, the most dramatic of which are the events of terrorists and their murder videos. The Public Diplomacy section of the State Department in 2003, under the former head of the J. Walter Thompson advertising agency, undertook 'the biggest public relations effort in the history of United States foreign policy . . . to show the United States to the world as a tolerant and open society' (Snow 2003, pp. 24–5). Democrats in the US Congress called the 'open society' part of that description into question, at least inside the country, in February 2005 when they accused the Bush administration of 'covert PR' amounting to domestic propaganda when they alleged that it paid journalists to promote a certain policy.[8]

This government/PR connection is in line with the opinion of Habermas (1989) who notes the negative effects on the public sphere of involvement by an interventionist state. He argues that the social welfare state and business together diminished the public sphere. They have, in his memorable phrase, 're-feudalised' it: these elites present pre-determined opinion to the public when once it was the public who formed opinion. As argued above, the interventionist state continues in the USA, readily using PR.[9] Dartnell (1996, p. 291) estimates that US business is regulated by 116 government agencies and programmes, and that it is represented by 500 PR firms and 3,000 trade associations in Washington, DC. One of these firms, Hill and Knowlton, was shown to be involved in false stories about Iraqi troops removing 312 babies from incubators in Kuwait in October 1990, just before US involvement in the Gulf War. McNair (1995, p. 185) calls this 'public relations of the type frequently used in wartime – what is sometimes referred to as "black propaganda"'. Snow also notes the long inter-connection between US promotional industries and government overseas interests: 'The United States has a one-hundred-year history of marrying commerce with politics and tapping public relations to "brand" America abroad' (p. 25).

Cutlip (1995) traces these linkages back to the founding of the US state. In his history of PR, he starts the first chapter titled 'Hype for colonies, colleges and the frontier' with

> Utilization of publicity and press agentry to promote causes, tout land ventures, and raise funds is older than the nation itself. In fact, the US talent for promotion can be traced back to the first settlements on the East coast in the 16th century.

He uses the terms 'public relations' and 'propaganda' interchangeably throughout his first three chapters which deal with the colonial and then the revolutionary foundations of the USA. His Chapter 3 (pp. 34–51) is about the ratification in the newly independent country of its constitution: the title is 'Greatest public relations work ever done'. It starts with the sentence 'The power of propaganda to mobilize public opinion was relied on heavily in the history-making campaign to ratify the United States Constitution in 1778–9.' He ends the chapter with 'But truly, winning ratification of the United States Constitution was "the greatest public relations work ever done".' He writes that 'The exaggerated claims that often characterise publicity' began then in the USA. Many immigrants came from Europe in response to them (p. 2). The channels for publicity by colonists and their London backers were: advertisements in newspapers; press releases; pamphlets; favourable sermons; the staged event (an Indian chief was brought to London in 1734, p. 8.); poetry competition in *The Gentleman's Magazine* in 1735 (p. 8); and charity fundraising (for a school in Virginia, p. 10). Cutlip talks of all this as propaganda creating 'high, unrealistic expectations' (p. 9).

From the perspective of a history of ideas, US PR grew up into its modern shape, fearing a breakdown of social order brought about by the strengthening of democracy. Central to this was a conservative concern that the masses were 'getting into the saddle' and the bourgeois elites were losing control. Labour unions worried conservatives from the 1880s onwards. Cutlip (1995, pp. 204–5) describes the violence against organised labour and notes how PR was – is – used against them: 'Much of public relations history . . . is woven into this unending struggle between employer and employee that today is fought with publicists, not Pinkertons.' Bernays was aware of this mood, shared it (Tye 1998, pp. 91–111) and was noted for it. Lasswell (1927, p. 2) wrote about Bernays that he was a member of a 'new propaganda, or publicity, profession'. Gustave Le Bon (1896, *The Crowd: A Study of the Popular Mind*) thought that the human unconscious was a significant motivator of action and that the unconscious was converted into a civilising process in the hands of elites, but that mass democracies threatened this civilising power of the superior few. The masses were the 'crowd'; Sighele (1898, *Psychology of Sects*) wrote of its suggestibility, and of less psychological self-control of people in collective movements. Wallas (1908, *Human Nature in Politics*) wrote to challenge what he called the intellectualist fallacy which asserted that reason played a major role in politics. He argued that politics consisted largely of the creation of opinion by the deliberate exploitation of subconscious, non-rational inference. Trotter (1916, *The Instincts of the Herd in Peace and War*) put emphasis on instinct as a human motivator. Lippmann (1922, *Public Opinion*) doubted the involvement by a mass democracy in the rational debate needed to form policy and direct a government; instead the governing elite should use symbolic systems such as film to persuade.

Carey (1995, pp. 80–4) includes Lasswell in this conservative pessimism. He quotes Lasswell's entry in the 1934 *Encyclopedia of the Social Sciences* to the effect that 'the one means of mass mobilisation which is cheaper than violence, bribery or other possible control techniques' is propaganda. It was essential in a democracy because 'men are often poor judges of their own interest'. Mattelart and Mattelart also note (1998, pp. 26–7) that Lasswell regarded propaganda as necessary for 'governmental management of opinion'.

> For Lasswell, propaganda was henceforth synonymous with democracy, since it was the only way to generate the support of the masses. Moreover, it was more economical than violence, corruption or other comparable techniques for government. Since it was a mere instrument, it was neither more or less moral than 'the crank of a water pump'. It could be used for good or ill.

The media was useful for 'circulating effective symbols' to a passive audience.

Bernays and Ivy Lee

Edward Bernays (1892–1995) and Ivy Lee (1877–1934) are widely regarded as the two founders of modern public relations – but both are embarrassing nominations for modern PR people. Bernays was influenced by his uncle Sigmund Freud, by the new emphasis on mass psychology as a social control technique, and by his work for the Creel Committee. Sproule (1997, p. 18) says that he associated PR with propaganda after the end of the First World War. Bernays's second book was *Propaganda* (1928). Today the readers of such a title would expect a critique: in Bernays they find praise.[10] The first chapter is entitled 'Organising chaos' and opens with these two sentences:

> The conscious and intelligent manipulation of the organised habits and opinions of the masses is an important element in democratic society. Those who manipulate this unseen mechanism of society constitute an invisible government which is the ruling power of our country.

He has a caution about the misuses of this manipulation, but this caution is subordinated to its contribution to 'orderly life' (p. 12) and he ends positively: 'Propaganda will never die out. Intelligent men must realise that propaganda is the modern instrument by which they can fight for productive ends to bring order out of chaos.' Bernays maintained these views until at least the 1980s.[11]

This consistency, while irritating other contemporary PR people who sought respectability for their trade, would perhaps have earned a smidgin of admiration from a 1929 critic. An *Inquiry* magazine review of Bernays's book *Propaganda* observed 'that we should be a whole lot better off if all propaganda were offered undisguised – that is, with full revelation of the promoting interests' (see Olasky 1984). Emphasis on the reduction of social 'chaos' was the theme of his first book, *Crystallizing Public Opinion* (1923). Bernays refers to Lippmann's influential *Public Opinion* (1922) and notes (p. 38) that 'the significant revolution of our modern times is not industrial or economic or political but the revolution which is taking place in the art of creating consent among the governed'. He takes from Lippmann at least two foundational ideas for his PR philosophy. The first is Lippmann's new concept of stereotype as the basis for influencing public opinion; the second is how Lippmann's 'pseudo environment' (human nature plus social conditions) and 'pseudo facts' concepts (pp. 15–29) can be actively used to influence people.

By managing stereotypes through news creation, Bernays writes that the public relations counsellor 'is the pleader to the public of a point of view' (p. 57). The counsellor must represent the public to his client and vice versa, must understand how public opinion is formed and maintained (p. 76). He must understand social psychology and, in particular, stereotypes (p. 99), which are the mental phenomena used by people in the formation of public opinion, because the PR counsellor works through them (p. 162). This counsellor creates news (p. 171) to strengthen, weaken or amend stereotypes. They include categories of people (capitalist, boy scout, chorus girl, woman lawyer, politician, detective, financier (p. 98)), slogans (President Theodore Roosevelt's 'square deal' (p. 163)) and visuals (the US flag).

Bernays was comfortable with these social psychological processes: he was practised in recognising and harnessing them, and his pioneering talent was to relate them into a body of PR knowledge. He moulded them into 'an art applied to a science' and used them for clients in commerce and in politics, these two fields combining as when he lobbied Washington in 1951 on behalf of the United Fruit Company against a Guatemalan president with land reform policies.[12] The processes were subsumed into the larger one of propaganda, which is 'a purposeful, directed effort to overcome censorship – the censorship of the group mind and the herd reaction' (p. 122). In this way, he appears to make PR a sub-set of propaganda, which was a larger and positive societal process of manipulation; propaganda makes for order through the promotion of 'good' ideas, values, events, people. The 'good' is not defined but the implication is that that which serves order in society is 'good'. Tye (1998, pp. 264–5) concludes that Bernays refined PR to make it become more effective in creating consent, sometimes for benign purposes, but that he remains 'a role model for propagandists'. Finally and in terms of the history of ideas, the role of the PR person described by Bernays is reminiscent of Gramsci's 'organic intellectual' whose task was to build support for 'progressive' causes in a 'war of positions' against opposing interests. Cassidy (1992) is explicit about the Gramscian connection in the case of social movements and their media relations.

At the same time (after the First World War), the psychologistic basis of PR was also being emphasised by Ivy Lee, often named as the other founder of modern PR. Ewen (1996) reports Lee saying in 1921 that 'publicity is essentially a matter of mass psychology. We must remember that people are guided more by sentiment than by mind' (p. 132). Later that year in a lecture on PR at Columbia University's School of Journalism, he invited his audience (p. 132) to 'come down and let us show you our library, see the extraordinary collection of books on psychology, all the elements that go into the making of crowd psychology, mass psychology'. He added: 'You must study human emotions and all the factors that move people, that persuade men in any line of human activity. Psychology, mob psychology, is one of the important factors that underlay this whole business' (p. 132). Lee was not alone in his reference to the emotional for Snow (2003, p. 25) quotes Goebbels, the Nazi propagandist, as saying that 'There is no need for propaganda to be rich in intellectual content.'

Lee's contribution to PR development was earlier than Bernays but is not so much referred to as Bernays's who wrote fifteen books.[13] Lee is credited with urging leading US capitalists, known to political critics as 'robber barons' in the last quarter of the nineteenth century, to be more communicative about their businesses. He was successful in this to the level of more open PR, but there is doubt about his influence in opening up core business functions such as production planning and pricing to any public scrutiny. More of a legacy was his usage of press releases and conferences, providing more rather than less information, and listening to press and public opinion rather than dismissing it. His *Declaration of Principles* put it as 'All our work is done in the open' (Hiebert 1966, p. 48). Before Lee, it was 'the public be damned'; afterwards, it was 'the public be informed'. Hiebert in his sympathetic biography of Lee details this technical contribution, but regrets the company Lee had to keep. He writes (p. 316): that 'less ethical contemporaries used his techniques to create an image as a façade to cover the truth' and editorialises that 'much that parades under the title of public relations today is nineteenth century press agentry in bankers' clothing', and 'as a result Ivy Lee and his present day counterparts while serving a useful function in society still suffer from a widely held and deep-seated suspicion of being fixers, propagandists and ghost thinkers' (p. 317).

The more generous judgements about Lee and Bernays can also be made about contemporary, conscientious PR people. Both these foundational figures served their principals well, were sought out but claimed more than they could deliver. Their contribution to relations between the public and business was at the technical level of more efficient PR. Tedlow (1979, p. 201) in his survey of US business PR concludes that 'This pattern of essentially peripheral influence of PR can be traced down to the Watergate scandal' and that PR people 'who have self-consciously set about to reform their employers as the first order of business . . . most likely met with failure more often than success'.

Today few PR people or writers would enthuse about the closeness of the propaganda/PR relationship and there is an unspoken but palpable feeling that Bernays, particularly because of his literary legacy, is an embarrassment. So is Lee, for shortly after Hitler came to power in 1933, he worked for the German Dye Trust to improve US–German relations. He met senior Nazis including Hitler (Hiebert 1966, p. 288), which led to the charge that he was a Nazi sympathiser. At the same time, Bernays was told over dinner by a journalist witness that his book *Crystallizing Public Opinion* was in the library of Goebbels.[14] But the intellectual climate was moving against Bernays and Lee. The cultural and political mood towards propaganda was changing. There was a growing rejection of propaganda as acceptable communication and the rejection was sourced in the European and US experience of the rise of fascist dictatorships in the 1920s and 1930s, and then, later, of the Cold War from the late 1940s to 1989. These experiences stripped away any positive connotation from the idea and practices of propaganda (and, by implication, of any communicative manipulation). Propaganda came to be perceived as the practice of Nazis and communists, anti-democrats, oppressors and murderers. That Western governments practised – and practise – propaganda, at least against their external enemies, is another reason for disassociation.

In the light of this historical experience, PR had no future by the 1960s as a popular, accepted concept, or practice, or business in liberal, democratic societies if it was defined as linked to propaganda and manipulation.[15] Whether the connections between PR and propaganda are organic or not, what is clear from this retrospection on the age of Bernays and Lee is how time gives its own gloss to ideas about PR.

Habermas and other critics

This is no fracture of the PR/propaganda link for Habermas. He (1962, pp. 193–6), in his historical analysis of the development of liberal public opinion and of the 'public sphere' concept (a rational, disinterested public opinion, accessible to all citizens), argues that PR was publicity to advance the political interests of business (see also Carey 1995, Ewen 1996, Raucher 1968, Tedlow 1974) as advertising was publicity to advance its market interests. As such it was outside the public sphere and a negative influence on it. He notes the contribution of Bernays and equates PR with opinion management done through stressing public interests and de-emphasising, if not hiding, private business ones. He thought pro-business PR was US in origin and came to Europe after 1945, dominating the public sphere.[16] PR managers insert specially designed material into the mass media and create events to gain its attention. It is a form of social engineering done with communications to gain the consent of public opinion for capitalist interests. If historically and conceptually, the public sphere was a notional space where there was universal access to rational, disinterested debate about matters important to liberal societies, PR was one development to politicise that space in favour of business interests, and to corrupt it by, in Habermas's phrase, 're-feudalisation', i.e. the substantial exclusion of the public from public policy-making, but its apparent involvement through the device of 'demonstrative publicity'.[17]

Habermas further theorised on the public sphere concept in *Between Facts and Norms* (1996) and is more explicit about PR than in his 1962 text, but without any diminution of his critique. He regards 'mass media and large agencies' as the most conspicuous elements in a public sphere. They are 'observed by market and opinion research, and inundated by public relations work, propaganda, advertising of political parties and groups' (p. 367). This description develops Habermas's 1962 position, for it admits a role for public relations inside the public sphere, albeit still negative. Social actors in a public sphere include 'Journalists, publicity agents, and members of the press' and they 'collect information, make decisions about the selection and presentations of "programs" and to a certain extent control the entry of topics, contributions, and authors in [a] mass-media-dominated public sphere' (p. 376). 'These official producers of information are all the more successful the more they rely on trained personnel' (pp. 376–7). These more explicit references to PR propaganda in Habermas's later work correspond with the rise of the modern European PR industry. Holub (1991, p. 6) also critiques PR, the mass media and party politics as negative factors in the late twentieth century that put the disinterested exchange of ideas under threat. Webster (1995, p. 101) argues that PR is degrading the public sphere because it disguises its sources and is not disinterested.

Herman and Chomsky (1988) posit a 'propaganda model' to describe the behaviour of the US mass media, which serves the interests of social and political elites by the 'manufacture of consent'. They note the influence of Lippmann's view that propaganda is 'a regular organ of popular government'. They used case studies to show that various 'filters' (including PR material supplied by business and government, and PR people as 'flaks' disciplining journalists) leave only 'the cleansed residue fit to print' (p. 2) in the media. Gandy (1982) developed the idea of the supply of PR material by 'the modern public relations firm' on behalf of 'those with economic power' to the media into the concept of 'information subsidy' (p. 64). The media accept the material because it reduces their publishing and broadcasting costs. PR 'plays the central role in the design and implementation of information subsidy efforts by major policy actors' and about this subsidy, he says that 'the source and source's self-interest is skilfully hidden' (ibid.).

The most robust restatement of the 'manufacturing consent' thesis is by Stauber and Rampton (1995, pp. 205–6) who note that 'PR campaigns do not invite individuals to become actors on their own behalf but treat them as a targeted, passive audience' and that positive uses of PR 'do not in any way mitigate the undemocratic power of the multi-billion dollar PR industry to manipulate and propagandise on behalf of wealthy special interests, dominating debate, discussion and decision-making'.

Herman and Chomsky (1988), Gandy (1982) and Stauber and Rampton (1995) are identified with US liberal scholarship. From the conservative tradition, there is the argument of Olasky (1987) who declares that he writes from a pro-business stance for 'political conservatives and libertarians' (Preface) to warn, *inter alia*, that corporate PR is 'designed to minimise competition through creation of a government–business partnership supposedly in the public interest'. He calls this corporate collaborationism.

Carey (1995) associates PR with what he calls 'corporate propaganda': it is about 'taking the risk out of democracy' – the risk to big business. 'Commercial advertising and public relations are the forms of propaganda common to a democracy' (p. 14). Corporate propaganda has two objectives: to identify free enterprise with 'every cherished value', and to identify interventionist government and strong trade unions 'with tyranny, oppression and even subversion' (p. 18). He identifies what he called grassroots and treetop propaganda – the latter aimed at other, non-business leaders of society (p. 88). Carey argues that after 1900, when the reputation of US business was low, public relations was used by business more; he observes the careers of Lee and Bernays.

Raucher (1968) notes that the Ford motor company in the same period, the early twentieth century, was doing 'regularised press relations'; had a customer and dealer magazine *Ford Times* from 1908; used film, exhibitions, factory tours and car-racing before the First World War. 'All these activities might have been called PR, but they were not. Ford did not establish a public relations department until the 1940s' (p. x). The President of the Chicago and Alton Railroad suggested, while discussing 'proper relations between railways and their patrons', that publicity could eliminate complaints by revealing the problems the company faced (p. 33). Raucher notes (p. 6) that 'publicity' referred in the early twentieth century in the USA to advertising and press agentry, and to any activity that made information public. The title 'public relations' was not used in the name of the company generally considered to be the first, independent PR agency, which operated in Boston, New York and Chicago from 1900 for about ten years: its founder called it 'Publicity Bureau' (pp. 11–15). Its founder George Michaelis is unlikely to have heard of 'public relations'. He wanted to distinguish himself from an advertising agency and cast around for a proper descriptor: 'publicity expert', 'specialist in relations with customers' and 'corporation advisers' were all used to describe a service run in part by ex-journalists for 'collecting factual information about clients for distribution to newspapers' (p. 13). Michaelis, however, had some attitudes that PR people will recognise today. He saw the value of promoting publicly that he employed high-status people, e.g. Harvard graduates, and that he had high-status clients, e.g. he was a fundraiser for Harvard University. The latter adopted behaviour that some modern PR people will recognise: they would not pay the fees billed. Another educational institution client – MIT – did. It was new; of much lower status than Harvard, and needed the exposure.

Raucher (pp. 7–11) illustrates the operational development of early PR through a career sketch of the man identified as an early example of the modern corporate and marketing press officer for a manufacturing company. Ernest H. Heinrichs worked for Westinghouse from November 1889 and worked there until at least 1914. He appeared to be called 'press agent' or 'advertising agent for the Westinghouse concerns' rather than 'public relations officer'. The company was headed by George Westinghouse who developed the alternating current distribution of electricity. He felt he was losing a sales and promotional battle with the Edison company who developed the direct current distribution. Heinrichs was instructed by his boss to release the achievements of the company to the press '"because the truth hurts nobody" . . . but misleading, garbled statements invariably do, and I want you to prevent misrepresentation whenever you can'. Heinrichs was known as The Baron to Pittsburgh newspapers.

Carey (1995, p. 88) argues that there was another stage of manipulative PR development in the Depression of the 1930s when business used both violence against workers and 'a protective screen of public relations activities' in their industrial relations. After the Second World War, there was also a shift to more PR in the USA (pp. 26–7). Carey's references are mostly to US and Australian PR, and in the introduction Lohrey, his editor, writes: 'As an Australian politician for almost fourteen years I have had direct experience of the methods by which government reactively and continually place business interests before public interests.' He introduces the negative concept of 'democratic propaganda'. Earlier, Pimlott (1951, pp. 206–7) had picked up on the connection between business and PR. Fones-Wolff (1994, pp. 5–6) notes that the process continued after the Second World War.

> At the national level, business organisations like the Advertising Council and the National Association of Manufacturers orchestrated multi-million dollar . . . campaigns that relied on newspapers, magazines, radio and later television to re-educate the public in the principles and benefits of the American economic system.

Marston (1963), the author of an early US textbook, writes, however (p. 308), in a section headed 'Government public relations efforts propaganda' (*sic*): '[Governments] have needed to keep their own citizens happy through internal information, or propaganda.'

Tedlow (1979) concludes that PR is corporate propaganda after his review of its use by US business. 'Scholars from various disciplines have discerned a movement away from physical force to persuasion as the chief method of social control in twentieth-century America. Public relations can be seen as part of this movement' (p. 202). Marchand (1998) is explicit. He tracks the use of PR by US business between 1900 and 1950 to legitimise itself in the face of the various charges of monopoly, size, remoteness, profiteering and social irresponsibility. He quotes (p. 82) a PR man at AT&T, one of the first businesses to be PR active, in the early 1920s as saying that he aspired

> to make the people understand and love the company. Not merely be consciously dependent on it – not merely regard it as a necessity – not merely to take it for granted – but to love it – to hold real affection for it.

Packard (1981, 2nd edn, pp. 177–8) notes that PR people were 'mind moulding' on behalf of business, alongside the 'Hidden Persuaders' of the advertising industry. Sproule (1997) classifies PR as propaganda in his review of the latter's relationship with US democracy. He uses the phrases 'mind managers', 'engineered persuasion' and 'opinion engineering' without quotation marks when he writes of propaganda. Gloag (1959, pp. 142–3) classifies PR as a 'technical operation of increasing importance in democracies'. He takes Ivy Lee's definition of PR as publicity (including advertising) for an idea or institution and concludes that 'Once the idea . . . is launched, it moves like a snowball rolling downhill, gathering weight and volume.' Korten (1995) notes the close connections between business, PR and a 'corporate-dominated' media, while Nelson (1992) chronicles the use of PR firms by global businesses to protect their markets and open new ones. Miller (1999a, p. 2) in her study of Hill and Knowlton argues that generally 'recent histories of post war opinion management have overestimated the power of public relations' but she concludes (p. 194) the agency's 'campaigns affected the general public but mostly by affecting its own clients and people who already thought like they did'. Mallinson (1996, p. 10) notes the rise of modern PR in the USA, evolving from a press agent function 'with an element of propaganda' to a form of mass marketing. To some PR people, however, corporate propaganda is an obligation. Robert Dilenschneider (1999), a former CEO at Hill and Knowlton, writes in a newsletter for business communicators: that 'it is incumbent on business to sell aggressively the benefits of capitalism – to workers, at least – because the system is sure to be attacked'.[18] The PR people in the public sector also see the virtues of selling: 'Liz Hurley knows exactly how to sell herself and the NHS [National Health Service] should do the same.'[19]

The Grunigian paradigm

Standing outside this succession of authors who were either PR professionals or academics from other disciplines is the US scholar James

Grunig.[20] He is the most influential thinker about PR since Bernays. He inherited, by way of public perception and conceptual construct, the linkage of PR to propaganda, a linkage powerfully theorised by Bernays in *Crystallizing Public Opinion* (1923) and *Propaganda* (1928). Grunig and Hunt's (1984) four-part typology was a historically sensitive and conceptually nimble rejection of that link, and it is still the principal basis of the contemporary academic and operational paradigm about PR.[21] It does, however, involve the admission that much PR is propagandistic. Their model equates PR with this quality in its press agentry, public information campaign and two-way asymmetrical forms, all three of which they classify as asymmetrical PR. Grunig later wrote that 'such a mindset [the asymmetrical] defines public relations as the use of communication to manipulate publics for the benefit of the organisation. "Persuade" is a softer word often substituted for "manipulate" but changing the word does not change the mindset' (1989, p. 18). More recently (Grunig *et al.* 2002, p. 312), Grunig has clarified his position by saying that persuasion has always been part of the two-way symmetrical model, and that persuasion is not rejected as long as it is symmetrical (p. 316). This sensitivity towards the concept of persuasion is often found in modern PR thinking and the source is persuasion's approximity with its 'black sheep cousin' propaganda.[22] Grunig and White acknowledge (1992, pp. 38–42) that asymmetrical PR 'steers' towards 'unethical, socially irresponsible and ineffective actions', and that it 'has dominated' the practice of PR. Elsewhere Grunig (1992c)[23] equates press agentry with propaganda. Grunig and Hunt, however, break the link with manipulation and propaganda by going on to posit a symmetrical PR that is two-way, balanced, dialogic communication and that is respectful of its public. 'We estimate that about 15% of all organisations today use the two-way symmetric model', and they are mostly big businesses regulated by government (Grunig and Hunt 1984, p. 26). The two-way asymmetric model is, therefore, widely practised. Miller (1999a, p. 27) notes about Hill and Knowlton, probably the most famous/infamous PR agency, that it 'did not seek the role of mediator between conflicting groups, instead privileging one point of view, that of the client'. The asymmetric is also still written about: see Saffir (2000) who says in his *Power Public Relations* that his subject is the 'aggressive engineering of perception' (p. xiii).[24] Austin and Pinkleton (2001, pp. 280–1) write about the consequence of this strained attitude to persuasion thus: 'After a long discussion of the importance of symmetrical practices and social responsibility, students of public relations often worry that engaging in persuasion somehow is unethical.' The consequence is that the Grunigian paradigm has come to have an asymmetrical relationship to persuasion, associating it with PR that is not 'excellent'. This contemporary approach, however, is at odds with some pre-1980s attitudes towards the PR–persuasion link. Marston (1963, p. 3) writes, for example, that the 'really important key word' in his definition of PR is persuasion and that PR people are part of the 'family' of persuaders, alongside lawyers, clergymen, school superintendents, salesmen and politicians. Price (1992) observes PR as persuasive social communication and describes it in relation to public opinion. He notes how political organisations and parties can 'communicate elite opinions downwards, serving as channels for informing, persuading, and activating members of the attentive public' (p. 77); and how decisions relying on public opinion 'are made through publicity and communication, but communication is just as much a tool for persuasion as for information gathering and as potentially useful for managing opinions as for soliciting them' (p. 91). Writing immediately after the Second World War, Merton (1946, p. 38) also sees these social communications as persuasive but detects two 'technical' differences from propaganda: they have more social interaction between persuader and persuadee, and they are more flexible in reacting to the case made against them than propaganda.

The rhetorical approach to understanding PR is a competitor to the Grunigian paradigm, but not so well established in the UK. It focuses on the symbolic exchange of words and visuals in PR messages sent out by organisations and groups to promote their interests in the political economy and civil society in order to analyse their meanings, their ethics and their effects. (See Toth 1992, pp. 3–17.) Such a focus is not the one adopted here. Instead, the rhetorical focus is secondary to it in the following way. The power relationships between the organisations and groups in the political economy and civil society, and with government, as expressed in politics and markets, and as scrutinised by media and public opinion are the primary focus for understanding why and how PR is produced. The starting point of this analysis is not the meanings and effects of symbolic exchange. It is the power relationships that generate these exchanges. If the Grunigian paradigm concentrates on the symmetries of organisational relationships for analysing PR, and the rhetorical approach privileges symbolic exchange between entities, the preferred concentration here is on power distributions among PR producers and consumers, and those observing their messaging.

PR intentions versus public compliance

So far this chapter has concentrated on the production side of PR and noted that the academic literature outside of PR (and some thinking inside it) judges that the intentions of public relations are propagandistic. The focus now switches to the consumption side of PR and how citizens and buyers of goods and services react to its messages. Do PR consumers in a liberal democracy such as the UK and USA comply with the intentions of the PR producers? This is a highly problematical question about which no clear conclusion is offered as the evidence is confused. Instead answers are tentative at the conceptual and empirical levels, and are in the form of inferences and speculations.

At the level of a review of the US PR academic literature, there is little extended discussion of the question for most of the scholarship focuses on PR production, not PR consumption. Some writers above suggest a clear PR production/PR consumer compliance effect about the work of the Creel Committee (Ewen 1996, Jackall 1995, Goldman 1948) but there is little data offered about compliance with New Deal PR and with capitalist propaganda. Karen Miller (1999a, p. 190) in her biography of the career of John Hill, the founder of the influential Hill and Knowlton agency, judges that 'Influencing public discourse and opinion proved the most difficult, for people were not unthinking recipients of H&K's messages.' The agency's influence was to reinforce existing opinion favouring its messages by sympathetic framing (p. 35) and release of persuasive information (p. 27).

In the matter of British government domestic propaganda after the Second World War victory in 1945, Crofts (1989) judges that some of the campaigns clearly did not win over working-class people. The 'information war' on terror following the Twin Towers attack in September 2001 is too contemporaneous for more than a first judgement but Snow (2003) infers compliance.

At the level of context, to continue discussing the production–compliance linkage without reference to pluralism and the mass media would be myopic. As argued in Chapter 3, modern PR has been expressive of a social context (accelerated pluralism) since the 1960s while much of the literature reviewed concerns earlier periods. In those periods, US and UK societies were pluralistic (e.g. trade unions, competing confessional churches, suffragettes) but to a much lesser degree. This puts the contemporary propagandistic production of PR in the following context; modern PR messages are subject to greater scrutiny in an increasing pluralism of interests and their propagandistic intentions (where known) meet with greater challenge in the media and in politics from competing interests. As a consequence, a better educated, more media-literate public may be less compliant than their parents' and grandparents' generations. In support of this proposition, it is possible to find groups of people who appear to want to consume PR propaganda, e.g. supporters of sports clubs, activists in political parties, members of fan clubs and readers of fanzines. Heath and Bryant (2000, p. 172) note that people seek out circumstances in which they know they will be subject to persuasion, and that, as well as agreeing, 'Persuadees ignore, resist and refute messages with which they disagree. They can be dynamic and may distort messages through selective perception, interpretation, and retention.' In a liberal democracy, such persuadees inhabit a social system that opens strong possibilities of non-compliance and communicative civic resistance; yet it is also an environment that encourages PR propaganda, a communicative mode designed to reduce the chances of non-compliance.

Any reflection on the context of PR production/consumption immediately throws up the complexity of ideas, emotions and circumstances involved. War, for example, engages so many feelings in a citizenry (fear, patriotism, idealism, deprivation) that tracking the impact of PR propaganda on the sources of those feelings is for the highest level of historiography and beyond the reach of this thesis. The First World War was, in the slogan of the time, 'the war to end all wars'. Could compliance with Creel PR propaganda generate a utopian hope? Did PR propaganda help President Wilson gain diplomatic support for the League of Nations, predecessor of the United Nations? President Franklyn D. Roosevelt presented the New Deal to the US people during the 1930s Great Depression. The PR propaganda came after his first election, but before and after his second and third victories at the polls. Were the policies promoted by PR already voted for by the majority of US voters? Given these complexities, it is not safe to go beyond a conclusion that PR production was – and still is – one powerful conditioning factor in the development of compliance and non-compliance by the public with beliefs, values, behaviours and policies promoted by dominant or subordinate interests in a liberal democracy.

At the normative level, the question of compliance with PR propaganda starts with a conversation about relationships between democracy and propaganda. Is the relationship a neutral, positive or negative one for democracy? What are the benefits and costs for society? (See Chs 6 and 7.)

Summary

This chapter looks at the nature of PR messages, and argues that they are propagandistic. This conclusion is reached after reviewing the US academic literature (and, in the next chapter, the UK experience of PR). This demonstrates that PR has been manipulative communications to promote business interests generally and certain federal government policies.

US PR grew up in an intellectual climate pessimistic about mass democracy's influence on public affairs. Its first use was to defend 'robber baron' US capitalism. It was then deployed effectively by the federal government in support of the First World War and of the New Deal. It became associated with 'corporate propaganda' and mass psychology as social control. Its US pioneers (Bernays and Lee) were supportive of these uses and saw PR's linkage with propaganda positively. However, after the US experience of the fascist regimes between 1919 and 1941, and of the Cold War with communism after 1945, PR had no future as a publicly acceptable activity in a liberal democracy unless the conceptual link with propaganda was fractured. That fracture was achieved conceptually by Grunig and Hunt in 1984.

Turning to the consumers (citizens and goods/services buyers) of PR propaganda, the question of their compliance is highly problematical. No clear answer is available but the role of PR as a conditioning factor in compliance is admitted, along with a likelihood that compliance is less in the accelerating pluralism since the 1960s.

The next chapter looks at the UK experience and Chapters 6 and 7 at the relationship between PR/propaganda and democracy.

5   PR propaganda in the UK

This chapter continues looking at PR as propaganda for the interests of its producers, but particularly from the UK perspective. Although Simmons (1991) has argued railways in Britain were doing what we call PR from the mid-Victorian period (lobbying, setting up an industry representative body,[1] talking to the press), it is generally held that the UK PR industry is younger than the US, getting established in the 1920s. Whether that is right or wrong, it is clear that early influential PR people[2] in the UK, all of whom were associated with either business, government or official bodies, viewed their work in a similar light to their US colleagues. They saw PR propagandistically: it was controlled communication for their goals of commercial, social and political management.

These senior PR people in the 1920s and 1930s sought control through communicating reassurance about the stability and progress of the UK when the country was facing economic depression, radical social change and turbulence in its foreign relations. These challenges included mass unemployment, an adult population with a nearly universal franchise, organised working-class interests, a growing welfare state, and a popular press and radio with national audiences. Like their US counterparts, they were aware of the very active use of propaganda by the totalitarian regimes of Mussolini, Hitler and Stalin; unlike them, they were concerned about their country's declining power in the world. They wanted to manage internally a public opinion, which was no longer made up of just the respectable middle classes and the aspiring working class, but of the great mass of working people as well. It was the unknown and perhaps uncontrollable power of a new, empowered mass public opinion that worried them.

They believed stability and continuity would come through 'education', information and positive feelings delivered by their propaganda, a term with mostly positive connotations until the 1930s and which increasingly gave way to PR.[3] They sought to project a confident and prosperous UK through the Empire Marketing Board and the British Council. PR for them was mass communication of official messages via newspapers, the BBC, advertisements and posters, lecture tours, exhibitions and conferences, and other events involving direct contact with the public. They were more likely to call their work 'publicity', 'propaganda' or 'public education' than 'public relations', a term that was largely unknown in the 1920s.[4] As time passed and the term 'propaganda' took on totalitarian connotations through its association with fascists and communists, 'public relations' was used more.

These early UK PR people would have welcomed what Deacon and Golding (1994, p. 4) later called 'the public relations state', government as active persuader of its citizens.[5] The idea of the modern state and mass persuasion are intertwined. Many PR people helped to build that state as they built up PR. Harrison notes (1995, p. 20) that 'the history of public relations in Britain, largely based on work done to explain government policies or promote government-backed bodies and services, reflects the public information, propaganda and persuasion phases' of PR development. This was PR as social engineering. L'Etang (1998) shows that the Institute of Public Administration, founded in 1922, saw PR as a means of communicating to the public growing state provision of social welfare, and as a means of feedback about public opinion. The National Association of Local Government Officers shared similar views about the link between PR, service provision and public opinion. They also saw that it was a means of enhancing their own work status. Black (1989, p. 200) believes that 'the first stirrings of organised public relations were probably the efforts made by the Insurance Commission in 1912' to explain the new concept of national insurance. It involved presenters going around the country telling employees and employers what national insurance was (Gillman 1978). There was a housing information office in the Health Ministry in 1922 (ibid.) and by 1939 'virtually every department in Whitehall has accepted publicity and/or public relations as a legitimate part of its functions' (Grant 1994, p. 248). Harrison (1996, p. 20) reports that, after the Second World War, many former government information officers started up in PR and advertising. Tim Traverse-Healy, one of the founders in 1948 of the then-Institute of Public Relations,[6] confirms this. He notes how the reforming post-war Labour Government (1945–51) believed that public relations was an aid to social improvement because it publicised to the whole nation the benefits of the new welfare state and nationalised industries.[7]

Grant also notes (p. 252) that the previous, minority Labour government of 1929–31 'were willing to use publicity' in the form of public information campaigns by pamphlets, lectures and meetings to further policy. Pimlott (1951) notes that the 1945–51 Labour government used PR to promote its social and economic reforms. Manning (1998) reports that Ernest Bevin as Minister of Labour in the 1940–5 wartime coalition government encouraged contact by his staff with labour and industrial correspondents because he wanted 'to utilise the press in his campaign to suppress industrial militancy in the coalfields' (quoting Bullock 1967, pp. 300–1). The phrase 'public relations state' – the publicity seeking state

(Deacon and Golding 1994, p. 4) – succinctly catches the readiness of modern UK governments to use mass persuasion for policy implementation, an example being the distribution of an advice booklet to the 25 million households in the UK in 2004 on how to react to emergencies.[8]

Public information campaigns by government, however, raise concerns for democracy. The campaigns range from the largely uncontroversial (e.g. anti-smoking, banning mobile-phone-use-while-driving campaigns) to topics still in political contention (e.g. more involvement with the European Union). They may be considered overwhelmingly beneficial – as in drink-driving or in breast screening – or highly controversial – as in signing the proposed European constitution; in all cases, it is their one-sided presentation, their national dimension, the difficulty of mounting any large-scale counter to them, and the fact that the government is the most powerful public communicator in the land that are causes of concern. They are conviction communications by the state, with no hint of the 'other' case to be made.[9] Their scale of public funding is also contentious: the UK government was criticised by political opponents when its £62 million advertising spend for the first three months of 2001 was up 157 per cent on the same period a year before, and was double that of the largest private sector spender.[10] The figures exclude any PR, and marketing expenditure, and thus understate public expenditure. Some of the delivery channels for public information are also an issue. Government advice on reading skills for illiterate adults has been inserted into the scripts of popular soap operas such as *Eastenders* and *Brookside*. Such insertion is a frequent[11] and a historic activity. After Second World War battles in the Atlantic against U-boats to keep the UK supplied with food, it was national policy by all governments to make the country self-sufficient. To this end, the Ministry of Food and Fisheries in the 1950s supplied the BBC radio programme *The Archers* with information designed to promote self-sufficiency.[12] Literacy and farming advice are benign but the principle of inserting official messages into entertainment in an unsourced way raises questions about how audiences are viewed and whether they are treated with the respect due in a democracy. Dozier *et al.* (2001, pp. 231–47) share these concerns and argue that respect for the audience returns if two-way symmetry is used in the mass delivery of public information: 'public communication campaigns need to shift away from engineering consent and towards more flexible goals and objectives that are negotiated in good faith with target populations'. Referendums are preceded by public information campaigns, and regulations on the conduct of the latter introduced in 2000 indicate recognition of their benefits and costs.[13]

Early PR in the UK

After the First World War, the UK was a less violent, more class-stratified, deferential, centralised, poorer country than the USA, but it was exhausted after four years of machine-age war, unsure of its world role. The UK political economy was enfeebled: that of the USA emboldened. The context for doing PR was different, even if the response of senior PR people was similar. In overseas politics, the UK's relative power was declining and two policy initiatives were framed to achieve their goals through PR. The first was the Empire Marketing Board (EMB) set up to promote trade with the colonies and the Commonwealth after the UK had failed to introduce preferential tariffs, and to make UK citizens more 'Empire Aware'. It was headed by Sir Stephen Tallents, a major figure in the development of PR in the UK. He wrote *The Projection of England* (1932), a pamphlet arguing (pp. 12–13) that England was under threat from other powers and must counter this by establishing supremacy in a 'new and complicated art – the art of national projection'. He lists 'national institutions and virtues' for projection, and examples include the monarchy, the navy, the London underground, a reputation for disinterestedness, a reputation for quality. The list is the 'standing raw material of England's esteem in the world'. He writes (p. 11) that 'today a people is known to its fellows' by cable, printing press, airwaves and screen, and must use these communications 'which science has provided for the projection of national personality'; that 'projection is world-wide' (p. 22); and communications media to include international exhibitions (p. 34). There is a need for a school of national projection (p. 41) with some official status that searches out material 'which can be turned to the advantage of England'; which seeks out opportunities to use such material; and which co-operates with BBC, press and news agencies. The school would have a centre for press liaison, cinema workshop and exhibition design centre (p. 43). National projection is likened to 'public liturgies' (p. 47). He takes up a modern PR theme when he writes (p. 47) that everyone in an organisation or group is involved with its PR – 'every customs official or porter' who gives good service to overseas visitors are national projectors and 'are adding thereby a trifle to England's invisible exports and winning for her if it be but a bit a mite of the world's good opinion'.

Tallents wrote as a concerned English patriot; he made England the object of projection, yet addressed his forty-eight pages to 'my fellow citizens of the UK in Scotland, Wales and Northern Ireland'. He was calling for several outcomes that today would be known as cultural diplomacy, public diplomacy, destination branding, national propaganda, diplomatic PR. Tallents also wrote as a British establishment figure. Here is the start of the biographical note about him in an 1958 guide of the then IPR:

> Sir Stephen Tallents, KCMG, CB, CBE, during a varied career in the Government Service first became concerned with PR work in 1926 as Secretary of the Empire Marketing Board (EMB). He was afterwards PRO to the General Post Office, and Controller (PR) at the British Broadcasting Corporation.

Tallents was the first president of the then-IPR in 1948. Another author developing PR theory was J.H. Brebner who in 1949 was one of the first UK practitioners to write about PR techniques. He drew a distinction between PR for small and large audiences, stating that both were specialisms which started 'as an attitude of mind, a way of regarding and approaching other people. Anyone who in his dealings with other people takes pains to listen well, understand well, and explain well, is putting himself into this attitude' (p. 7). He worked for the Post Office, the wartime Ministry of Information and later for the newly nationalised transport industries, and this suggests that he had PR for state bodies in mind as he developed his theory and practice.

Both Brabner and Tallents were professional progressives, wanting to promote British interests and institutions through the latest technology and techniques. Tallents saw film documentaries as such, and encouraged John Grierson and the nascent film documentary movement at the EMB and later at the General Post Office (GPO). The EMB staged exhibitions as part of a marketing strategy to increase consumer awareness of imports from the British Empire, and it was among the first to use the technique of indirect promotion for a product, i.e. it promoted pineapples by displaying tropical landscape, not the fruit.[14] The second policy initiative was the British Council, set up in 1934 after the failure of the EMB, with a wider 'soft' diplomacy remit. It started work when the European dictators Mussolini, Hitler and Stalin were building up totalitarian states. The Council was a sympathetic base from which to operate conventional PR techniques such as news management, and what later became known as corporate identity creation, arts promotion and event management.

Inside the UK, PR was taken up by many leading commercial bodies, both private and state. Lambert noted sixty years ago (1940, p. 178) that government departments and public utilities were also early users. In the private sector, Editorial Services was the first PR agency in the UK and was set up in 1924 to service growing demand. By 1933, it had handled 400 accounts, including home ownership for the Halifax Building Society. The Gas, Light and Coke company, later the North Thames Gas Board, developed the 'Mr Therm' marketing campaign in the 1930s. During this period, London Transport was active in the creation of its corporate identity through the famous underground map, posters, station design and carriage furniture. Earlier in 1902, another railway had played a pioneering role: the Great Central Railway appointed a media relations officer, though not with that title, who reported to the general manager (Simmons 1991, p. 267).[15] Southern Railways had a PR officer in 1925 and John Elliot was the first to bear that title in the UK. He had been a reporter for the *New York Mail* and came across PR there when he wanted information about the subway. He had to contact a public relations officer named I.V. Lee. The Southern, under Elliot, promoted its electrification programme through active media campaigns and by 1939 had gone on to use – if not initiate – techniques corporate and marketing PR professionals employ today: corporate advertising; a customer relations magazine; branding products (engines and whole trains) with logos and names; a distinctive station architecture; interior design of carriages; signage co-ordinated by colour and typeface; and lobbying (Moloney and Harrison 2004). The BBC had a controller of public relations in the inter-war years (Sir Stephen Tallents, previously with EMB, from 1935) and one of its famous voices, the wartime reporter Godfrey Talbot, who later became the first court correspondent, joined the BBC as press officer for the northern region in 1937.[16] ICI, British Overseas Airways Corporation (now British Airways) and the Port of London Authority made similar appointments. The GPO, which had a public information campaign in 1854 (Gillman 1978)[17] made many films, including the famous *Night Mail*. Shell Mex was also active in films and in branded visual design for its publications encouraging car-based tourism. L'Etang (1999, p. 15) shows for how long documentary film was seen as an effective PR technique. She quotes from one edition of the trade magazine *Public Relations* as an indication of the industry's attitude in the 1950s and 1960s towards film: '[t]he documentary uses its money to do a job of public relations and instruction'. PR people also noted after the Second World War how their skills could be employed 'as advocates on behalf of business' in the ideological battle over nationalisation of industries (L'Etang 2004b, p. 85).

As in the USA after the work of the Creel Committee in the First World War, in the UK the propaganda work done in the Second World War gave a strong impetus to the growth of PR. L'Etang (1998, p. 433) records how in 1945 there 'was no dismantling of the Ministry of Information but a transformation to the Central Office of Information'. Writing at the time Williams (1946, p. 130) argues:[18]

> An intelligent democracy must be prepared to make the fullest use of every available method of informing its citizens of what is essentially their business. Information is a weapon of democracy. But to refuse to use it is to turn one's back on one of the ways in which the enormously complicated business of modern government can be made comprehensible to the ordinary person. There cannot be public control without public understanding.

These comments are perhaps understandable from a journalist turned propagandist for the Ministry of Information during the Second World War, but it is nonetheless the language of social engineering, propaganda and guided democracy: the mind-sets of war were being transferred to civilian government. Few PR people with official status would go so far as Stephen Jolly, Master of the Guild of Public Relations Practitioners in the UK, and say that 'modern PR is born out of military propaganda after World War II' and that 'the use of force and the resort to spreading falsehoods are all that distinguish PR from military propaganda'.[19] Williams also writes (pp. 77–84) about 'the Growth of "Public Relations"' from the 1930s to post-1945 and in that description he makes no distinction between propaganda and PR. Kisch (1964, p. 92) makes the same elision, calling the Ministry of Information 'an instrument of state public relations'. Crofts (1989) provides an extended case study of what he called the Labour government's domestic propaganda between 1945–50 (see p. 67 below). He notes (pp. 250–5) that no previous UK government had allocated 'so great a proportion of its resources to the task of informing and cajoling its citizens'. The wartime propaganda machinery was only disbanded in March 1946 and was replaced by the Central Office of Information. Labour propagandised because it wanted to avoid coercion to achieve its economic goals of a positive trade balance, full employment and low inflation. It chose to persuade via propaganda and used conventional PR techniques such as media relations, corporate advertisements, film, lectures, talks, booklets and exhibitions (p. 13). Franklin (1998), in his analysis of news management by the first New Labour government (1997–2001), notes a centralised information policy controlled by Downing Street, and changes to personnel, who were 'expected to be more energetic in pushing the government agenda' with the result that 'the fourth estate risks being overrun by a "fifth estate" of public relations and press officers' (p. 4). Modern government PR people are indeed powerful and they have testimonials to their influence from unexpected sources. The revolutionary Irish leader de Valera is quoted as saying: 'Any government that desires to hold power in Ireland should put publicity before all' (Coogan 1993, p. 362). He went on to found his own newspaper group[20] in 1931 and it had an open link with the political party he led. He became prime minister in 1932.[21]

By the 1950s, relatively obscure firms used PR actively. Steelmakers Samuel Fox used film, as did Dexion in the form of employee communications to reassure workers about moving to factories in the new, unknown 'garden suburb' town of Hemel Hempstead. More prominent firms had been PR productive since before 1939: Anglo-Iranian Oil (predecessor to BP); Imperial Airways (forerunner of British Airways); ICI; Rootes cars; and the corner-house restaurants of J. Lyons. By the 1960s Shell had 200 people in its PR department. Outside of commerce, PR was well established in local government through the efforts of the officers' trade union and through encouragement from the learned body in the field. The London County Council and its successor the Greater London Council were noticeably active in PR. As local government delivered many planning, hygiene, leisure and regulatory services to the UK population, PR allowed message delivery and feedback from the public. Kisch (1964) binds these private and public sector uses of PR together into the judgement that both are the mostly hidden communications networks of big business and government. His case studies include the anti-nationalisation pressure group Aims of Industry; the defence of the oil industry; defence of the

British Empire in Africa; and laying the ground for commercial television companies. He saw PR as the communications aspect of the establishment defending and extending its interests.

A UK context

What marked out the early stage of British PR (up to the 1960s) was how it was a response to particularly British needs. In the first place, it was used overseas to strengthen the weakening UK and Empire international trade position, and to bolster British influence via cultural activities when fascist and communist ideologies were growing. Second, it was a communicative response to the expanding provision of social services. Moreover, it was associated with cultural productions that are still appreciated today. It encouraged a new art form, the film documentary, for its own motivational and educational purposes, and it promoted good visual and graphic designs, in what are now considered to be classics.[22] What it shared with US usage was patronage by business and government interests who thought of propaganda as socially purposive and legitimate, and who saw PR as inextricably linked to it.

Some literature throws a light on UK matters. PR propaganda as manipulation is discussed by Michie (1998). As a PR man, his book *Invisible Persuaders* is important in the UK literature: he admits that PR does social harm. He quotes (p. 4) a spin doctor: 'PR is very much an invisible art and it doesn't serve our purpose to reveal how much we manipulate journalists and the public.' The US author Saffir (2000, p. 304) concurs: 'The less the public knows about public relations techniques, the better they work. Another reason for soft peddling PR's real power is the fear of backlash.' A letter writer to Britain's *PRWeek* makes the same point about marketing PR: 'The most effective weapon in a marketer's armoury is now the accurately delivered message that lands at the heart of the editorial material so many assume is impartial.'[23] These are public admissions that are rare, if not unique, and few PR people are like Michie and take a balanced view of costs and benefits.[24] About this balance, he asks (p. 69):

> But what happens when [PR's] vigilance to protect [companies] against disaster and [PR's] positive policy steering turn into a campaign to distort the truth? What about companies which, in the face of environmental and political sensitivities, use PR for altogether more evasive purposes? It is in this quagmire that PR becomes an instrument of perversity and deception.

He turns to this question after making the case for socially beneficial PR: that PR puts information into the public domain and is a precondition for informed choice in a democracy (p. 57). He is critical (pp. 57–8) when 'a company really does only *act* according to the public interest, giving the appearance of heeding concerns and expectations rather than genuinely doing so'. He adds: 'In such circumstances, PR becomes the means by which the wool is pulled over the public's eyes, the propaganda by which a company's profits and power are protected.' He believes this propagandistic PR is more likely to happen in 'broader corporate PR' outside of take-over battles for companies and outside of PR about financial matters. He draws attention (pp. 81–92) to the PR called 'greenwashing', which he describes as 'the process whereby a company, rather than earning a good reputation, buys one. It can involve anything from simple window-dressing to undertaking a much more fundamental shift in opinions towards issues and industries.' It is 'one of the most pernicious uses of public relations'. His description is a wide one, covering changes in both marketing tactics and corporate strategy. The examples Michie gives are critical of chemical, oil and tobacco companies, car makers and nuclear energy producers. His examples include a campaign to change public attitudes against environmental groups; setting up apparently independent advisory boards; commissioning research from sympathetic scientists and academics; and funding an anti-green writer. Michie argues that these activities amount to a corporate 'green backlash' against the environment movement. Gabriel and Lang (1995, p. 136) make a similar point about corporate behaviour, but in their case towards staff and consumers, when, in the early 1990s recession, 'neither the employees' jobs nor the overall product quality matters as much as the maintenance of an effective image and an intensified public relations exercise to keep the confidence of shareholders and fund managers'.

Alistair McAlpine (1997), a UK businessman and political activist, goes beyond noting deception by PR. He urges it on the 'image twitchers' (his soubriquet for PR people): 'By using half-truths and convenient words, the image twitcher's job is to make certain that the world knows that the employer is well armed' (p. 154). The political journalist Nicholas Jones (1999, p. 11) writes about the miners' strike in 1984–5 as 'textbook example of media manipulation' by non-industry interests.

As in the USA, the historic, principal use of PR in the UK has been the manipulation of information by PR producers to alter thinking and behaviour in their interests. Robins *et al.* (1987, p. 16) nominate PR as one of the 'active persuasion industries', along with advertising, in nation states of late capitalism where information management is 'inherently totalitarian'. PR is certainly an active persuasion industry; indeed the argument here is that it is a propaganda producer. But even if the judgement that the intention of its producers is 'inherently totalitarian' is not challenged, that view comes up against the complex questions of compliance by PR consumers (see Ch. 4, p. 55). Miller and Dinan (2000) analyse the role of PR in bringing about the 'tilt to the market' through privatisation and deregulation policies for the UK economy in the period 1979–89, noting that 'the PR consultancy industry in Britain has acted largely for business interests and has had a key role in ensuring the success of particular types of business activity' (p. 29). Crofts (1989) is one of the few authors to offer evidence of non-compliance and his view is a caution against a premature judgement that PR effects – as opposed to intentions – are totalitarian, or effective in any sense. His study of British government propaganda after 1945 shows that many official information campaigns had mixed success; e.g. the 'work or want' one alienated working-class support while the job recruitment campaign for the Lancashire cotton industry was successful. Many people recognised propaganda and rejected it unless it fitted with their own predispositions. Other factors also worked against the government: counter-propaganda – e.g. the British Housewives' League; the Opposition in Parliament and the country; the size of COI and departmental publicity budgets; the uninspirational character of official campaigns. About the latter, Crofts notes (pp. 243–9) that the UK's financial dependency on the USA meant that the British government could not enthuse its own voters with appeals to democratic socialism. Crofts concludes (p. 252): 'It has not been possible to find any causal connection between these campaigns and the attitudes and behaviour of those segments of the population at whom the recruitment and production propaganda was directed.'

More evidence of resistance to official propaganda/PR comes from the 'no' vote by Danes in 2000 to joining the Euro. The losing 'yes' campaign had the following support: 70 per cent of Parliament; 98 per cent of business; nearly all trade union; and forty-six out of forty-eight media outlets.[25] Resistance to propaganda also takes the form of reluctance to admitting producing it. Taylor (2002, p. 437) notes that spokespersons for democratic governments have always been nervous about having their work described as propaganda, which is 'something which other, usually more unscrupulous, people do whereas they merely communicate "factual information" and "tell the truth"'. The chair of the 1993 CIPR working party on redefining PR wrote (Newman 1993) that 'Our working party discovered that there were good historical reasons for the professional body to seek comfortable notions like "mutual understanding" and to avoid ideas of management and persuasion' (p. 12). The Institute wanted to distance itself from the fears caused by Packard's book *The Hidden Persuaders* (1981), and from Bernays's ideas on engineering consent. 'It was also frightened of being associated with propaganda' (p. 13).

PR as propaganda

Most academics writing about PR, including influential modern PR academics, and some non-academic writers (Bernays, Carey, Doob, Crofts, Ellul, Ewen, Gandy, Goldman, Grunig, Habermas, Hawthorn, Herman and Chomsky, Hiebert, Jackall, Jefkins and Yadin, Kisch, Korten, Kunczik, Lambert, Lasswell, McAlpine, McNair,[26] Marchand, Michie, Miller, D., Miller, D. and Dinan. W., Miller, K., Moore, Nelson, Olasky, Robins *et al.*,

Pimlott, Salter, Stauber and Rampton, Tedlow,[27] Tye), conclude that PR has been manipulative communication in the very great majority of its practice, or they have conflated it with propaganda. A senior British PR man notes the elision: 'For what is perceived as propaganda by some is labelled public relations by others. Some commentators see no distinctions between the two as to purpose or practice.'[28] Parsons (2004) in a guide to PR ethics notes conflation: 'In the name of strategic persuasion, public relations practitioners have, over the years, resorted to a variety of techniques that hover on the border between persuasion and blatant propaganda, or between the truth and lying by omission' (p. 105). In her history of British public relations, L'Etang (2004b) is nuanced in her judgement about distinctions. She notes that, until 1955, the 'concepts' of PR and propaganda 'were still being used interchangeably and apparently unproblematically in the IPR journal' (p. 82). She judges (p. 14) that generally PR academics do not engage in 'conceptual discussion about propaganda' except as PR's pre-history, and that therefore 'academic public relations has acted to support the public relations professional agenda rather than to analyse what is clearly a fundamental espistemological and moral issue'. The same equivocation is found in *The Encyclopedia of Public Relations* (Heath 2005, p. 656) where the propaganda entry ends with difficulties of separation: 'It [propaganda] often blends seamlessly with legitimate public relations practices, and it is highly likely that this trend will continue into the foreseeable future.'

Bernays in his memoirs (1965, p. 294) observed that in 200 years the meaning of propaganda had turned completely negative. But he still wrote about his 1928 text *Propaganda*: 'In this book I called public relations the new propaganda and expanded the thesis of *Crystallizing Public Opinion* [1923]'. The last paragraph of *Propaganda* (p. 159) finishes with the judgement that 'Propaganda will never die out.' Less prophetically, Moore (1996, pp. 79–97) argues that 'public relations is fouled up with propaganda: it ranges over the ground between compulsion and free persuasion'. It becomes propaganda, he believes, when it is imperative in tone, offers no alternative facts or views and is formulaic. Grant (1994, p. 11) has the phrase 'tampering with the human will' when considering propaganda. Jefkins and Yadin (1998, p. 12) appear confused about the relationship. They say of PR, advertising and propaganda that 'The lines of distinction are sometimes too fine to distinguish' and on the same page that PR and propaganda 'could not be more different'. Ten years earlier, however, Jefkins, who was one of the first and most popular of UK textbook authors on PR, gave the reason for the distinction: 'The popular belief that public relations is a form of propaganda nullifies its purpose and destroys its credibility' (see Traverse-Healy 1988, p. 10). Traverse-Healy also reports (p. 11) that White, a distinguished British PR academic, 'argues that . . . propaganda and public relations activities are essentially the same in nature and in their use of information and that both can be misused'. Only Grunig has offered a developmental model for transformation towards a propaganda-free PR. All but one of these authors (Crofts) sees the PR/propaganda relationship to be a negative or problematic association.

There has been little literature refuting the elision of PR and propaganda, which is embarrassing to most PR people on the few occasions when they philosophically talk of their work. The topic is, moreover, avoided by the great majority of PR writers.[29] The Americans Kruckeberg and Starck (1988) note that the historiography of PR in the USA is under-developed: in the UK it has only just started. Mostly, they argue, the development of PR is treated as the Whigs treated history: a progressive evolution to better times. They cite the views of the respected PR authors Aronoff and Baskin (1983) that PR evolves through three stages: manipulation, information, and mutual influence and understanding. 'Significantly, they note that while the stages generally have been sequential all three have coexisted from the beginning' (p. 8). They conclude that 'it would be grossly unfair to paint a picture of public relations today as consisting of hucksterism and propaganda as it was often practiced in the past. Yet, to many people, the distinction would be blurred' (p. 7). Evolution of the two terms is also shown in a comparison of usage over time. Compare two quotations, published forty-one years apart. Albig writes in 1939 (p. 289): 'In America, propaganda has accompanied each great mass movement. In the agitation preceding the Revolutionary War, a number of propagandists, notably Sam Adams, were effective inciters to revolution.' McKinnon *et al.* write in 2001 (p. 557) on 'Political Power through Public Relations' and say 'Since the birth of American democracy, public relations practices have played a key role in shaping our politics. . . . Samuel Adams organised committees of news correspondents to disseminate anti-British information throughout the colonies.' That respectful tone towards PR is still heard today: a prominent US public relations counsellor writes 'This is a profession rooted in the history of this country. . . . Public relations has played an essential role in . . . [the] democratic process, which is now reaching people worldwide.'[30]

The critical writers about PR generally develop their conclusion of manipulation or propaganda without precise definitions of these phenomena, relying instead on their structural analysis of unequal power in the political economy and/or on their experience of PR. The alternative methodological approach is via definitions. Some of these illustrate the date of their origin by including activities today conventionally argued not to be propaganda, i.e. advertising and PR. For Lasswell (1934, pp. 13–14) 'Propaganda in the broadest sense is the technique of influencing human action by the manipulation of representations by words, pictures and music' and 'Both advertising and publicity fall within the field of propaganda.' Albig (1939, p. 285) cites Lumley's definition, which characterises propaganda as a cluster of attributes centring on hidden promotion as regards sources, interests involved and methods used, with 'the results accruing to the victims'. Jowett and O'Donnell (1992, p. 4) define propaganda[31] as 'the deliberate and systematic attempt to shape perceptions, manipulate cognitions and direct behaviour to achieve a response that furthers the desired intent of the propagandist'. They posit propaganda as an extreme form of one-way communications imposing attitudinal, cognitive and behavioural outcomes on people. O'Shaughnessy (1996) lists characteristics of propaganda as bias,[32] intent to influence, high-pressure advocacy, simplification and exaggeration, ideological purpose, avoidance of argumentative exchange, and reluctance to give and take views.

On these definitions, PR, past and present, has been – and is – either a component of the larger propaganda phenomenon or equates with it. For definitions with origins in the twentieth-century US and UK history of ideas, propaganda was mostly interpreted until the 1930s as a positive or, at least, a neutral social phenomenon; but less so with each decade. An influential UK witness to the positive nature of propaganda was the documentary film-maker and social commentator John Grierson who did much of his work between the wars. Grant (1994, p.18) notes how he saw propaganda in a positive way as an empowering, educative agent that increases citizens' knowledge and decision-making capacity in a democracy. Gloag (1959, pp. 142–50) does not write of PR as propaganda but he takes a directive, top-down view of 'this technique of opinion-moulding'. He says that 'More things must now be explained to people who . . . make goods and consume them, and upon whose skill and industry a country's prosperity ultimately depends.' During the Second World War, urging patience on people as a patriotic duty 'became one of the function of public relations'. The academic Crofts takes a sophisticated view about the PR and propaganda relationship (see p. 64 above). In his 1989 study of British domestic propaganda, 1945–50, he uses the term in its historically earlier sense of propagating ideas and beliefs (p. 12): the pejorative overtones are 'not intended in this history'. He understands it to mean any attempt by government or other organisation to create, or to maintain, states of mind conducive to a required end. He notes that governments prefer the term 'information services' (ibid.). 'Information' (ibid.) is a component of propaganda; is a selection of facts and hopefully the truth but rarely the whole truth. He quotes an anonymous other: '"Public relations?" Don't be fooled by the grandiose title: it is simply propaganda in a dinner jacket' (ibid.).

There is, however, a qualification to the PR and propaganda identity. Propaganda is fired by its makers, so to speak, as 'the magic bullet' of communications in three strengths. Jowett and O'Donnell (1992, p. 8) make a typology of propaganda that allows such a differentiation. Propaganda is 'white' where its source is known and the information is accurate: the examples given are the Voice of America radio network and the BBC overseas. It is 'black' where it is credited to a false source, is misinformation, passes on lies and deceptions, and is based on emotion alone. Cold War propaganda is an example. In between, there is 'grey' propaganda. On this shading, PR is 'white' or 'grey' propaganda and will be described here as 'weak' propaganda.

Grierson's positive attitude to propaganda was linked to his progressive politics and was in competition with another, more pessimistic, view of UK society after the First World War. This pessimism reflected the conservative US intellectual climate of the same time.[33] For conservatives, propaganda was a negative phenomenon because it leads, through the susceptibility of the common people, to the 'herd instinct', and because, in the wrong hands, it also leads to loss of control by elites. Both positive and negative approaches were understandable in the 1920s and 1930s when the meaning of the term was in transition; both permitted their proponents to use propaganda – one to further a progressive ideology, while the other to sustain a conservative one. The word's positive connotation, however, was first undermined by the success, ironically, of UK and US official propaganda campaigns at home and abroad in favour of the First World War (1914–18). If governments could propagandise successfully in wartime, they and other interests could do the same in peacetime. Later, the sight of totalitarian propaganda suborning debate and public opinion in fascist and communist regimes finally relieved the word of positive meaning. Taylor (1999, p. 66–7) noted its growing negativity, and that with the rise of the Soviet Union and Fascist Italy there was 'This growing association of "propaganda" with falsehood and the manipulation of opinion.' He reports – perhaps wryly – that after 1918 it had been seen retrospectively as the 'fifth arm of defence' of Britain in the First World War and that the British were regarded as good at it, but that they were rather precious about their reputation: 'What other nations were doing may have been propaganda but the British told the truth.'[34]

Positive attitudes to propaganda, like Grierson's, informed – and still inform – many public information campaigns. It is hard to mount a sustained critique of the 'Drink More Milk' campaigns of the 1920s and 1930s as a threat to liberty (Grant 1994, pp. 194–224). The motivation behind these particular campaigns was an amalgam of many influences, including Whitehall departmental self-interest and dairy trade politics, but it did include a health education concern about low nutritional levels among the population. Taylor (1999) argues that modern campaigns are propaganda (pp. 243–4) where they benefit the source as much as or more so than the audience and gives anti-smoking and drink-driving ones as examples. He notes, more broadly, that advertising 'has become the acceptable propaganda of late twentieth century free market enterprise democracies' and it is done openly for gain. People are thus more tolerant of it than political propaganda, 'which is why the latter seeks euphemistic aliases such as "political advertising", "information policy", and . . . "spin doctoring"'.

In these ways, public campaigns have to be seen in terms of the political and social discourses of their times when official pronouncements were authoritarian in tone, and education and literacy levels were lower than today. One-way communications with the public were the norm. People were not expected to speak back. The 1960s saw the end of such silence and deference by the public; since then, while the urge to propagandise remains strong in elites and in government, compliance with propagandistic messages by the public in the social environment of accelerated pluralism is much more in doubt. Where the propagandistic intention is evident as in advertising, people are aware and then wary.

Thus the term 'public relations' replaced 'propaganda' in the UK and USA as the popular descriptor for persuasive mass communications, excluding advertising. What has dogged PR people and theoreticians ever since, however, is whether the semantic substitution reflected a change of meaning and practice. Is PR re-badged propaganda? PR people want the two concepts and practices to be different. Indeed sometimes they want the difference so very much that the strength of their wish makes their language propagandistic: 'Public relations is different to propaganda. We must see that these distinctions are understood by all.'[35]

Summary

This chapter continues to look at PR propaganda by business and government, this time in the UK. Modern PR has been established in Britain for at least eighty years and its early, influential founders shared the same fear of social change as their more established US colleagues, and the same resort to manipulative PR as social control. Propaganda still carried positive connotations in the 1920s and 1930s but these were turning negative throughout the period after its use by US and UK governments in the First World War; and then by fascist and communist states up to 1939. PR is shaped by the political economy in which it is found and early UK PR was influenced by specifically British circumstances. It was a public communications system able to tell the population about new national state services; it often took the form of filmic, visual and graphic work, some of which is still appreciated today; it was market support for large, prestigious businesses, state commercial bodies and Empire countries. It was used to promote trade and diplomatic policies overseas by projecting a positive identity of the UK. It was very much official and establishment communications.

Overall, PR in the USA and UK has been, and still is, manipulative communications, or weak propaganda – more 'ordering' and 'telling' than 'listening' and 'talking', with a selection of supportive facts and some appeals to emotion in the message, presented many times without the source being identified. Three sources of evidence confirm this conclusion: the academic literature looked at in this and the previous chapter; the current PR paradigm that classifies much PR as propaganda (Ch. 4); and its low reputation with public opinion as self-advantaging communications by others to be treated with caution by recipients (Ch. 2).

6   Can PR and democracy co-exist?

If public relations messages are both propaganda and the 'voices' of interests competing over material, ideological and reputational advantage in a market, capitalist, liberal democracy, how does PR relate to democracy? After examining in the last two chapters the relationships of public relations to interest groups, pluralism and propaganda, the focus now shifts to PR and forms of government. Such a focus is important for at least two reasons. First, it is a common critique of PR that it diminishes democracy; second, people in liberal democracies often offer as a primary definition of themselves that they are democrats. Thus how PR touches democracy strongly affects perceptions about it by citizens. It is not good public relations for public relations to be dismissed as a threat to democracy.

Combining the words 'public relations' and 'democracy' positively is an extremely rare word coupling and only seen by this author in the title of Davis's book (2002), and as a mention in some US textbooks that make the linkage through pluralism. The addition of 'propaganda' to the combination, in other than a negative manner, has not been written about by other authors, maybe for the good reason that the three concepts (PR, democracy, propaganda) cannot be demonstrated to co-exist in either a beneficial way, or in a neutral way.[1] Thus it may be concluded that in theory democracy excludes PR and propaganda. There are, however, reasons why the relationship (democracy to PR propaganda both as theory and as practice) has to be argued out and observed, regardless of the consequences for PR's reputation. Indeed this book rests on the assumption that the most important question about PR is its relationship with democracy.

The first reason for looking at the relationship is the evidence that the spread of the apparatus of democracy (universal adult franchise, elections and secret ballots) is not inconsistent with public relations practice. The development of a fuller British democracy in the twentieth century has happened alongside a developing PR practice since the 1920s. The use of this early PR before the 1960s by dominant business (L'Etang 2004a, pp. 351–2) and by political interests, both reforming and conservative (Crofts 1989; Cockett 1989) has not stopped the delivery of the important public goods of national and civic freedom, health, education, welfare provision and equality rights to the British people. PR flourishes in other liberal democracies such as the USA, Canada, Australia, New Zealand, Japan; in the countries of Western Europe, and increasingly of Eastern Europe; and of South and Southeast Asia. There is evidence of PR practice in China as it marketises its economy, and cautiously grants more individual freedoms. In the UK, it has quickened its pace of development in the last twenty years with new aspects – celebrity culture; corporate branding; social responsibility programmes, issues and crisis management, and corporate reputation management. PR effects, the consequences of PR, appear at least not to diminish existing democratic forms.

The second reason is the pervasiveness of PR. The citizen, the consumer, is surrounded by it; and is either aware or not. The concerned democrat has to take note and account for the pervasiveness and the varying levels of awareness. The third reason for exploring the relationship is that the pervasiveness of PR makes it easier to see its weaknesses: its often invisible sourcing; the easy access to it by dominant forces (big businesses, governments, political parties, royalty); its biased selection of facts buttressed with emotional appeals; its insistent tone of 'telling' rather than 'saying'; its listening in order to 'tell' more effectively; its conviction that it is 'right'. It would, however, be an inadequate response just to 'lament' the 'PR turn' and pass on. PR is too much part of our promotional culture for that to be intellectually acceptable at both the level of ideas and of evidence. There is, moreover, a traditional and longstanding response by PR's professional and trade bodies to the PR propaganda/democracy link. It is that PR increases mutual understanding and goodwill in society by communicating to publics, and so implicitly helps democracy, though this extension to democracy is rarely, if ever, made explicit in the UK.

This response is rejected here as an idealism that cannot be sustained conceptually and about which the evidence is extremely thin. It is a foundational, 'article of faith' position for thinking PR loyalists, and a psychological comfort for the great majority of PR producers. Instead the link argued here is that PR as the 'voice' of rival interests competing for advantage is a form of public communication consistent with liberal democracy. It is not argued that PR is a necessary condition for democracy or that there is a conceptual equality between PR propaganda and democracy. The latter position would be a confusion of categories for PR is a promotional mode that appears to be consistent with a form of government characterised by public debate, and by elections with universal suffrage. Seeing PR as either a condition for democracy or as democratic communication in action are maximal positions about the relationship that veer towards over-theorising and idealism. It is not, however, argued here that there is a negative correlation between PR propaganda and democracy where the existence of more of the first means less presence of the second. Such a mutual exclusion could not explain the pervasiveness of PR in modern liberal democracies, nor how historically in the UK and USA there has been a growth of PR in the last century, and more evidence of democracy. Instead what is presented here is two forms of co-existence: PR propaganda and a type of democracy surviving together (neutral co-existence) without benefit to democracy; and PR/propaganda producing benefits for that democracy (beneficial co-existence).

PR and democracy in neutral co-existence

Before examining PR propaganda in a neutral relationship with democracy, it is necessary to look at types of democracy, and then its components. Posner (2003) sets out two ideal types of democracy – a deliberative, Athenian and idealised category, and a representative, pragmatic, elitist one. He gives identifying characteristics of the two models when he sets out (p. 156) that in deliberative democracy 'people think and debate and vote as citizens' compared with the 'everyday politics of horse trades and interest groups' in representative democracy. He notes (p. 194) that the first category is a co-operative model and the second is competitive, and this distinction follows from his economistic model of politics as a market analogy with political parties and governments 'selling' policies to voters who 'buy' some rather than others with their votes in elections. Posner draws out a further consequence of the representative model (p. 189) with the statement that 'In economics as in political markets, the buyer does not design the product: he chooses from a menu presented to him by sellers.' The argument here rests on a representative model of democracy where parties and governments have policies and take actions that are responses to the particular interests in the civil society and the economy which they (parties/governments) want to represent at any particular time. These parties/governments are obligated by constitutional law and culture to seek this representative role through the approval of a plurality of votes cast in secret ballots. Such a model sits well with the idea of PR as the 'voice' of competing interests in an economic and value pluralism. While, for some of the time, these 'voices' are talking to each other, the rest of the time they are talking to government (as lobbyists) so that government will represent their interests through favourable policy and action. Interests have to draw the attention of governments (through PR 'voice') to their preferences while governments (and parties) are deciding which interests to represent through policy and action.

An example is the announcement of a campaign by the Food Standards Agency (FSA) in September 2004 to reduce salt consumption by the UK population, and the immediate challenge to it from the Salt Manufacturers' Association (SMA). Both sides used media and websites for 'voice'. The FSA launched a campaign around Sid the Slug under the slogan 'Too Much Salt Is Bad for Your Heart'. A supermarket joined in with ads about their 'assault on salt', and a food manufacturer with 'never been so unsalted in my life'.[2] The SMA claimed, via a PR agency, that they were being wrongly represented, i.e. the evidence about salt and blood pressure in particular was incomplete, and a week after the initial FSA announcement it complained to the Advertising Standards Agency about the Sid the Slug character, which implied, the SMA alleged, that the slug-killing property of salt applies to people. The SMA called at the same time for the public funds to be diverted from the campaign to treating patients who are 'hypertensive'. A wider round of 'inter-voicing' came within two weeks when another supermarket announced a labelling scheme for 300 popular products, listing salt content. The SMA replied that such listing was inadequate for understanding the complexities.[3] Then in the next month (October), there was a SMA media release on the 4th; one from the FSA on the 12th; a reply to that from the SMA on the 18th; and another release by them again on a different topic (a case study disputing FSA advice) on the same day. In November, there were two more media releases from the SMA, one attacking 'weak science' and the other a pro-salt case study about pregnancy, and another in December. By March 2005, there were another two, making ten in all from January 2004. In the same period, the FSA published the same number, and its website rates the salt subject as a 'top search item'.[4]

Another example from September to November 2004 was some trade union leaders claiming that the government was not representing (in pension employment protection policies) the interests of 'working people' in the UK, 6 million of who were union members. They made these statements before the unions met for their annual Congress at which Prime Minister Blair replied that he was talking for 'hard-working and hard-pressed families'.[5] Not all PR 'voicing', however, is from interests to government; much is among competing and co-operating interests.[6] One of the most historic, visible and still potent examples of inter-interest conflict is the one between capitalists and organised labour. It still employs class conflict images of 'dinosaurs' and 'back to the 19th century' in its periodic bouts of statement/ counter-statements.[7] Another longstanding bout of 'inter-voicing' is between Baby Milk Action and Nestlé over marketing baby foods, a competition for communicative advantage lasting twenty years. The campaign group criticises the company's PR and has a webpage 'Nestlé's bogus arguments'.[8]

These examples illustrate differing aspects of a representative model of democracy and raise questions about the nature of their PR 'voices'. For example, the SMA represents its six member firms while the FSA is charged with working in the interests of the good health of the UK population. The SMA could be portrayed as a 'special interest' in the negative sense often used about US businesses whose sectional interests are advanced at the expense of a national, broader interest. But about breadth of interest, the SMA noted that the Department of Health had published an incomplete finding on the health effects of salt, so creating doubt whether there was unanimity of official, expert opinion about the national interest. These differences of sectional/national interest and of competing expert views make the point that PR 'voices' come from, and are contested by, constituencies that are variously constructed by either numbers involved, or by economic influence, or by agreement on message content. Indeed, not all interests are after material advantage. Witness the intense competitive 'voicing' in the Anglican Church between liberals and evangelicals over homosexual priests, their use of the media, and see there a struggle for advantage as combative as any secular contest (Bates 2004). All these differences influence the authority and credibility of the 'voices'. They are also a reminder that to model PR as a set of 'voices' for interests is to describe a promotional mode in operation.

The differences also allow us to separate the mode from a judgement about the worth of the 'voices'. The work tasks for the PR person concern the efficiency and effectiveness of individual 'voices' in message production and transmission; for the PR academic, the tasks are assessing those operational aspects as well as assessing whether all interests in a policy area are 'voiced', and the relative influence of 'voices' on civil society, the political economy, and therefore on democracy. Hagen (1992, p. 21) notes how pluralism of message sources and contents is a basic concept for what he calls 'dialogue democrats', those concerned with 'facilitating decision-making processes built on inter-active and rational persuasion between the members' of social movements. The simile of interests as mountains of different height and mass is useful here for more understanding. The 'voices' coming from, so to speak, the top of Everest in Nepal and the top of Snowdon in Wales are heard more or less loudly by more or less people over more or less distance. If a democracy is seen as a level land accessible to all, the size and position of mountains matters. The examples above also serve to highlight another feature of interest representation: the Posner model used here is an ideal type in the Weberian sense of a cognitive model that coheres completely through full internal consistency. It is not found in practice; rather the model's role is to be a 'perfect' evaluative tool for measuring field data. The model lets us see that there are Everests and Snowdons of interests, and thus 'voices' of different reaches. Finally, the examples and the simile remind us that interests and their PR 'voices' can be related to the concept of the marketplace of ideas (see p. 32). This is a further simile to represent the competitive pluralism of ideas (as well as associated evidence, values and behaviours) found in liberal democracies. Those ideas are 'voiced' by PR techniques, not by them exclusively, but by them frequently. The example above of salt consumption and health throws up the following competitive ideas, related data and values – the threat to human health from various consumption levels of salt; the variety of expert opinions; the evaluation of producer and consumer interests in a representative democratic political economy; the power resources of those interests; the place of patient groups in the debate; the role of government as referee, mediator or arbiter in relation to interests.

The argument at this stage has been to present PR propaganda 'voice' as a technical component of the promotional culture that has a neutral effect on the democracy in which that component works. PR is a major communicative expression of competing interests, and any analysis of benefit or cost to democracy therefore has to principally focus on the strength and distribution of the interests in question. The argument presents PR as value-free technique, operating in a micro- and macro-culture (PR as part of the promotional culture; competing interests as part of the democratic culture). Two references elaborate on this technical and cultural perspective. McNair writes (1996, p. 52) that 'mass democracy is inevitably populist in which appearance and image, as well as policy substance, have a role to play'. Schlesinger and Tumber (1994, p. 271), in their work on the criminal justice system and news sources, find evidence 'for the existence of an inescapable promotional dynamic that lies at the heart of contemporary political culture'.

PR propaganda and democracy in beneficial co-existence

Can we argue that PR is in a beneficial relationship with representative democracy? That it is a type of communication which aids debate in civil society and in the political economy? Two quotations from otherwise fervent critics of PR are supportive here. John Stauber, co-author of *Toxic Sludge Is Good for You* (1995), makes a distinction that allows this thesis some evidential and intellectual space on which to stand. In a radio talk for the Australian Broadcasting Corporation[9] in 1997 about 'Corporate PR: a threat to journalism', he makes the distinction between 'public relations' and 'the public relations industry' (pp. 1–2). He adds

> Obviously I'm up here doing public relations; anybody who tries to address the public in any way, at any level, who tries to get a message out, is engaging in public relations – small 'p', small 'r'. Democracy is very dependent on people learning the art of rhetoric, learning the art of communications and being able to communicate their ideas and persuade others.

He makes a symbolic distinction between PR in capital letters and pr in lower case; between big 'PR' and small 'pr'.

Miller, who regards PR as propaganda, notes (1997, p. 76) that

> public relations and promotional politics can be viewed as either positive or negative for democracy but it is difficult to see the promotional dynamic in wholly negative terms when it provides some of the very few opportunities for the powerless to answer back.

He argues (p. 67) that 'the rise of public relations as a specialism was a response to the modest democratic reforms' of the end of the nineteenth century. About contemporary society, he notes (p. 65) that it 'has become more promotional and this quality parallels and is intertwined with . . . the expansion of the role of the media in societal decision-making and development'. Support for beneficial PR also comes from Jon White, a British PR academic who takes a Grunigian view. He makes positive claims: public relations activities contribute to group performance through getting support for their positions by persuasion.[10]

A liberal egalitarian perspective about civil society provides a conceptual framework for PR in a beneficial relationship with representative democracy, and a review of its essential features shows how that linkage can be constructed. Kymlicka (2002) develops this perspective as the combination of two ideas: a liberal commitment to individual freedom or chance; and an egalitarian commitment to eliminating disadvantages in the distribution of resources and opportunities. He argues that people's inequalities due to effort, risk, savings and consumption are permissible but inequalities due to circumstances beyond their control such as individual talents,[11] race and class should be remedied or compensated for. He calls this perspective the 'equality of resources' variant of liberal egalitarianism and bases it on a commitment to distributive justice, with roles for the state and civil society as agents of resource redistribution.

He situates this redistribution in a context of citizenship, and thus produces a civic setting in which individual citizens should be concerned with providing more social justice in their society by their involvement with the state, and with the associational life of their civil society. Involvement with the state is via participation in representative democracy and in official administration; and with civil society, it is through public and private interest groups, NGOs, trade unions, cause groups, social movements, religion, artistic and recreational groups. He argues that what these voluntary associations in civil society need from the state are a legal framework for association, and an assurance (p. 94) 'that all citizens have an equal opportunity to participate in civil society . . . and that no-one is excluded from associational life as a result of poverty, ignorance, discrimination or harassment'. Rosenblum and Post (2002, p. 8) support the Kymlicka thesis, noting 'the responsibility of government to provide groups and associations with sufficient public goods and entitlements to commit them to publicly imposed order and cooperation'. They list public funding for parochial education and cultural reproduction as examples. The thesis of egalitarian pluralism argued by Cohen and Rogers (1995) also buttresses Kymlicka. They want (p. 28) equal representation of groups in an associative democracy and argue that 'an outcome is legitimate only if it emerges from a process of representation and bargaining in which all interests have substantially equal chances of being heard and influencing the outcome'.

A normative theory of equalising PR resources

Can these general statements about a polity theorised as tolerant of and supportive of people associating to further their interests, facing few or many external obstacles to their combination, be made specific to public relations? Application to public relations starts with a normative statement that it is a responsibility for such a tolerant and supportive state to reduce the communicative inequalities that exist amongst groups representing the values, behaviours and material interests of their members and supporters. A normative theory of PR therefore states that differences in the communicative resources of organisations and groups needed for PR should be made equal by all meeting the threshold for effective messaging in the pluralist competition over values, behaviours, ideas, resource allocations and reputations that exists in market, capitalist, liberal democracies. Looked at in terms of PR-specific theory, this equalisation thesis takes Gandy's (1982) concept of big business providing information subsidies to journalists through their PR productions, and expands the concept of subsidy out of the realm of resource-rich business to all interests that do not come up to a minimum level of PR operational capacity. Gandy conceived of an information subsidy as internally funded by a business for its private benefit *vis-à-vis* markets, media and politics. The PR equalisation concept, however, is based on external funding from outside the organisation or group for the public benefit of markets, media and politics adequately hearing its messages. The thesis should be applied to non-profit-seeking organisations and groups wanting to contribute openly to matters of public interest. The thesis does not argue for an absolute equality of PR resources, but rather a distribution that meets a threshold level of capacity and which is proportionate to the organisation's or group's contribution to public interest discourse. Proportioning the subsidy is possible by dimensions of membership; public support; financial resources; existing PR resources; media interest; and the importance of the topic being discussed.

This equalisation should be made because inequality of communicative resources (as well as other resource types) is manifest in liberal democracies, and grossly asymmetrical distribution of resources weakens such polities. Witness the inequality of messaging resources between business and trade unions historically found in societies like the UK and USA (see p. 45). Unemployed people have traditionally found it difficult to 'voice' their interests about job protection, retraining and social benefits given that they are by definition resource-poor and dispersed.[12] Other groups with less communicative resources conventionally include pensioners, the rural poor, immigrants, asylum seekers, the disabled, victims of transport crashes, patients' support groups for rare diseases. In the London Borough of Tower Hamlets one estimate[13] was that of the 700 voluntary groups there, only 8 per cent lobbied local councillors, community relations officers and members of regeneration bodies. They do not talk of 'doing PR'; rather they advocate and persuade. It was estimated that another 10 per cent did PR recognisable to industry professionals, using annual reports, executive briefings, media relations and public speaking. These resource-poor groups are often represented locally in councils for voluntary services, and receive from them some PR training. These local councils are in turn enabled by national bodies such as the National Association of Councils for Voluntary Services and the National Council for Voluntary Organisations.[14] Could voluntary service councils subsidise PR agencies to offer free PR advice, as legal aid centres support lawyers offering legal advice? Could legal aid centres have PR advice sections in them? Could citizens' advice bureaux offer PR advice?

PR resource equalisation is already on the agenda of the voluntary sector; the argument here is that it be systematised and expanded into a communicative equality to promote social justice. Such equality need not be focused exclusively on the social disadvantaged. Poor communications resourcing is not uncommon in other sectors, and non-commercial groups wanting a PR 'voice' for new technologies (e.g. nanotechnology), environmental practices (e.g. renewable energy sources) or lifestyles (e.g. trans-sexuals) could be given a communications subsidy. The media also has a training role *vis-à-vis* resource-poor groups, as Goldenberg (1975) observed in a study of them. The UK media takes up that role via the Media Trust, sponsored and supported by media organisations and PR firms. Its purpose is 'to help charities communicate' and it trains them in PR.[15]

What form could the equalisation of PR resources be if undertaken by the state? Approached from a civic education point of view, the subject could be included in media education curricula at secondary schools in two ways: PR as a societal practice with benefits and costs in relation to politics, media and markets,[16] and as a promotional practice that can be recognised in much media content. Professional skills of communication auditing, message construction, channel choice, media relations, lobbying, better written and spoken English for public communication could be taught at FE colleges or delivered on site to needy groups as knowledge transfer. University degrees could make another contribution to this practice development, but with more emphasis on PR sociology and PR effects. Philanthropic foundations could contribute alongside the state. A similar contribution could come from subsidised courses offered by Britain's Chartered Institute of Public Relations, perhaps in partnership with public providers. The National Consumer Council, which is 80 per cent publicly funded, could build awareness of PR effects into its education programmes. It has goals which facilitate that extension: 'The consumer interest in communications relies on universal and affordable access to public service broadcasting' and it is concerned that 'many people, especially those on low incomes, may be excluded from access to some communications services'.[17]

Beyond education and training and awareness raising to achieve a communications level playing field lies the more radical step of state oversight and regulation, with or without statutory underpinning. A starting point for developing such a regime is the observation that the UK print advertising industry is self-regulated by the Advertising Standards Authority[18] (ASA) but within a framework of over 170 statutes, and with the Authority able to ask the Office of Fair Trading to take court action in the case of serious breaches of its codes. If this component of promotional culture (print advertising) is deemed to need scrutiny, what is the case for exempting a component more pervasive and more frequent? The regulatory regime for PR could have an equalisation of resources dimension, whereby it would publicly report (at the very least) on asymmetries of communicative resources in cases where it thought the public interest was significantly disadvantaged by such a condition. Who would be the institutional regulator? It could be an adjunct to the ASA or the Office of Communications (Ofcom) that regulates television, radio and telecommunications. The CIPR is a possibility but a remote one for, as the representative body for individual PR persons, its claim to be disinterested about promoting PR resources would be tainted.[19]

In the UK, regulatory intervention in the operational conditions of public debate has been known since the Political Parties, Elections and Referendum Act (2000), which empowers the Electoral Commission to appoint lead campaign groups known as 'designated organisations' on either side of a referendum. The Commission can then subsidise these groups with up to £5 million of public money, and give them free postage for campaign literature and free use of public rooms.[20] The duties of Ofcom, which is a statutory corporation, also abut onto regulating public debate: one of them is a duty to 'balance the promotion of choice and competition with *the duty to foster plurality*' [author's italics].[21]

If this principle of public subsidy for parties to a national referendum, and the duty to foster plurality in public debate, were applied to situations where PR 'voices' were seriously unequal, the consequence is PR campaigns by civil society and by market-development groups paid for out of public monies. This is a step beyond a regulator publicly monitoring unequal PR resources. It would be an innovative public policy, and a controversial one. It would extend the regulatory power of the state into a new area.[22] Such arrangements for PR by public subsidy in significant public debates could not avoid difficulties of inclusion and exclusion for some values and behaviours, and for groups that 'voiced' them.[23] Paedophilia is an example. It is hard to see how a group advocating legal status for this sexual orientation could be publicly supported. The case for resource equalisation argued here rests on a normative theory of PR that seeks communicative equality for groups in public debate. Such a theory is grounded in liberal values of free expression through open debate and in tolerance of different views when these views are themselves grounded in concomitant liberal values of respect for human beings and their right to give informed consent. If reasoning prohibits subsidised communication resources for paedophile groups, how does it fit with support for voluntary euthanasia? Or human cloning? These different examples are raised to indicate how the proposal advocated here of public subsidy for PR propaganda would soon be caught between the upper and lower grinding stones of communicative equality and tolerance of difference. Such challenges of balancing incommeasurables are mediated in liberal polities all the time. What is new is the introduction of the notion of PR resource equalisation to inject PR communicative equality into public debate.

PR and civil society

The argument for subsidised PR has rested so far on a conceptual construct, liberal egalitarianism, taken from political studies and pressed into the particular services of the case for a reformed PR. Another concept can be taken from political studies to add to the reform case. Civil society is an important social location for public relations. The voluntary associations that are outside family, not in markets and separate from the state generate much messaging. The variety is great – cause groups, charities, learned societies, sports and leisure clubs, non-governmental organisations, trade unions and religions. They exist to indulge their members' interests and, usually, to promote them. They seek new members. They contest the views of other groups (pro- and anti-foxhunting). They are numerous in the same policy area.[24] They want to influence markets (food for healthy living), and governments (ramblers over access to open country). They proselytise materialist views of the world (anti-famine campaigners) and metaphysical ones (faith groups). Their PR 'voices' are frequently heard – in leaflets through the door and in the streets; in media stories of alarm and protest; in parish magazines; through petitions; and at rallies, marches and stunts. They are often unconventional and creative in their PR and may be treated as 'outsider' groups with which government will not consult on policy-making (Fathers4Justice).[25] They use the Internet for campaigning and organising[26] and if Graham's judgement (1999) is correct they will use the Internet more because 'by its very nature, it has a tendency to promote reinforcement of interest and opinion among the like-minded' (p. 83). He notes a social consequence of these multiple PR voices, for the Internet 'is more likely to increase social fragmentation than it is likely to promote social consensus' (ibid.).[27] Some groups specialise in non-violent direct action (residents' groups blocking roads); some are violent.[28] Not all groups, therefore, in civil society are benign. Other examples are organised paedophile groups in the UK, and the Ku Klux Klan in the US South. It was also in North Carolina that Schulman and Anderson (2001) showed how a family of local capitalists exercised paternalistic control over an 'unincorporated town' of textile mills, providing local services and stopping unionisation.

Edwards (2004) reviews the history and contemporary condition of civil society, and presents thinking about it that relates to the conception of PR as a resource promoting communicative equality in areas of public interest.[29] He notes (pp. 78–9) that a modern idea of civil society (connected with the fall of communism) focuses on 'the value of voluntary associations in curbing the power of centralising institutions, protecting pluralism, nurturing constructive social norms, especially "generalised trust and co-operation"'. This view is called 'neo-Tocquevillian' (after the French aristocrat who observed US democracy in the 1830s) and is linked to communitarianism, localism and liberal equalitarianism. It recognises the effects of unequal resources on the working of civil society and thus focuses 'on the structural obstacles that prevent some groups from articulating their interests'.[30] The consequences of these obstacles are that (p. 97) 'The persistence of serious inequalities and insecurities endangers civil society as a democratic enterprise and places too much influence in the hands of elites.' He wants (p. 99) government to encourage public debate involving marginalised groups through putting more information about public and private finances, policy-making and employment practices into the public domain. He also wants more public spaces (community centres, libraries, universities) for meetings, and more access to public broadcasting. The argument here adds to Edwards's list of reforms with the proposal of more access to PR training and education in order to equalise communication resources between elite groups, and those representing marginalised interests and views.

Public relations and the souring of pluralism

UK public relations has formally claimed since 1948 'to establish and maintain goodwill and mutual understanding' between organisations and their publics, and, since the early 1990s, to manage reputation to that harmonious end. These are the dignified claims made for the practice and the industry by its representative body, the Chartered Institute of Public Relations, as its contribution 'to business, government and democratic society'.[31] If the PR industry (and function) was a noticeable role player for promoting those social goods, it could be said to create trust, the feeling in citizens and consumers that other individuals, alone and collectively, regularly behave in the benign way expected. There is little evidence, however, that the general public or particular publics accept the first claim about goodwill and understanding, while the jury is out on the effectiveness of the second about reputation. This book rests on an assumption that the perceived gap between PR claim and PR performance is accounted for by the efficient (rather than dignified) role of public relations in the political economy and in civil society, i.e. to give 'voice' to particular interests as they seek to maximise their advantage. This 'voicing' is at odds with the dignified role attributed to official definitions of PR by its representative bodies; hence the disjuncture between efficient and dignified descriptions. PR fulfils its efficient role within an over-arching social context of promotional culture. This role means that public relations adds to an 'argument' culture in the UK and other liberal democracies; produces little 'goodwill and mutual understanding'; and so reduces trust creation (see p. 173). Think about Greenpeace and Shell; Tesco supermarkets and local farmers; BBC and SkyTV over the television licence fee; railway workers and train companies over safety; and UK universities and the National Union of Students on tuition fees. Listen to fast food chains arguing against an obesity tax; business wanting less regulation; successful banks arguing against profiteering charges.

This communicative 'argy-bargy' is a structural consequence of two features of market, liberal democracies: promotional culture in which most communications are self-advantaging (Wernick 1991), and the public wrangling that flows from the 'marketplace' of ideas, values, behaviours circulating in public debates. These features produce what Tannen (1998) calls an 'argument culture'. She writes of it: 'Our spirits are corroded by living in an atmosphere of unrelenting contention – an argument culture . . . which urges us to approach the world – and the people in it – in an adversarial frame of mind' (p. 3). She draws a distinction between the positive of *making an argument* in public for a point of view and the negative of *having an argument*. Her argument-makers are the media, journalists, politicians, academics and emailers. She writes about US society, but the tone she ascribes to its politics and civil society, as bitter and corrosive arenas of negative and destructive argument, can be heard as well in UK society today. Examples are tabloid contempt for politicians, trade union attacks on executive pay, and frivolous claims for compensation. PR is a megaphone for this tone, adding to a cacophony of pleading and preening to public life in the UK today. The PR 'voice' is usually assertive in either a defensive or offensive way, often to a combative point. Indeed, Susskind and Field (1996, pp. 1–9) explicitly blame PR for its contribution to what they call an 'angry public', a characterisation which can be related to the argument culture in that anger is a cause of public argument. They assert that the public is angry because 'business and government leaders have covered up mistakes, concealed evidence of potential risks, made misleading statements, and often lied' (p. 1). They note that these leaders 'attempt to blunt or undercut the public's concerns by dredging up countervailing "facts" or rebuttals from pseudo-independent experts and unscientific polls. They commit to nothing and admit to nothing' (p. 9). Ironically in the face of their critique of PR, Grunig *et al.* (2002, p. 312) assert that Susskind and Field's book is 'a manual on how to practice the two-way symmetrical model in a conflict situation'. Weidenfeld (1998) also picks up on the role of communication in conflict situations. He reviews eleven national case studies and concludes that 'communication and the potential for dialogue have to be improved' (pp. 11–12) among mediating institutions involved in normative conflicts in modern societies. He recommends that 'greatly increased efforts at creating and strengthening mediating structures in the communication between

differing value and normative situation in the world is of foremost importance' (ibid.).

In these ways, PR 'sours' pluralism, and a poignant example is the
Anglican Church's public wrangling in the media over the Bible and gays.[32]
There is a debate to be had whether the 'souring' condition is more serious
in the USA, and whether the UK has the less acute state of a 'grumble
culture'. The discomfited PR professional in either country can, however,
take comfort from the status of PR as a set of neutral promotional techniques. It is expressive of embedded societal forces using its 'voices' to
argue or grumble. Civil society is one of those forces and Edwards (2004)
has noticed its vices as well as its virtues (see p. 84 above). Civil society is
the 'land of difference' (p. 61) and can be a raucous and jostling environment. He writes (p. 64) that it often reaches consensus based on the lowest
common denominators amongst interests; it encourages soundbites,
slanging matches, and it witnesses the rise of moneyed special interests. It
results in 'inequalities in public voices and participation'. Moreover, 'civil
does not mean with all politeness' (p. 67) – it means peacefully; without
violence trying to resolve disagreements, using methods from street protests
and satires to debate and non-violent direct action. Civil society is a better
human condition than civil war but its 'voices' often speak harsh and cruel
thoughts and words.

Summary

Previous chapters argued that public relations is weak propaganda
'voicing' interests competing for advantage in a market, capitalist, liberal
democracy. This thesis raises the most important question about PR – how
does it relate to democracy? The relationship can be viewed as either a
neutral or a beneficial co-existence. The first view theorises democracy as
of the representative, rather than of the deliberative, kind where interests in
society are pitted against each other. PR is a major communicative agent in
the wrangling and horse-trading for advantage (material, ideological,
legislative, reputational) between organisations and groups representing
interests. The media publishes these competitions. Many contemporary
competitions focus on the power of the state to regulate industry and individual behaviour, alongside the historic contest between labour and capital.
Empirical support for neutral co-existence comes from the observation
that, in the last century, PR has flourished in the UK and US democracies.
PR started in the UK in the 1920s and concurrent with its growth there,
the democratic apparatus has developed as has access to public goods
necessary for a minimally civilised life. PR propaganda from capitalist and
governing elites may have hampered these developments but has not
prevented them. As the democratic apparatus (universal franchise, free elections, secret ballot) is introduced to other countries, PR practice spreads.
PR effects appears to be consistent with democracy.

PR has a beneficial co-existence with democracy from the perspective of liberal equalitarianism, which argues for a diminution of discrimination between individuals through a redistribution of resources in the name of social justice. The chapter applies the redistribution specifically to PR resources in order to move towards communicative equality in public debates. The aim is equal 'voicing' among interests in a representative democracy. The means is twofold: monitoring differences of PR resources amongst interests, and then private or public subsidy to transfer more of them towards resource-poor, non-profit-seeking interests. A conception of civil society also argues for a redistribution of PR resources.

However, PR 'sours' pluralism through endless public argument, and tends towards a culture where 'having arguments' takes precedence over 'making arguments'. PR also expresses the negative side of civil society where special pleading predominates and reinforces structural inequalities in it.

7   Is PR damaging democracy?

The previous chapter argued that PR propaganda has either no effect on democracy; or that it has a beneficial effect. A possible third outcome of the PR and democracy relationship is negative effects on democracy. These effects include: the PR 'voices' of dominant groups in society are heard more than those of less dominant groups; PR gives advantages to special interests at costs to the public interest; and this asymmetry of communication expresses and reinforces unequal power relationships. Other effects are that PR 'clutters already-choked channels of communications with the debris of pseudoevents and phony phrases that confuse rather than clarify', and that it 'corrodes our channels of communication with cynicism and "credibility gaps"'.[1]

A starting point for the negative-effects thesis is an anti-capitalist critique that PR has traditionally helped financial capitalist and big-business interests maintain their dominant position in the political economy of liberal democracies. Statements of this position can be found in Carey (1995), Ewen (1996), Marchand (1998), Miller and Dinan (2000), Olasky (1987). The basic proposition in the negative-effects thesis is that capitalists are an elite (if not a class) who control the accumulation and distribution of funds needed by business for profitable growth, and that this control makes them as powerful as, if not more powerful than, elected governments, and certainly more powerful than other interests (if not classes) in liberal democracy. This financial capitalist elite[2] maintains its dominant position over fund ownership by generational self-perpetuation through marriage, education and common culture. The political class is related to these elite capitalists through marriage, education and culture. Adonis and Pollard (1997) argue that the economic and social distance between the British elite and the poorest is growing.[3] In these ways, the anti-capitalist critique argues that there is a ruling class above and beyond democratic control (Scott 1991). Frank (2000), in a critique of US market populism and capitalism, cites PR as the communication technique to give US business from the 1930s onwards the legitimacy it lacked with the public because it lacked 'soul' by seeking profit and treating people as means (pp. xiv, 37–9, 222–6). He quotes Marchand (1998) who had earlier chronicled how a PR narrative of care and concern was constructed by portraying the business corporation as a public servant; a good neighbour; friend of family life and 'plain folks'; and holder of small town values. In fact, Marchand repeats in his introduction the fable of Lambert Hollow, an imaginary, isolated US Midwest town joined to the rest of the nation by the Pennsylvania Railroad.[4] He summarises (p. 3) US business attitudes in the first third of the twentieth century as 'The corporate quest for social and moral legitimacy spurred an array of public relations.'

In operating their control, the capitalist elite has access to professionals such as investment managers,[5] deal makers, accountants, lawyers, marketeers, and public relations agencies. Hill and Knowlton is one such, and Miller, K. in her history of it (1999a) argues that it could justifiably claim to be the most important public relations agency ever (p. 1) for it has represented some of the largest businesses in basic sectors (steel, tobacco, aviation) of the largest economy in the world. Her title of *The Voice of Business* is therefore well chosen. The agency was well attuned for the ideological defence of business in 1933 for its founder, John Hill, was 'a conservative ideologue' (ibid.) who believed that unions and government had no role in business. However, when clients' needs required government regulation or involvement, the agency was able to justify interfering in markets, as it did in favour of dairy farmers and aircraft manufacturers. Hill and Knowlton did marketing PR but became most known for public affairs campaigns. It 'amplified the voice of business, as opposed to fostering dialogue between competing groups' (p. 4). Hill is quoted as saying that 'The role of public relations in the opinion forming process is to communicate information and viewpoints in [*sic*] behalf of causes and organisations. The objective is to inform public opinion and win its favor' (p. 4). Hill embraced two-way asymmetrical PR and Miller quotes its anti-strike ads for the steel companies as 'the antithesis of the symmetrical model because they all too often antagonised rather than creating dialogue' (p. 27). Miller is ambiguous about the effect of the agency's campaigns on public opinion but argues that their influence was principally indirect in that they reinforced clients' beliefs and those who thought like them, bolstering executive morale in battles with unions and government (pp. 189–94). Hill and Knowlton was a major user of community relations programmes for the steel industry (pp. 59–66): they were self-interested, 'providing the industry's point of view' (p. 63), argues Miller. Gandy (1982) has also identified another PR technique that suits business interests: the information subsidy (PR people preparing briefs for journalists) is one frequently used method for heavily influencing, if not controlling, media scrutiny and comment about capitalism. It is a technique for resource-rich organisations as it reduces the cost of information collection and delivery to journalists. Moloney (1996) has identified commercial lobbying – the hiring of lobbyists – as another PR technique expressive of dominant influence. He argues that these hired lobbyists are 'corporate accessories' employed by big businesses (the borrowers of capitalist funds) to defend their interests against any hostile government policy or regulation. Business has the resources to hire them and they are successful enough in promoting business interests to be rehired over the lifetime of successive governments. These lobbyists, their employers and capitalist fund managers beyond them are beneficiaries of current neo-pluralist thinking about the political economy that privileges, but in a challenged and fractured way, the general business interest above others in UK society (p. 138). An example of a challenged business interest is British tobacco manufacturers who have their marketing constrained by health regulations and public opinion.[6] L'Etang (2004b) has shown how British PR had its origins in a mixture of the marketing needs of business and the promotional needs of government; and how it was first staffed by men close to the establishment, if not in it.

Davis (2002) elaborates PR's role in modern UK power structures in some detail and he takes a view that is a weak version of the anti-capitalist critique. He looked at how, in the 1980s and 1990s, financial and business interests used PR in relation to the media and how trade unions did the same. He concludes (p. 180) that the first decade 'might be seen as a period in which corporate and government PR effectively privatised a number of policy debates and established several areas of unchallenged consensus'. The second decade had a different balance: 'a period in which alternative interest group PR began to break into established elite discourse networks and to use the media to bring policy debates more into the public sphere' (ibid.). What makes this conclusion a weak version of the anti-capitalist critique is Davis's judgement that there has been some movement towards communicative equality for resource-poor and marginal groups, a position that earlier authors in that school do not admit. But he is very cautious about this progress: 'despite such developments, pluralist optimism should remain muted' (ibid.). This book is close to Davis's position but on the side of more optimism. Its optimism is based on a longer time period that goes back to the 1960s. It argues that British PR has been on a long journey away from the exclusive servicing of dominant business interests and of government, towards more inclusive use by subordinate interests.[7] It notes that there is an established history of public interest lobbying by concerned citizens, e.g. patients, families and sympathisers protested to keep open a hospital for chronic illness in southern England in 1948 (Lindner 1998). PR's former employment by elites was inimical to more democratic control, for its major consequence was that most 'voices' in a political economy and civil society were less heard from in public policy debates and decision-making. If Davis is hesitant about the future, he does at least offer to others a methodology for increased access by subordinate groups (2002, pp. 173–4).[8] Grunig *et al.* (2002, p. 330), however, are more assertive that PR helps the less powerful in society but only offer a generalised methodology based on professionalism, knowledge and empowerment.

Davis's work is media focused. PR, however, has one powerful element among its array of techniques that is not and it is this mode (lobbying)[9] which causes most concern about negative effects on democracy. That concern is frequently expressed in the USA where 'government by special interests' is a commonly used phrase in its public discourse, a phrase that expresses a dilution of Lincoln's ideal of government by the people for the people. The precise concern is this: powerful interests will gain undue access to and influence over elected policy-makers by giving candidates money to campaign for political office.[10] In the UK, the concern is muted because of the strict limitations on election spending. Nevertheless, lobbying did increase from the 1980s[11] as the neo-liberal Thatcher governments privatised the nationalised industries and deregulated markets as major reforms to establish the supremacy of free markets. These policies led to a search for commercial advantage and market positioning by established and emergent capitalists as the assets were sold off and a new political settlement for doing business laid out. Jordan (1991) has tracked the costs and benefits of the rise of hired lobbyists. Concern about their influence in UK politics peaked with allegations of malfeasance involving money-for-influence in the early 1990s, and these led to the appointment of the investigative Nolan Committee and its first report in 1994.[12]

Political lobbying generally in Western democracies has a poor reputation (expressed in phrases such as 'influence peddling', 'corridor creeping') with the general public and sections of the political class, and the scepticism embedded in that judgement is justified. It needs, however, to be tempered by the knowledge that lobbying is unavoidable in a liberal democracy and specific examples of big business unduly or illegally (through bribes) influencing policy are hard to prove. A major reason for this indeterminancy is that policy-making is subject to so many formative influences – e.g. party policy; party factions; civil service advice; ministerial enthusiasm; parliamentary pressure; media pressure; public opinion – that allocating causality to one variable is near impossible.[13] In the popular phrase 'lobbyists are often pushing at an open door'. There is, therefore, no established methodology for influence allocation. Moreover, Moloney (1996, p. 147) notes that even lobbyists are cautious about assessing their influence: 'Hired lobbyists themselves invariably hesitate to claim a clear, causal relationship between their efforts and lobbying outcomes. They do not claim a formula for successful lobbying.' There is, however, one unambiguous conclusion: lobbyists are employed on the staff of businesses, or are hired in when needed, to provide many support services (e.g. monitoring, contact point) connected with public policy. Businesses are thus repeatedly making the judgement that their lobbyists are influential enough in policy-making to be worth their salaries and fees. As the aphorism has it, lobbyists are like advertisements: half are effective; but which half?

Power and PR

Lobbyists should therefore be seen as valued aides, extra resources, auxiliaries for the pre-existing power of business, especially big ones, in liberal capitalist democracies. Lobbyists working for companies do not create power for the business interest: they project through persuasive communication the power of their employers in order to sustain or increase it in the face of hostile government policy or any other challenge (e.g. from environmentalists or foreign competition). They are also used by non-business interests as well (many voluntary-sector organisations have honorary or paid government relations officers) but the focus here is on business because it is the single largest bloc of interest in a political economy where the economic system relies on capitalism for production of goods and services. This judgement about the power of business is captured by the neo-pluralist perspective, first associated with Dahl (1961, 1971, 1982, 1989), and Lindblom (1997). Marsh and Locksley (1983, pp. 1–21) also noted that the power of capital was 'qualitatively as well as quantitatively different' from other groups. Dunleavy and O'Leary (1987, pp. 293–7) confirmed that for neo-pluralists 'business interests occupy a position of special importance compared with other social interests when it comes to influencing public policy-making'.

Lindblom concludes that elected governments respond to this bloc of influence with varying degrees of business-friendly policies. He also notes (1997, p. 141) that inequalities of wealth limit access to public relations people and to the media. Together, it is this tendency of partiality by government towards business, and limited access by other interests, that link lobbying PR with negative effects on democracy. Business employs lobbyists to make elected governments more partial to its interests (e.g. in the UK to set high barriers to workplace recognition for trade unions; to set corporation tax at a low level for casinos). Media relations PR is used for messaging in favour of capitalism and markets as the optimum paradigm of ideas and practices for wealth creation. These messages are sent out from business 'peak' organisations such as the Confederation of British Industry and the Institute of Directors, and from capitalist-supporting think tanks such as the Adam Smith Institute and Social Market Foundation in the UK. Lieberman (2000, p. 149) notes how American right-wing think tanks have 'turned themselves into roaring publicity machines with direct links to public policy and idea formation'.[14] This ideological reproduction via PR has a historical profile in Britain. L'Etang (2004b, pp. 85–7) notes the lobbying by the Economic League, the Aims of Industry, and by the Mr Cube campaign, all against the nationalisation of basic industries policies of the Labour Government from 1947 to 1951; and how British class structures shaped PR practices.[15]

The analysis of power by Lukes (1974) can also be related to uses by business of public relations. The essential point of the business/PR connection is the 'voicing' of business-supportive messages designed to influence ideas, attitudes and behaviour in a polity (a political economy combined with its civil society), and to influence policy-making by elected governments. This connection raises the concern that there are non-business or anti-business interests which are so under-resourced that they cannot create a PR 'voice', or, if they can, they are not heard or adequately considered. Lukes explores three ascending dimensions of power by which its holders make their preferences prevail. Barrow (1993, p. 153) regards this hierarchy as supplying 'a successively broader approach in which to understand the operation of state power'. Lukes's three dimensions can be summarised as noticeable conflict among interests; controlling agendas for public debate and policy-making; and conditioning the beliefs and thoughts of others. Lukes associated these three dimensions with decreasing levels of public visibility of the power exercised. More power is associated with less visibility of it. The visibility levels can in turn be associated with different PR types and their effects, and can be called the visible, the indeterminate and the invisible levels of public relations. PR lobbying can be related to the indeterminate level of visibility because it is hard for those observing to know when it takes place. Lobbying as direct personal influence on policy-makers usually happens in private and seeks to create a policy bias in its favour, and so actively shapes the political agenda in a hidden way. This creation of bias to shape agendas is the central feature of Lukes's second dimension. Lobbying, of course, is done by most interests and groups in a liberal democracy and as such its consequence, the mobilisation of bias to shape agendas, is not a concern specifically related to business. In a representative democracy, such mobilisation is a constant aim of all interests and groups. Rather it is the amount of mobilised bias generated privately via PR lobbying by the single most powerful interest in a liberal democracy (business) that makes for concern.

Moreover, business, as a set of ideas and as a practice, is so constitutive of known liberal democracy that it has structural power to affect the circumstances in which it operates. This power is Lukes's third dimension. It is the power of dominant groups to condition the thinking of others, an important one when big business is mistrusted.[16] It is the power to keep conflict latent in situations where there is 'a contradiction between the interests of those exercising power and the *real interests* of those they exclude', even when the excluded may not express or be conscious of their interests (1974, pp. 24–5). Lukes calls this a fully sociological form of power: 'Indeed, is it not the supreme exercise of power to get another or others to have the desires you want them to have – that is to secure their compliance by controlling their thoughts and desires?' (p. 23). Shanahan (2001) offers an elaboration of this unconscious, embedding process. He argues that there exists today a sociological propaganda that is different from the overt and expected kind from known sources (e.g. Goebbels,

Kissinger, Stalin, Voice of America). This new form is embedded in social contexts 'which produce persuasive messages and promote receptiveness to those messages, somewhat automatically' (p. 6). Study of this sociological dimension concentrates less on techniques and on producer/receiver personality than did previous study of conventionally defined propaganda. Shanahan (pp. 4–5) agrees with Ellul (1962, p. 63) that sociological propaganda is 'penetration of an ideology by means of its social context'; and also with Doob's (1935) idea of unintentional propaganda that happens in situations where social control is exercised via suggestion. Shanahan also notes that, in the USA since the Second World War (1939–45), propaganda analysis was displaced by communications research 'for within the context of the struggles for democracy against fascism and communism, to focus on propaganda was simply, though perhaps ironically, ideologically unacceptable' (pp. 8–9).

PR is a communicative agent of structural power in that it produces messages that are visible but which have an intended but undeclared conditioning effect on their consumers: they condition others into thinking that the message contents are the natural order and are 'common sense' (McLellan 1979, p. 185). PR productions creating these outcomes are part of what Marxists call ideological reproduction – the maintenance of ideas over time and over social classes that uphold asymmetrical power relationships amongst interests in a society. These ideas produce thoughts and attitudes that give legitimacy to dominant groups and keep them in power, and are an exercise in what Gramsci called cultural hegemony (p. 186). Pearson (1992, p.123) cautiously endorses this role of PR in producing capitalist legitimacy; 'In earlier ages, the response to potential economic crises [by capitalism] was the reallocation of material resources – a greater sharing of economic benefits. In current times, the appropriate response takes place in the realm of ideas.'[17]

In these ways, PR messages for business and governments – and in the case of the UK, monarchy – are so frequently originated by their sponsoring interests and then repeated through so many media that they reproduce structural power for these dominant institutions through the creation of unthinking acceptance. Davis (2002, pp. 174–5) writes, for example, that 'government sources employ PR operations that are literally a hundred times larger than alternative sources acting in civil society. For simple economic reasons, therefore, elite institutional sources are likely to dominate as information subsidy suppliers over a long period.' He also notes (p. 175) that business elites in the UK have enough control over sources of business news that 'journalists are left in the position of reporting outcomes or recording those conflicts that financial elites choose to play out in the media'. The argument here is not that there is no challenge from non-dominant interests to the structural power of dominant interests. Abercrombie *et al.*'s thesis (1980) of ideological and material challenges from counter-interests is accepted. In our field of study, it is seen empirically in the PR messaging of anti-capitalist, political oppositional, and republican groups; and outside of politics in the messaging of novel forms of marketable products and social entrepreneurship.[18] These groups either do not know how to send PR messages, or transmit them incompetently, and thus the interests they represent are not adequately heard and debated in the political economy or in civil society. It is this shortfall in PR messaging (low volume and frequency, and lack of persuasive technique) that creates communicative inequality.

The argument above has associated lobbying PR and ideological reproduction PR, through their indeterminately visible and invisible aspects, with the second and third dimensions of Lukes's typology of power. PR also provides evidence for Lukes's first dimension of power – power expressed in the public struggle amongst interests. This is power as visible behaviour and the least sociological, in his terms. PR is the communicative sign by which this behaviour is observed (the media relations of negotiations; published leaks about private lobbying; photos with the powerful; staged events such as conferences and stunts; and campaigns of protest). This PR expresses amounts of power in the visible outcomes of explicit conflict, and in Lukes's typology the less powerful who are involved in it are unaware of how the issues in conflict are on the controlling agendas of other, more dominant interests. In his study of the media relations of trade unions, Manning (1998) draws a conclusion that offers some support for Lukes's thesis: in achieving union aims, control of material and political resources is more important than successful access to the media, even though the latter sometime enables growth of political resources.

The matching of PR via its types of production and their effects to Lukes's tripartite hierarchy of power is supportive of the negative-effects thesis of PR on democracy. It has been shown possible to match PR to all three of his dimensions. The matching with the visible communicative behaviour of organisations and groups in pluralistic conflict (his first dimension) is the least concerning in relation to democracy: visibility of PR messaging (in the media, corporate literature, sponsored events, conferences and demonstrations) and its effects by one interest allows the possibility of counter-messaging from opposing interests for material, policy, ideological or reputational advantage. Power countervails power, resources permitting. More concern flows from the second dimension, which focuses on the policy agenda over which the lobbying PR of pluralists competes, and the process by which that agenda is influenced. This touches on the power of strong PR producers to influence through private lobbying what is on that agenda and what is excluded. This is the power of PR lobbyists to be gatekeepers of hidden agendas of organisations and groups. Most concern, however, comes from the role of PR in the maintenance of structural power to condition beliefs and thoughts, which is Lukes's third dimension. The PR messaging is visible but its contribution to ideological reproduction goes unnoted, for the messages are seen as speaking about what is presented as the natural order of social arrangements. This is communication that conditions awareness among citizens about power distributions in their polity in favour of existing power holders. In this way, PR weakens libertarian and equalitarian values in democracy, and closes down opportunities for critical public debate.

The Lukes typology applied to PR is a caution to the view that, on balance, the positive effects of PR to a liberal democracy outweigh the negative ones. Indeed, the matching reduces the cogency of the normative position taken in this book that PR as communicative equality will benefit a liberal, representative democracy (see pp. 79–84). If PR for dominant interests is the communicative agent for maintaining their power through mobilising bias, influencing agendas and through conditioning thought, will more visible PR by subordinate groups reduce the agenda influencing and structural power of dominant groups? The contribution of PR messaging and its effects to the reinforcement of asymmetrical power distribution amongst interests makes the task of neutralising its negative effects a most demanding one.

Neutralising negative effects of PR on democracy

Conceptually and empirically, it is difficult to argue that PR is going to disappear, or diminish in liberal democracies such as Western Europe and North America. Rather it looks set to increase as the pluralism of values, attitudes, ideas and behaviours seen since the 1960s takes hold in upcoming generations of citizens and consumers. Whether the return of the Christian fundamentalist and neo-conservative Republican administration in 2004 will halt pluralism in the USA is moot. The very prominence of US fundamentalism will of itself provoke a countervailing response in the USA (and elsewhere) as liberal interests rethink their ideas and policies. This contestation between fundamentalism and liberalism as rival paradigms for whole political economies and civil societies will in itself generate more PR 'voices'. Even if pluralism is checked, the paradigmatic competition with neo-conservatism makes more, not less, public relations likely.

Neutralising the negative effects of PR (increasing or not) already happens at many social locations, and through both individual and collective behaviours. Vigilance about the presence of PR is the agency for neutralisation, and it takes many forms. It can be regarded as the first act of citizen and consumer resistance to promotional culture, and it is theorised here as a stimulus to critical thinking and action that counters any PR effects tending to compliance through fraud, deception or conditioning thought. The rest of this chapter and much of the following chapters on politics, markets and media will explore these neutralising phenomena, but they will be introduced here as twofold: the culture of vigilance by the public in a democracy in their roles as citizens and consumers, and institutional aides to that vigilance. In politics, that vigilance is expressed through the scepticism, wariness and scrutiny of individual citizens in their role of voters, and if offering themselves as candidates, in their role as elected representatives. It is summed up in the aphorism that 'external vigilance by the people is the price of liberty'.[19] In markets, that vigilance is expressed in the legal aphorism *caveat emptor* (buyer beware). The corporate and individual ethics of PR producers reduces empirical untruthfulness and deception in PR messaging. Any remaining untruthfulness, and more importantly biases invisible to the employed PR person, are checked by watchful consumers of PR in politics, markets and in media output.

The anatomy of this vigilance towards public relations is seen in many social forms and locations. The pluralist competition is itself a neutralising phenomenon; organisations and groups are monitoring their operating environments to locate allies for co-operation and opponents for challenge. In PR language, this is the boundary-scanning function done as a first step in the identification of issues to be managed. This is the beginning of the dialectical process of communicative power countervailing communicative power. Where the resource threshold is below the level of an effective minimum for PR 'voice' to be able to message, the equalisation subsidy should be applied (p. 79). But it is outside of PR 'inter-voicing', the exchange of PR messages amongst groups and organisations,[20] that most monitoring is done. These extraneous sites are individuals as members of media audiences, as citizens, as consumers of goods and services, as elected representatives; and are also their aggregation into stakeholders or publics.

An individual's vigilance towards PR is part of his or her general vigilance towards other promotional forms – advertising, marketing communications, political messaging between elections and electoral propaganda itself. It is tempting to believe that populations that have had democracy and mass-market economies for 150 years are now characterised by individuals with cultural habits of caution towards public messaging; but it is tempting in a way that brings complacency too close. Personal debt levels and selling frauds are reminders of continuing gullibility by consumers, as is the demand for celebrity news. The effective scrutiny of PR by individuals is founded on their PR literacy, which is the ability to directly recognise PR messages in corporate writing, speech and behaviour, and indirectly when it is embedded in journalism.

Where general media literacy about broadcasting and print is taught in schools and colleges, PR literacy may well be an indirect consequence. But public relations is now such a pervasive component of promotional culture that it deserves its own pedagogic space in media and civic literacy programmes. As with all these forms of literacy, PR literacy faces daunting challenges to educate younger people, especially in front of the Niagara of persuasive yet seemingly reasonable material about which it seeks to develop a new critical awareness. A multi-strand and long-term strategy is needed. The curriculum could build on the work of the 1930s Institute for Propaganda Analysis in the USA, which developed seven propaganda indicators.[21] Schools and colleges are the prime locations for these programmes. The role of PR degrees is different: PR graduates are, hopefully, skilled PR producers who accept the contested role of PR in a liberal democracy and who are ready to debate its benefits and costs.[22] The industry and representative bodies for public relations should be providers of PR literacy skills as well. They often claim that PR has social benefits (increasing goodwill and mutual understanding in society; expressing pluralism) but they are hesitant to discuss publicly its costs. Their position amounts, to turn the language of PR on itself, to asymmetrical communication.

At the level of vigilance towards PR by institutions, scrutiny by the media is the most proclaimed and often the most effective in terms of alerting the public to a PR presence. The protection takes two forms. There is first a professional rivalry, and frequently a dislike between journalists and PR people (see Ch. 2), which is proclaimed almost daily in the print media.[23] This rivalry is an important emotional motivator of scrutiny by the media. Apart from this professional 'turf war', there is a functional tension between the two groups: journalists want unselective access on their terms to people and information inside organisations and groups; while PR people offer access on the selective basis of promoting their principals' interests. If journalists are, classically, 'gatekeepers' to the media, PRs are 'gatekeepers' to their organisations and groups.[24] The two roles cancel themselves out and the information immobility that results is released by negotiation: the exchange of favourable publicity in the media for information that makes a story. Journalists may be obliged to engage in this exchange but their instincts are to evade it, and its 'gatekeepers'. In terms of their informal constitutional role of scrutiny of the powerful, the dishonest and the secret – their vigilance on behalf of democracy – the questioning and evasion of the PR function is at its heart.[25] Unfortunately recent journalism, at least in the UK, has weakened its vigilance role by adopting a co-operative attitude towards PR. This is seen on the celebrity and entertainment pages of the press, where there is an open and admitted exchange of publicity-for-access (see p. 161). It is possible to be relaxed about this co-operation on the grounds that it is 'only' celebrity news. If that position is judged not to be complacent, the co-operation of financial journalism and business PR (Davis 2002), and the closeness of political journalism with political news management, is a clear cause for concern about vigilance by the media (Jones 2002). This PR-isation of the media is discussed more fully in Chapter 11. The National Union of Journalists could have a scrutiny role as well, but its stance is ambiguous for it recruits PR people into its press, PR and information officer section, and has published guidelines for their ethical practice.

Government in a liberal democracy is also a site of vigilance about PR. Not only is it the largest producer of PR in such a polity (with 1,000 information officers messaging for the UK government), but it is also the largest recipient of PR communications, via lobbying, media releases, conferences, speeches and stunts. Its task with these messages is to distinguish between the special interests encoded within them and the wider public interest. Local government has a vigilance role as well and it is seen in its consumer protection, fair trading, accurate weights and measures functions. There are also government-funded consumer education agencies to be counted in, such as the National Consumer Council and the Food Standards Agency.

Other institutions provide vigilance of PR as well. There are 'watchdog' bodies such as privately funded consumer champions (*Which!* magazine in the UK) assessing promotional claims made for goods and services; and anti-PR industry bodies such as PRWatch in the USA and SpinWatch in the UK. Universities are sometimes critical, and publish and hold conferences to that end; but this critical activity is not frequent, largely because academics, at least in the UK, are not adequately engaged with PR as a serious topic for analysis (see pp. 165–7).[26] There is also the question of the critical distance the academy should maintain between itself and the object of its teaching and research. This distance is under tension when the academy benefits from recognition by outside professional bodies. The example in British PR is that validation by the CIPR aids student recruitment and encourages employers to offer work placements. Finally, in the realm of the possible but not very probable, an official regulatory body to police PR could be set up[27] or PR monitoring could be added to the tasks of the existing Advertising Standard Authority. The existing industry bodies in the UK (the CIPR, the PRCA and the Association of Professional Political Consultants (APPC)) could devise a common code of conduct that emphasised the dangers of unethical PR. The CIPR represents some 8,000 PR producers in the UK, and its vigilance role could be strengthened by a more rigorously applied discipline over members.[28]

Summary

There is a negative-effects thesis about PR and democracy. It is that dominant PR 'voices' are heard more than those of subordinate interests, and that this asymmetrical communication expresses and reinforces unequal power relationships in a democracy. The anti-capitalist form of the thesis takes a determinist view that no reform of PR will change the power inequalities, on the grounds that changing the communicative agent will not change its principal. Less determinist critiques see some halting progress towards more communicative symmetry, especially since the 1960s; while the neo-pluralist perspective suggests that business communications are dominant in liberal, capitalist democracies, but in a challenged and fractured way.

The analysis of power by Lukes (1974) can be applied to PR: competitive messaging in public conflicts amongst interests fits his first dimension of power expressed in visible conflict; lobbying (usually private) to mobilise bias in order to control political agendas is evidence of his second, less visible dimension of power; while PR which conditions people's thinking to accept asymmetrical power distributions is supportive of his third dimension, which is 'fully sociological', unnoticed structural power.

Vigilance about PR's presence is the neutralising agent against its negative effects on democracy. Vigilance is exercised by individuals as media users, as citizens and as consumers under the role of *caveat emptor* (buyer beware). Media and civic literacy are important for the reproduction of this vigilance by individuals. Vigilance, however, is also institutional. The media has a professional and constitutional role here, although its effectiveness is hampered by growing media dependency on PR materials. Government is vigilant as well in its role as legislator and executive because the state needs to evaluate lobbying by special interests, for the latter need to be assessed against the broader public interest. Consumer watchdogs and anti-PR groups are also invigilators. Whether, however, the more private or hidden forms of lobbying PR and the intangible consequences of PR as a cultural reproducer (PR for agenda shaping and for entrenching dominant groups) are observed and then checked effectively is a problematic and worrying issue for democrats.

8 Ethics, social responsibility, stakeholders

There is some amusement to be had from the phrase 'public relations ethics'.[1] It is, indeed, a risible oxymoron when it describes much past and present PR practice. There is some hope, however, that the phrase will lose a little of its paradoxical connotation. This hope has its source in the conception of the better PR practice argued for in this book – more communicative equality in the political economy and civil society. In the meantime, the wry smiles of the present come from observers noting the assertion of PR people that their work aims at the creation of goodwill, mutual understanding, good reputation and trust.

If, however, PR and propaganda are the same, how can PR be ethical? To make that argument, a separation is needed between two entities: the values, behaviours and data about the causes and material interests that are the subjects of PR propaganda; and the PR propaganda techniques themselves. The formulation of the question in this way alludes to a broader issue: can propaganda ever be justified in a democracy? Turning to the subjects first, supporters of those subjects (e.g. some profit-seeking product, some social cause, some political policy) exercise judgement that they are right and good in some moral or normative sense and truthful in some empirical or material sense. In the PR context, these supporters are producers of goods and services, social activists, politicians, aggrieved individuals (and maybe celebrities). They are involved actively with the values, behaviours, data, causes and material interests that they espouse. They seek to display commitment and conviction in a way that maximises attention and advantage. They are 'true believers' in the objects of their commitments and convictions. They are ready to be communicators of conviction, or to employ specialists to be so.[2] Examples of those intense judgements are found across the political economy and civil society. In politics, politicians offer 'visions' of the 'good society' and in liberal democracies they and the media sometimes say that democracy is a public good of the highest order. Scammell (2000, p. 43), reviewing relations between the media and democracy, says that democracy is a cause worth propagandising for. She writes that, from some theoretical perspectives, there are 'entirely legitimate propaganda functions for the media'. She lists propaganda by democratic states against enemies; propaganda for democratic education; and for competing candidates at elections. Jowett and O'Donnell (1992, p. xi) note that advertising can be presented as the 'most prevalent form of propaganda in the US'. Doob (1935, pp. 207–35) lists causes that attracted the support of liberals and leftists, and which he classified as propagandist. The New York Society for the Suppression of Vice, the American Association for Social Security (state pensions) and the National Association for the Advancement of Colored People are what he calls 'propaganda societies'. Street (2001, p. 109) notes about the UK that 'Certainly, political parties and interest groups engage legitimately in propaganda exercises.' Cutlip[3] nominates the founding of the American Republic as a cause worth propagandising for. The British Government used propaganda in the First and Second World Wars to further their war aims, and many Britons today would say that its use in the latter war was fully justified. Since 2001, the UK and USA have used propaganda to promote their ideas of good government and good society in the face of dictatorship and terrorism. In peacetime, political parties proclaim that their promises, manifestos, policies are 'right' for the nation. These examples are from politics. From the marketplace, business managers believe that their products and services are superior and the 'best' on offer (e.g. new cars, slimming diets, digital equipment,[4] drugs, new food[5]). In civil society, religious fundamentalists proclaim the Bible as literal truth. It can be assumed that the Catholic Church believed that it was doing right and good when it set up the Office for the Propagation of the Faith in 1622 as part of the Counter-Reformation against Protestantism.

These judgements, made in whatever area of social activity, are the opposite of the dispassionate, sceptical and conditional ones made in deliberative, discursive environments, such as the academic life at its best. The judgements are arrived at by a mixture of reasoning and emoting in unknown quantities. Holding and publicising these judgements of conviction cannot be denied to politicians, producers of goods and services, activists and aggrieved individuals if they are within the law. Observers of this process who live in liberal democracies will hope that they are observing judgements arrived at by reason, supported by evidence and by positive, nurturing emotion, but they will be disappointed about others' judgements an unknown number of times. The outcome is judgements made by individuals in organisations and groups, and held with commitment and conviction, that the chosen values, or behaviours, or causes or material interests are right or good or true – or all three – for the appropriate domain (economic, moral, social) in which they operate. A liberal democracy is the polity that tolerates and encourages these publicly stated judgements and convictions within the law.

At this stage, enter PR people. The argument so far has looked at the subject to be propagandised. Now PR people face four professional decisions before messaging:

1   to make a personal judgement that the values, behaviours, causes and material interests, to which they apply their promotional skills are right or good or true or that they are not;
2   to decide whether they can or cannot make such judgements for reasons of organisational position or their own capacity;
3   to decide whether they avoid making such judgements, even though they have the position and the capacity; and
4   to decide whether they accept or not instructions to send PR messages from their superiors even if they judge the subject of the message to be wrong, bad or untrue.

Before all these judgements, PR people are in the same position as other professionals: advertising agents, marketeers, accountants, engineers. All face the choice of associating their skills with the cause, value, behaviour, interest in question. But it can be argued that, for PR professionals, the activity of themselves speaking the words of rightness or goodness or truth gives a particular personal dimension to their choices that is not present when the engineer, for example, sees another car leave the production line or when the marketeer publishes a trends survey. When they send messages, PR people utter words that are right, good or true, or not.

Awareness of communication ethics has been more on PR teachers' curricula, and maybe on professionals' minds, since the late 1980s in the UK. It is not, however, a novel awareness. Merton noted the link in his 1946 study of the psychology and techniques of a successful US war bond drive. He wrote of the 'practitioner in propaganda' but the work is that of today's PR person, and this contemporaneousness can be appreciated if national lotteries are in mind when his comments are read.

> The technician . . . must decide whether or not to use certain techniques which though possibly "effective" violate his own sentiments and moral codes. He must decide whether or not he should devise techniques for exploiting mass anxieties, for using sentimental appeals in place of information, for masking private purpose in the guise of common purpose. He faces the moral problem of choosing not only among social ends but also among propaganda means.
>
> (1995, p. 271)

Ethics in PR practice

Once the decision to message has been made, the focus of action falls on the PR person. How do they exercise their skills ethically? The first response is to ask how public relations is conceptualised. Marsh (2001) posits a more effective PR as two-way symmetrical communications relationship and develops an ethical framework on that foundation. Parsons (2004) is less foundational about basic assumptions and defines (p.10) PR ethics as 'the application of knowledge, understanding, and reasoning to questions of right and wrong behaviour in the professional practice of public relations'. She distils the recognition of ethical matters by PR people down to the application of five values (p. 142): veracity (truth telling); non-maleficence (no harm doing); beneficence (doing good); confidentiality (respecting privacy); and fairness (social responsibility). She then operationalises (p. 152) these five values into a model of best practice: gathering all pertinent information; defining problems; identifying professional values; applying the values; analysing one's loyalties; making decisions; double checking them; acting. Such models of good practice (and others, like those of the CIPR and National Union of Journalists)[6] are to be applauded.[7] It is also notable that, since the 1990s, there has been more attention by PR people and teachers to ethical practice. In the UK, this attention, it could be speculated, is a reaction to business scandals (e.g. the BCCI collapse; endowment mortgage and pension mis-selling); the climate of political sleaze that led to the Nolan Committee report in 1995; and the 'spin' phenomenon from the mid-1980s. This period was one of strong growth for promotional culture and therefore for public relations. Those years witnessed the dominance of capitalist economics; the deregulation of markets; the rise of possessive individualism expressed in a widening and deepening culture of retail consumption; and state mismanagement such as the poll tax and over-budget military equipment procurement. Market and official excesses led to a critical public opinion that wanted more social responsibility, and business and public sector regulation. Public relations professionals worked in this climate and PR teachers in higher education became noticeably more explicit about ethics.[8] This awareness is a positive development in relation to moving towards enacting communicative equality, for unethical PR is an act of deception against colleagues who seek to communicate honestly, and against citizens and consumers who seek accuracy and truth in public messages.

But models for ethical PR practice have the weaknesses of all formulas for moral behaviour: they divide social complexities into bounded categories and they reduce philosophical complexities to simplicities. The conflict between the values, behaviours and interests of capitalists and employees in market economics is a frequent site for observing the weakness of best-practice models. For example, a business is taken over by new owners (venture capitalists) and, within a week, they sack hundreds of employees.[9] They issue a statement to the media that includes the following: 'We regret the impact that these intended closures will have on our people and will make every effort to re-deploy as many people as possible elsewhere.' Two difficult questions for a media spokesperson of the new owners immediately come to mind. How is 'regret' shown by the new owners and how can its authenticity be evaluated? What does the phrase 'will make every effort' to find other work for the sacked staff mean in relation to a business's search for higher profits? Should profits be lower so that more jobs are saved?

Several organisational factors put PR people into difficulty. The first is that the majority of them are in low-ranking to middle-ranking positions in private or public bureaucracies, and they have on them the contractual obligations to carry out the lawful and reasonable instructions of superior officers in their organisations, or to be disciplined. These obligations are the expression of weak job tenure in unregulated labour markets where employers' legal rights are stronger than employees'. PR people also have on them the more 'invisible' influences of work culture that often dampen down expressions of dissent, and encourage the comforts of group thinking. For PR people in agencies, that the situation is often more fragile for their employment may directly depend on work from the client whose PR messages they want to query ethically. These restraints are common to other organisational staff such as marketeers, engineers, accountants and solicitors. There is, however, one definition of the role of PR people in an organisation or group that makes ethical matters acute for them. Parsons (2004, p. 7–8) alludes to it when she writes: 'As the interface between the organisation and its public, and arguably the keeper of the organisational reputation, the public relations function has an even more important role as *the social conscience of the organisation*' [italics are this author's emphasis]. This is an arduous work role to take on, combining a difficult task with high probability of failure.

In his review of fifty years of US business PR, Tedlow (1974, p. 201) found that PR people 'who have self-consciously set about to reform their employers as the first order of business . . . most likely meet with failure more often than success'. Most PR people do not have the status in organisations to engage critically with dominant coalitions; and only a few have the capacity to undertake such a career-limiting and ethically challenging project. Regular reading of the PR trade press suggests that there have been few exemplars. Successful PR people (those with high position, status and salary in their organisations) are more likely to be communicators in a *realpolitik* mould than in an ethical one. They are successful because they have gained more communicative advantage for their organisation or group than disadvantage. No doubt their search is moderated by the social responsibility of their employers or of their cause, and then by their personal ethics. If the work setting is a charity, the expectation of an observer would be that personal ethics and social responsibility impinge more steadily on the search for communicative advantage than in a profit-seeking business. Reading the literature about PR people; listening to PR professionals talk of their jobs; hearing the experience of students coming off a year's placement and their reports of lying; all these sources suggest that doing PR is dominated by trying to achieve corporate and group goals, with social responsibility and ethics being an operational consideration but not a bar to their fulfilment. This ranking flows ineluctably from the position of PR people as agents for an interest or a cause, working either for reward or out of commitment.

In optimum circumstances, PRs are conviction communicators, personally believing in their PR propaganda, which has been produced responsibly and ethically. These circumstances produce what Jensen (1997) calls 'hemispheric communicators'. He describes them (p. 68) as

> people who because of their defined role in society such as lawyers, advertisers, lobbyists and public relations practitioners express messages that speak to only half the landscape. Like the shining moon, they present only the bright side and leave the dark side hidden.

Their justification is, he argues, that they are 'an important informational engine for society' (ibid.), putting into it information that would not otherwise be known. In an echo of the role of *caveat emptor* in scrutinising PR messages (see Ch. 6), he says that message receivers expect 'hemispheric' messages and are 'on their guard' against them (p. 69). Jensen also notes that messages from competing institutions 'contain information that balances the whole picture' and that 'critics abound in an open democratic society to challenge assertions and to present other data and views' (ibid.). Sternberg (1994, p. 91) echoes Jensen's point about one-sidedness. She says about business language generally that: 'it is wrong to castigate sales pitches and advertising for not providing the whole truth: that is simply not their function'. For her, *caveat emptor* 'can be seen as a pithy reminder of the purpose of much business language: it is securing sales, not producing general consumer advice'.

More emphasis on ethics will make PR shine a purer light on its hemisphere of conviction, but it cannot direct the beam towards the other half. The self-advantaging nature of PR propaganda ensures that. So PR producers will always be neighbours to ethical torment.[10] Atkinson in his survey of PR ethics (2004, pp. 427–35) has summed up accurately:

> The role of the corporate communicator remains challenging. There will continue to be a requirement to 'soften' or 'control' the effect of 'bad' news whether financial or otherwise. There will continue to be pressure to create the perception that all is fine even when it is not.

Social responsibility

PR messages reflect the interests of those who send them. Since the middle 1990s, PR producers have been sending noticeably more messages about the socially responsible intentions and behaviours of their organisations and groups towards their stakeholders. These socially responsible intentions and behaviours can also be called corporate ethics in action. The most frequently asked question by consumers and observers of PR is whether these intentions and behaviours are genuine. Parsons (2004, p. 157) asks this question from the perspective of PR ethics: 'When is ethics about the right thing to do and when is it about making an organisation look good?' The question can be rephrased into a statement that couples intention and profitability. Business in the Community does this with 'Companies with a code of ethics generated significantly more economic added value and market added value in the years 1997–2000 than those without codes.'[11]Another rephrasing, germane to this argument, is: 'when are statements of and progammes for social responsibility genuine, and when are they window dressing?'[12] Christian Aid (2004)[13] put the point succinctly:

> companies make loud, public commitments to principles of ethical behaviour and undertake 'good works'. . . . It sounds and looks like a modern version of selfless philanthropy and no doubt in many individual cases is. . . . The problem is that companies frequently use such initiatives to defend operations or ways of working which come in for public criticism.

In the corporate governance field, Day and Woodward (2004) also find a gap between statutory obligation to disclose information and reporting practice by some companies. They note the difference between substantive and symbolic disclosure about employee information.[14]

In the face of this range of behaviour, the detection of genuine or fraudulent intentions of individuals in dominant positions in organisations and groups is methodologically difficult to operationalise. It is hard to imagine that more than a handful of very cynical postholders will say, even privately, that their intentions and actions are to deceive. Triangulation of detection methods will capture more authentic and trustworthy evidence than will respondent statements but, even then, there will be much more doubt than certainty. On the other hand, the benefits of having, and of admitting to, genuine intentions and actions are substantial and cost free, for being seen as socially responsible is likely to attract sales and reputation,[15] donors and supporters. It has traditionally been assumed that cause groups have honest intentions (i.e. that the League against Cruel Sports does genuinely want to abolish foxhunting), but whether their actions, and more so those of interest groups that have material interests to further, are always responsible is now a more frequently asked question. Business interests are asking it now,[16] and the behaviour of Greenpeace, in their successful PR campaign with Shell in 1996 over quantities of toxic material in the oil buoy Brent Spar, is their first point of query. Other questions are about the destruction of crops by Friends of the Earth in their campaigns against genetically modified crops, and about the alleged assaults on laboratory staff by animal welfare extremists.

This current focus on the social responsibility of non-business interests comes after attention to business behaviour, and indicates that the origin of ideas about corporate social responsibility (CSR) lay in attempts to correct alleged abuses by business. The consequence of this attention is an important point made by Andriof *et al.* (2003): being responsible to stakeholders puts business in society. Previously business was, so to speak, just in the economy. Its dual location now in both the economy and society has the benefits, for business critics, of more regulation of capitalism via new responsibilities, and the potential disadvantage that government could retreat from welfare provision and incentivise business to supply it. CSR, therefore, has complicated business life: Surma sums this up (2005, p. 5) as businesses assuming roles as 'collective moral actors'.

Since the middle 1990s, it has been the combination of businesses assuming social responsibility and their consequent stakeholder policies that have brought about the involvement of PR departments in programmes of corporate social responsibility (CSR). This stakeholding thinking places a business in a network of non-market, and non-commercial, relationships with the 'significant others' in its operations. The business, usually large to medium-sized,[17] typically develops 'community relations' programmes with the people around its offices and plants, or offers sponsorship of a good cause in the local civil society.[18] In the case of customers, suppliers or business-to-business relationships, the firm pledges itself to environmentally sustainable policies or to high-standard labour practices in developing economies. These policies have cost consequences and, where they involve actions beyond what is required by law or international treaties, they are subsidies paid out of shareholders' funds to promote social responsibility. There are a range of reactions by an individual business to these costs: they are necessary to meet the higher obligations of corporate citizenship, or religious or humanist morality; they should be refused on the grounds that it is immoral to take funds away from shareholders without their explicit permission. This last position is taken by Friedman (1962, p. 133) who argued that the sole social responsibility of business is to make profits within the law and in 'open and free competition'. This minimalist position on business social responsibility is developed by Sternberg (1994), Henderson (2001) and Halfon (1998). The latter argues that objectives of CSR can be 'fundamentally at odds' with the capitalist system. He cautions business to scrutinise the ideology of activists, to ask whom they represent, and to whom they are accountable.

There is a middle and instrumental position in this range of reactions to paying the corporate responsibility subsidy and the many references in PR textbooks to CSR invariably take it.[19] That position is: it is enlightened self-interest for the business to examine each CSR proposal pragmatically, and to pay the subsidy in return for later benefits of better corporate identity and reputation; more goodwill from suppliers; and more sales by impressed customers. This middle position reduces to the slogan 'ethics is good business'.[20] L'Etang (1996b, p. 92) maps these responses to being socially responsible in philosophical terms: where there is the calculation of benefit, there is utilitarianism (action for good consequences); where there is the imperative of duty, there is deontology (action as moral imperative).

PR as the 'voice' of CSR

Where do PR producers enter into CSR programmes? They sometimes administer small-scale programmes and more often write reports about it.[21] They help create the 'blaze of publicity' (Micklethwait and Woolridge 2003, p. 180) in which business now operates, and which has disadvantages for them. They work against a background of cynicism that in the UK's case (Dawkins 2004, p. 110) shows up as 70 per cent of the public thinking that 'industry and commerce " . . . do not pay enough attention to their social responsibility"'. One reply by them on behalf of their business principals is that companies are heeding needs beyond their own commercial ones voluntarily. In so 'voicing', however, business is implicitly making a distinction between CSR and philanthropy, because publicity about giving (CSR subsidies) to stakeholders is self-interested, and this runs against the private and silent altruism of philanthropy. Maybe it is that distinction which the public pick up on.[22] PR people, however, can have no principled objection to this publicity for they produce communications for self-advancement, and cannot avoid that task. The creation of communicative advantage is their core work. It is unknown (and perhaps unknowable) how many PR producers communicate CSR ethically, believing their messages to be good and right and true, and not 'window dressing'.[23] This book, however, does not take the idealist or cynical view that all PR persons believe in their organisations' or groups' social responsibilities or that none do. Rather, it takes an intuitive view that mixed judgements are made privately by PRs. The virtuous outcome for the PR professional doing CSR communications is a concordance of self-advantaging communication and benefit to others; the immoral outcome is self-advantaging communication and deception of others about benefits for them.

There is, however, a weakness in the concordance argument above for it glosses over the professional and personal difficulties caused by the non-alignment of the ethics of the PR person with the corporate social *irresponsibility*, the 'window dressing'[24] of the organisation or group he or she represents. What is the right action if he or she is in conflict? If the PR senses that the organisation is being deceitful or over-stating in its intentions and behaviour, even if there is some benefit to others, how is he or she to establish the validity of his or her intuition? An example is a business giving sponsorship monies to a football club that has racist supporters and about whom the club authorities are passive or complicit. Another case is an oil company giving monies to the indigenous people in an oil field as part of a covert settlement with a corrupt national government. Parsons (2004, pp. 157–62) suggests one answer by separating out public relations ethics and organisational ethics; but as she says that they are 'inextricably intertwined' (p. 162), she does not provide a basis for right behaviour. Which takes precedence? Roberts (2003) describes the dangers of non-alignment and so introduces the dilemma for the PR person of having to choose between individual morals and corporate behaviour. Roberts fears that talk of corporate ethics is just 'talk', i.e. a new form of corporate self-presentation associated with public relations. 'In this form, corporate social responsibility is cheap and easy: a sort of prosthesis, readily attached to the corporate body, that repairs its appearance but in no way changes its actual conduct' (p. 250). PR as prosthesis weakens the force of ethical sensibility in a corporate body, allowing for business as usual. What will stop this weakening is the grounding of business ethical capabilities in employees' sensibilities. Roberts argues that ethics are an individual matter (p. 251) '(f)or the corporate body is devoid of sensibility and, in this sense, is incapable of responsibility; ethics in business will always be a personal matter and the sensible corporation will always need to be built and grounded in individuals'. What Roberts presents here is the PR equivalent of the soldier's dilemma about obeying illegal, immoral orders. There are intractable and incommeasurable complexities in these dilemmas (i.e. the corporate cause is good; the means are wrong; the ethics of the PR person are at odds with the means) that show up the limitations of PR ethical codes. They are reference books that simplify. Beyond them lie torments of the individual conscience, caught in competing moral and material pressures. There are also the complexities created by organisational size. Will PR people in small and medium-sized businesses in frequent contact with stakeholders find it easier to develop sensibility than if they worked in big businesses? It is a commonplace that personal relationships raise levels of sensibility in individuals.

The PR producer is involved with corporate ethics in another way as well: it is the linkage through personal ethics to the moral and philosophical values of his or her employer or client (as opposed to the linkage to social irresponsibility and 'window dressing' discussed above) and therefore the balance between the individual and organisational. If the PR person judges that the organisation (or group) is being socially responsible for utilitarian reasons of benefit to self and others, what is the right balance between self and others? Is the evidence disproportionally in favour of the organisation? How are these concerns acted upon? L'Etang (1996b, p. 92) suggests a social audit but the difficulties of methodology and variations in organisational status between the PR and the dominant coalition will usually be considerable enough to make an equitable audit infrequent.

This reference to auditing is a reminder that supporters of social responsibility by business in society often see themselves as a progressive movement with a development agenda. Hilton and Gibbons (2002) exemplify this for they have developed the concept of corporate social leadership in succession to CSR. They give as examples the African distribution network of Coca-Cola delivering health education material, and Nike helping teachers in deprived inner London to eradicate bullying. The UK government is also an enthusiast, having set up in 2004 an academy to 'help managers integrate CRS into their organisations'. They set out six core characteristics, one of which is 'questioning business as usual'.[25] Few CSR enthusiasts, however, are as fervent as one New Zealand businessman who evangelises as follows: 'Out there in consumerland, customers are yearning to have relationships with companies.'[26]

The text above couples references about CSR to both 'organisations' and 'groups'. This again reflects a growing perception about the need to review the social responsibility of cause, interest and pressure groups, when, for example, they close down public facilities or destroy property (close roads while occupying cranes; vandalise staff cars). Such behaviour is a consequence of the promotional bidding to media news desks by groups in order to secure publicity in a competitive environment. It is the 'grumble' culture turning into the 'stunt' culture.

Finally, while sceptics among customers and observers argue about the balance of altruism and self-interest in CSR, it is extremely rare for the recipient stakeholders to say anything other than 'thank you'. For voluntary services, the CSR subsidy is income to support their needy clients, as their mission statements require, and their acceptance of it is no doubt in line with their ethical codes.

Stakeholders

The beneficiaries of socially responsible (or corporately ethical) behaviour by organisations and groups are usually – but not always – their stakeholders.[27] These beneficiaries are individuals (e.g. consumers, and donors to charities) and organisations (e.g. suppliers to a business) whose actions affect, and are affected by, the beneficent organisations and groups. The theory posits that businesses, causes, interests and pressure groups have to manage their relationships with those external entities that can influence the achievement of their goals. In this light, being socially responsible to your consumers who support charities is self-interest in the form of prudence, knowing that they can affect you. The relationship is utilitarian in that it distributes benefits to the subject and object in order to maximise the interests of both parties. It is the precautionary principle applied to the sustainability of communications with outside influentials in order to ensure longer-term organisational survival. It is mutuality in the form of enlightened self-interest. Moss and Warnaby (1997b, p. 61) describe this mutuality in business strategy terms: 'goal setting in such organisations will normally involve an attempt to balance profit maximising or satisficing imperatives against the anticipated social costs of the alternative strategies that might be adopted to achieve these goals'. Relations with stakeholders are also evidence of organisations and groups using co-operation[28] as well as competition in their search for advantage. Positive stakeholding relationships increase the security of the parties by sharing benefits. The

firm supports the village football team, and the local people work enthusi-
astically for the firm. The local wildlife trust helps the largest factory on
the industrial estate monitor its level of pollution, and so the environment
is cleaner and legal costs to the firm are avoided. This mutuality makes for
a quite rare happening – co-operative PR outputs. Stakeholding is thus a
form of social inclusion and so it diminishes barriers to expertise/analysis
flowing into and out of organisations and groups. Heath (1994) implicitly
argues for this diminution when he makes the argument that, from the
perspective of an enactment theory for organisations, external and internal
stakeholders are theorised as interdependent entities, and as not independent ones.

But not all stakeholders are treated beneficially or inclusively by the
organisation or group. Effects on the organisation or group lie at the heart of
the relationship with a stakeholder. So competitive or aggressive behaviour
by the stakeholder will be replied to in an appropriate PR tone. This threatening behaviour is seen in hostile takeover battles of one business by another
and the PR 'voicing' in the financial media. It is standard behaviour in the
PR of industrial disputes. Stakeholder theory, however, is not sufficiently
developed with regard to PR messaging to distinguish among stakeholders
who are allies, or neutrals or opponents of organisations and groups.[29] Most
PR usage of the theory assumes too easily that stakeholders are allies.

Like corporate social responsibility, the rise of the stakeholder thinking
in British PR is found in the 1990s when it started to displace the term
'publics' to describe the 'significant others' who influence and are influenced by the organisation or group. The term was first heard in the USA in
the 1950s and 1960s when firms were gauging their reaction to trade
unionists and early consumer activists.[30] Stakeholder thinking thus has its
origins in the theory of the firm (Freeman 1984), and has at its core the
assessment of risk in the dependent relationships that influence, positively
and negatively, the achievement of strategic goals. Freeman signals this
dependency when he uses the preposition 'in' after 'stakeholder', i.e. 'A
stakeholder in an organisation is any group or individual who can affect or
is affected by the achievement of the organisation's objectives.' In terms of
the history of contemporary ideas about the political economy and civil
society, it is a reaction (see Hutton 1999) to the paradigm of possessive
individualism and neo-liberal economics in UK thinking since the middle
1970s. Indeed, stakeholder thinking has become part of the British PR
paradigm, along with two-way communications. There is also, happily for
PR producers, the benefit from its adoption of more work: more stakeholders lead to more messaging to them and about them (e.g. in annual
reports), just as more CSR programmes lead to more PR. Indeed messages
about beneficence to stakeholders are a major component of a related and
growing PR activity – corporate branding (see Ch. 10).

The major benefit of stakeholder (and older 'publics') thinking for the
PR producer is the supply of a recipient for the PR message: when the

stakeholder is identified the message can be constructed and channelled. In this way, stakeholders are essential to effective PR propaganda. After that, the benefits diminish. In PR thinking, the concept raises four questions, in addition to lack of calibration when identifying ally, neutral or opponent status as set out above. The questions are: How do you define a stakeholder? What is the relationship with 'publics'? Are internal and external stakeholders different in their power effects? And is government in a category of its own?

Developing PR stakeholder theory

Stakeholder thinking has a contingency-based methodology when it becomes PR practice. You identify the stakeholder only when the circumstances indicate – actually or potentially – that outward or inward communication to or from the other entity will influence your organisation or group. For example, a university will not communicate with the local authority as a stakeholder until it seeks planning permission from them; an overseas aid charity will keep messaging with corrupt governments to a minimum if it wants more subscriptions from home donors. More dramatically, are trespassers stakeholders[31] of a farm when they refuse to leave the land after being asked a dozen times by the owner? Reversing the process, are stakeholders only that status when they are conscious of their position?[32] In these ways, the contingency and agency basis of stakeholder thinking gives it an amorphous quality that is operationally inefficient for the PR person analysing communication needs. It provides inadequate answers to the questions 'Who will influence us tomorrow?' 'How can employees be stakeholders if they are part of the organisation?' 'Is everybody a potential stakeholder in us?' 'Do they know they are stakeholders?'[33] 'When does affecting us become threatening us?' There is also a disproportionality about stakeholder thinking that is operationally unhelpful. In the farm example above, in what way does it help the farmer when he is talking to the media, to group the trespassers and his permanent staff in the same relationship category? Spicer (1997, p. 253) gives an uncertain answer when he writes 'The most common characteristic used by decision makers is an assessment of the stakeholders' potential power to influence the decisions of an organisation.'

Also problematic is the relationship with the older and largely discarded concept of 'publics'. That term had the value of reminding PR people that their work was connected with public opinion, even when it was not done in public, as with most lobbying. It made associations with other notions such as 'public affairs', 'public realm', 'public domain', 'public interest' and the Habermasian 'public sphere'. It therefore associated PR with the sense of its messages being spectated on, being observed; of PR being one of three parties in communicative acts – message sender, message receiver, process observer. This terminological erasure of a public dimension is a significant loss for the argument of the previous chapter (pp. 92–6) where the visibility of PR is a condition of its acceptability in a democracy. The 'stakeholder' term loses that sense of visibility for it does not connote a public–private dimension. Its principal, if implicit, connotation is reference to positive or negative effects. This referencing fits well with a part of the thesis of this book, namely that PR seeks advantage by the promotion of positive communicative effects. But it hurts that other part of the thesis which posits that truth statements in PR messaging come from their dialectical clash in public debate, consciously entered into (Ch. 6). There is also the point that use of the term 'stakeholder' is in danger of losing that grading of publics which was at the centre of Grunig's situational theory (Grunig *et al.* 2002, p. 324)[34] about them, and which is valuable for doing PR. For example, publics are latent, with the potential to be manifest; policy active as well as passive. Another under-developed aspect lies in the lack of sensitivity about organisational boundaries. Is stakeholder theory sensitive to the differences between employees, contractually bound to the organisation and in a servant–master relationship, and customers, free agents in a market, and often called 'sovereign'? They represent very different categories of effect. Adding these points together suggests that PR thinking about stakeholding needs more development if it is to guide good practice.

There is finally the question of whether governments are stakeholders in organisations and groups in the same way that other social entities are. Governments can certainly affect organisations and groups through fiscal and regulatory policy, and do so to the point of threatening their survival. Non-government stakeholders can threaten organisational existence but rarely in the sovereign way of governments against which there is ultimately no constitutional defence. A business can be threatened by another in a hostile takeover bid; employees can strike against their firm; a cause group can interfere with building a by-pass road. These actions, however, do not have the sustained potential for continuous damage that a government with executive and legislative power can have, albeit a liberal, democratic one. Witness the consequences of taxing the profits of pension funds; of awarding defence equipment contracts to home or overseas companies. Observe the seminal marginalisation of the tobacco industry and how it is obliged to warn that its product kills its consumers.[35] Note new messaging from food manufacturers as public policy develops on obesity.[36] The relationship with government is not the stakeholding one of affecting or being affected by another business, trade union or pressure group, the essence of Freeman's definition. It is of a different order of effect: it is the relationship of guarantor to the organisation's existence. Elected governments with strong executives and centralised administrations, as in the UK, are very powerful. They are Leviathans, but perhaps democratic ones. In the last twenty years, British governments have dismantled the industrial public sector; reduced the power of trade unions;

favoured markets over monopoly and cartels; preferred consumer interests rather than producer ones; introduced the 'big bang' of competition into the City of London; reformed the education and public housing systems; decreased the taxing powers of local councils; and introduced regulation into all these areas of national life. Stakeholder relationships in these private, public and voluntary sectors were not able to combine their common interests to halt the flow of policy: they have only shaped its margins. Constitutional stakeholders will lobby to limit this power but they have to accept its decisions as the consequence of elected government.

Summary

This chapter reviews three aspects of PR work that have become more central since 1990. There is more awareness of the ethics of public relations in the UK since business and political scandals from the 1990s. PR ethicists, however, have to confront the relationship of PR and propaganda; and then their personal relationship with the client or the employer for whom they produce messages. If PR producers judge, after introspection and regard to others' opinions, that the organisation or group they represent is a good, right or true interest, they are able to communicate in good conscience. The next step for the ethical PR person is to follow professional rules or formal codes of conduct so that they individually produce PR messages in a moral way. There is, however, a third consideration. PR propaganda is always self-advantaging communication, making PR people 'hemispheric communicators', those who draw attention to the positive values and behaviours of the interest they represent and not the negative. PRs have to decide whether they are morally comfortable with this imbalance. If not, they should not enter public relations work.

Communicating messages about CSR is work that links corporate values to the ethics of individual PRs very directly: it is the language of collective and individual responsibility to others. CSR came onto the PR agenda as a reaction to neo-liberalism, and because of the rise of environmentalism and the sustainability principle. Applied to business, it is an emphasis on corporate citizenship, placing businesses, especially big ones, in 'society' as well as in the 'economy'. The most frequently asked question is whether CSR programmes are good intentions turned into benefit for others; or whether they are 'window dressing'.[37] Increasingly these questions are asked of causes and interests as well as business. A broader question is whether their existence allows government to transfer welfare provision from the public to private sector.

CSR by business, beyond legislative and contractual obligation, is a subsidy paid out of shareholder funds to outside interests. Most PR textbooks take an instrumental position that such programmes represent enlightened self-interest, promising future, rather than present, benefit. If CSR is 'window dressing', the PR person is confronted with ethical questions.

These are complex inter-twinings of moral judgements by individuals, operational knowledge of the programmes, status and power inside organisations, and work cultures. If, however, ethics and social responsibilities are believed to be grounded in individuals rather than corporate bodies, the PR producer cannot avoid them.

CSR programmes are usually directed at the stakeholders of an organisation and these latter are defined as those who do or can affect an organisation and those who are or can be affected by it. Stakeholder theory recognises the interdependence on others of those who produce PR. It is the precautionary principle applied to public relations. The term was used in PR from the 1990s and has its origin in theories of the firm. It has largely displaced the earlier term 'publics' in PR discourse. Its main advantage for doing PR is that it identifies to whom messages should be sent. Otherwise, it is under-developed theory for PR practice. It is a contingency-based methodology and therefore cannot predict friendly and hostile influentials; it cannot indicate their status along axes of activity or effect; it does not distinguish between types of influence, such as commercial or employee; and it puts the most important 'stakeholder', which is government, in the same single category as the least powerful.

9 Politics, corporate PR, campaigning

This and the next two chapters (Chs 10 and 11) look at PR effects on three important public institutions: politics, markets and the media. The argument so far has presented PR as a pervasive component of the promotional culture of liberal democracy, albeit with a poor reputation amongst the general public, and also amongst specific publics such as journalists and politicians, most of whom are, ironically, heavy producers of PR in their own interests. PR is popular, yet disparaged. The relationship of PR to propaganda was then examined and the conclusion was that PR is weak propaganda. But the oddity of propaganda flourishing in democracies, when the conventional view has it that propaganda weakens public opinion and elected government, led to an examination of PR effects on democracy. This incongruity is as concerning as it is reassuring. The argument now becomes less systemic, and looks at how PR impacts on individuals in their roles as citizens and consumers, and in their roles as members of organisations, groups and professions. Individuals can be seen as either PR consumers (receiving PR messages) or PR producers (constructing and sending them), and many people fulfil both roles. For example, individuals read about food and wine *and* are active in Friends of the Earth campaigning against genetically modified plants. People are shareholders in companies they work for *and* are also trade unionists actively campaigning against a move to money-purchase pensions.

More broadly in terms of the larger British culture, PR is widely perceived as having negative effects on important aspects of public life.[1] It is, for example, a universal reaction that the title of 'spin doctor' elicits a negative judgement on whatever entity or whichever person is doing the 'spinning'.[2] In the UK's case, this is because PR offends against a traditional, popular and conventional view of the British about themselves. It offends a certain idea of equality – the British sense of 'fair play'. To use a word common in the 1930s and 1940s, the British do not like 'flannel',[3] bland, fluent language that obscures problems. To use its substitute word of the 1980s and 1990s, they do not appreciate listening to 'bullshit'. To write of wanting 'fair play' and of disliking 'flannel' and 'bullshit' is to put the case colloquially. More formally, what the terms express when used about the core institutions of public life discussed here is twofold: a rejection of language as camouflage, and the need for unhindered access to transparent markets and to transparent political decision-making, via multiple, mass-mediated sources of accurate information. The concerns about PR come alive when it reduces, or is perceived to reduce, through manipulative communications, open access to three institutions that are near-universally viewed as important public goods. Those three institutions are: free markets that claim to give choice and value; a political system that claims to be democratic and representative; and a media that calls itself independent.

PR puts itself in the dock before public opinion when it favours powerful, sectional causes and vested interests at the expense of broader public ones. It is not that the public rejects PR because it is weak propaganda. They learn from popular culture that the terms are nearly identical or completely so, and that promotional presentations are consequences of the society they live in. Rather the complaint of the public is that the powerful use PR propaganda against the public interest (see Chs 4 and 5). The three institutions of the market economy, the representative political system and the mass media are the principal sites through which the public witness either promotional conflicts resolving in favour of the public interest, or in favour of powerful but narrow interests. They are also the principal social mechanisms through which the welfare of UK citizens is enriched or impoverished. The market and the political system together can be seen as forming, at a distance from the individual consumer and citizen, the basic societal platform on which material and ideological resources are collectively shared out to classes and groups, and so later made more or less accessible to individuals inside classes and groups. The mass media is important to this collective and, ultimately, individual distribution of resources because they are the 'binoculars' through which UK consumers and citizens can observe, evaluate, approve of or disapprove of that share out. UK consumers and citizens are wary of communicative manipulation by PR in any form which interferes in that distribution against their interests, and are watchful for an equitable share out of material and ideological resources. Their interests are served not by PR being 'banned' from liberal democracy, but by total PR production being in a state of PR communicative equality. This is where all interests are promoting themselves through factually accurate but biased, and emotionally moderate but positive, persuasive messages that are equally available to all citizens and consumers. These conditions for a socially beneficial PR (all PR production and consumption in a state of communicative equality) do not apply in the UK today (see Ch. 7).

Looked at exclusively from the viewpoint of PR consumption, this normative view can be characterised in another way as the 'auction house' model of PR. It is one in which citizens and consumers need accurate information and substantial confidence in communications before they commit themselves to: buying in markets; assessing the honesty of the public policy decision-making process; participating in politics; or believing what the media say. This characterisation can be developed further. The auction catalogue (the mass media) should be current, accurate and should publicise all organisations and groups making an offer to the public. The goods and services up for auction (public policy-making; market products; interests, causes) should be open to inspection. People putting things into the auction (politicians, businesses, campaigners) should be honest and contactable (accountable). There should be no price-fixers, market riggers, hidden persuaders (monopolists, unknown public policy-makers, undeclared interests) manipulating offerings.

Importantly, this auction house model is cast from the viewpoint of PR 'consumers': the people who are at the receiving end of PR, citizens and market consumers. It is not a model from the viewpoint of PR 'producers' and 'players'. Its focus is on the effects of PR. The PR literature in the UK (academic and professional) lacks this perspective to a great extent, being technical in tone and focused on organisational needs. The critical literature from media and cultural studies only touches on PR effects in a fragmentary or illustrative way. Indeed, it is a surprise how little attention PR as a distinct mode of message production for the media receives in mainstream academic work. There is room for a PR effects literature alongside the media effects one. It would fill gaps in understanding about how and why PR is produced and consumed. An example, from consumer behaviour, would be how marketing PR influences consumers as conceptualised in the nine roles Gabriel and Lang (1995) set out.[4] Chapter 10 explores markets and PR but here politics and PR are examined first, for effective markets depend on the legal framework established by politics and government.

Politics and government

It is hard to distinguish between PR and much of modern politics. The working styles and job contents of spin doctor, lobbyist and politician are merging, making the distinctions of less presentationally conscious times harder to grasp. The history of special advisers to UK ministers since the 1960s, when they were first introduced in significant numbers, illustrates this merger. Blick (2004)[5] shows that their policy advice and implementation roles were primary under the 1964–70 Labour governments but that this primacy has declined under Conservative and Labour governments since 1990. He chronicles (pp. 266–7) their increasing numbers, which by 2002 had half (forty) of them doing PR for ministers all the time or part of it.[6] Another sign of conflation is how special advisers, lobbyists in public affairs firms, and politicians move around jobs: the core work is familiar at the three locations.[7] The contemporary cultural dominance of marketing and PR with their primary emphasis on self-interested display and exchange is a systemic reason for the conflation. How naturally in this culture a Labour Party publication for its members can attribute to a Prime Minister the words 'We have a good story to tell. We have got to get out and sell it.'[8] Another, more conscious, reason is the judgement by the Labour Party leadership since 1983 that it had to cultivate better relations with a largely hostile, pro-Conservative UK press. The consequence was that the party leadership, MPs, paid professionals and many activists dropped their often ambiguous, if not hostile, attitude towards the media and became more PR conscious. The party careers of Peter Mandelson, Alastair Campbell and Charlie Whelan are symbolic of this change.[9]

There is, however, a cost to politics in this increasing emphasis on the presentational. While increased emphasis on PR is a response to the need to maximise electoral support in a media-saturated, marketised democratic system, more of it done by government blurs the distinctions between policy-makers (elected politicians and senior civil servants), policy explainers (civil service information officers) and policy promoters (special advisers). This blurring makes it harder to identify what politicians have decided, and runs the risk of taking power away from politicians and transferring it to experts in presentation. Blick recounts (p. xiv) how Clare Short, formerly Secretary of State for International Development, told a House of Commons committee in 2002 that:

> Alastair Campbell [then chief press spokesperson for the government] is responsible for the presentation of government policy, and that soon becomes propaganda and there is a place for that. Once proper decisions have been made, then the government should put forward what it is trying to do as well as it can and communicate with the public, *but the two often conflate* [emphasis added by Blick].

This conflation (the merging of policy-making and policy presentation) is evidence of the high water mark of PR influence on modern UK government, compared with its start in 1911 when the Liberal government sent presenters around the country to explain the first public welfare benefits. In personal terms, it has made Alastair Campbell the most influential public relations person in British history. In governance terms, conflation makes PR an integral part of policy-making, and not a second-order matter of presentation. It leads to allegations that words and evidence about policy are 'sexed up' (exaggerated) in order to maximise political support. This is the work of PR people inflating the meaning and significance of policy, and was an allegation against Campbell in his dealings with intelligence experts over the 2002 September dossier justifying the decision to invade Iraq in 2003.[10] A year later, the Butler inquiry investigated the conduct of British intelligence over the war. After the publication of its report, one of the inquiry members said 'Intelligence and public relations should be kept apart.'[11] If they are to be, Blick shows that there is a lot of

PR work to be separated out. He notes (pp. 288–9) that the Central Office of Information (COI), which advises government on marketing communications, is 'the largest purchaser in this market'. Add to this the 1,200 press and specialist PR officials in the Government Communications Network (GCN);[12] another 300 staff in the Government News Network (GNN); the media work of special advisers; the news management operations of Downing Street; and the total capacity makes democratic government the most resourced, comprehensive and continuous PR operation in the UK. It is evidence of what Franklin (2004, pp 5–7) calls 'this ambition to package politics'[13] and what Deacon and Golding (1994, p. 4) name 'the public relations state'.

Conflation of another sort (between PR as information-giving by civil servants and as political advantage by ministerial advisers) is also evident. Blick (2004, pp. 266–7) reports how the PR role of the special adviser is seen as different from that of civil servants in Whitehall press offices. It is the difference between giving factual information and giving political explanation. Special advisers could 'add that extra dimension – to an extent be the Minister's voice'.[14] These two roles can be distinguished in a conceptual way but they are too fine to bear the brunt of practice. Indeed Blick's account is, in significant measure, a history of special advisers and permanent civil servants clashing over policy presentation from two competitive stances – those of government as administration, and of government as political competition. The Jo Moore affair exemplifies the tensions between the two roles.[15] Another area of greater PR influence is the Downing Street media relations operation since 1997. It was much strengthened by the setting up of a Strategic Communications Unit that operates a 'grid' system for releasing news whereby 'good news' stories come out in a co-ordinated way from across Whitehall for all media edition times. This was a news management system imported from the Labour Party, as was the 'rapid rebuttal' system of countering hostile media stories operated from the Research and Information Unit, also at No. 10.

From all this, it is clear that the basic motivation in public relations of self-presentation-for-attention-and-advantage is found in politics and government. The urgent and constant search for media coverage is shared. Politics assimilates from PR and marketing such attitudes and skills as: research into what electors want through surveys and focus groups; sensitivity about personal appearance; being 'on message'; event management; sponsorship; creating pseudo-events;[16] and constructing new corporate identities. There is an evident transfer of skills from mass marketing and corporate PR to politics.[17] The most common term for this is political marketing, and its most striking feature is the attempt to know what mass populations want. The search to understand mass public opinion and satisfy it is a relatively new political phenomenon, unknown before the Enlightenment and less than 140 years old in the UK.[18] Until the 1860s, political persuasion was not a mass process, instead taking the forms of

Establishment and professional class networking through personal contact, and of corruption with drink or money of householders who had the vote. In the UK, there never has been a golden age when politics and persuasion went separate ways, and there never will be. The incremental spread of the franchise; the rise of modern political parties from mid-Victorian times; and the development of mass persuasion techniques at the end of that period meant that politics and persuasion entered a phase of massification. Modern PR makes the connections manifest (see Franklin 1994, 2004; Jones 1995, 1997, 1999, 2002; Rees 1992; Scammell 1995) but the linkages are not to all politicians' liking. Tony Blair said in 2002 that his first government had overvalued PR (2004, Blick, p. 268), an irony coming from a politician near universally liked or disliked for his presentational skills. The irony, however, is not a new one – Harold Wilson, who was twice Labour Prime Minister and renowned for his presentational skills, is alleged to have said PR was 'degrading'.[19]

Whatever the personal judgements, politicians use PR because of its benefits to them. These advantages, and wider ones for democracy, can be summed up as attention-catching information flows from parties and government to electorate and public. PR is a major flow of persuasive information between rulers and ruled, and when democracy is seen as an information system about public goods, its contribution is important. PR makes connections between political elites and the mass electorate. McNair (1995, p. 191) elaborates this: PR and other political marketing techniques make politics a more attractive 'mass spectator sport' to an electorate who are adept at winnowing out manipulation and propaganda from useful information and opinion in political communications. However, whatever the benefits, there is little refuge from PR and the persuasive mode for modern democratic politicians: mass electorates oblige them to be more persuasive than they were in the age of limited democracy. Wernick's (1991) promotional culture is not partial: self-interested messages come from all sites in society, the political as much as the commercial. Schlesinger and Tumber (1994, p. 271) talk of evidence 'for the existence of an inescapable promotional dynamic that lies at the heart of contemporary political culture'. Franklin (2004, p. 5) writes about a 'media democracy' and that it is difficult to 'overstate the centrality of media to politicians' identity'. McNair (1996, p. 52) is correct when he notes that 'mass democracy is inevitably *populist* democracy in which appearance and image, as well as policy substance, have a role to play'. Democratic politicians have to behave as suitors as well as policy-makers. In these ways, mass-mediated persuasive messaging, much of it now called PR, has been merging with politics since the mid-Victorian period. It would, however, be wrong to think that in the pre-democratic period of politics, the aristocratic era, that politics was as impersonal as marble. In the 1780s, Georgiana, Duchess of Devonshire, is credited by Foreman (1999, p. 401) with being among the first 'to refine political messages for mass communications. She was an image maker who understood the necessity of public relations and she became adept at the manipulation of political symbols and the dissemination of party propaganda.'[20] At least eleven women canvassed daily (p. 157) for either Fox and Pitt in the 1784 Westminster by-election and what made Georgiana stand out was her persistence in canvassing and her readiness to relate directly to electors, getting out of her carriage, going into homes, eating and drinking with electors, buying from their shops and allegedly being kissed by them (p. 143). Foreman says (p. 158) she treated electors as her equals. Today we are more likely to say that she was a celebrity who knew how to manage events, if not stunts.

Politics, however, is about ends as well as means: PR is always a means to an end. The forms of presentation of PR and of politics are coalescing for politics is parasitical about where it finds its persuasive means. However, politics, as the non-violent resolution of conflicting interests, should be the master activity in relation to policy, with presentation a secondary concern. Politics deals principally in a currency of incommeasurable values, goals and behaviours, out of which equilibrium may or may not be produced. Presentational skills alone will never make for peace and justice in Northern Ireland, Iraq or the Middle East. Or for adequate dental services provided by the National Health Service. Only right policy makes for good outcomes, and so Clare Short is correct to warn of the dangers of merging policy-making and policy presentation.

Political news management and 'spin'

'Spin' and its 'doctors' are both new and old in UK politics: new because they are a New Labour style (soon copied by other parties); old because UK governments have always practised news management,[21] which is PR with a media focus. L'Etang (2004b, p. 151) writes of concerns going back to the 1960s about PR in politics. McQuail (2004, p. 326) notes an academic and journalistic opposition that amounts to a 'demonology of spin'. As a style, the Labour Party developed its news management in the 1980s to neutralise hostile media coverage. The development was more than the creation of the memorable metaphor of 'spin': it was a new attitude and behaviour towards the media on the part of Labour politicians, such as Peter Mandelson and later Tony Blair when he became party leader in 1994, and his chief press aide then, Alastair Campbell. Aggressive behaviour towards journalists; the withdrawal of respect for them as a Fourth Estate (a corps whose service to the unwritten UK constitution was to publish scrutiny of government); and no or little sympathy for the principal of editorial independence, are core elements of spinning.[22] The literature illustrates these features. Jones (1995, 1997, 1999), McSmith (1997) and Oborne (1999) describe how Mandelson, Campbell and Whelan, the three best known New Labour spin doctors, offered exclusives to favourite journalists; browbeat them by verbal bullying, swearing[23] and withholding information; spoke negatively about them to rivals and their bosses; humiliated them publicly. Indeed, New Labour spin doctors were sometimes aggressive towards their own side. Evidence for this is the critique by Ken Follet, a former fundraiser for New Labour, who asked (in July 2000) whether Tony Blair wanted to be remembered as the Prime Minister who made 'malicious gossip an everyday tool of modern British government' against its own members (Blick 2004, p. 12).[24] Two months earlier Labour MP Alan Simpson reported that a 'spin machine, a press publicity briefing machine' exists and that its job 'is to promote those that the [Blairite] project favours, and to quietly sideline or undermine those that it disfavours'.[25] He named the then-Cabinet Office minister Mo Mowlam as a target. Lord Hattersley, a former deputy leader of the Labour Party, reported that a Downing Street press officer phoned him to denigrate a minister about whom he was writing a profile.[26] Politics is indeed a 'rough old trade' for, in other spheres of public life, such behaviour constitutes harassment and discrimination, and is subject to workplace discipline and legal challenge.

Lloyd (2004a) further describes the Labour origins of spin. The makers of the New Labour project integrated the media into policy and campaigning, and moved away from seeing the media as an institution to which politics delivered messages periodically. He argues that New Labour does not regard presentation as important as policy content. 'But it was accepted that people had to be convinced if policies were to be successfully implemented and that meant using the media to inform them' (p. 88). The transition from Old to New Labour had to be done in public if the electorate was to be convinced that Labour had left socialism behind; 'The public acceptance of the process . . . was an integral part of the exercise' (p. 89). Moreover, the media had changed into a twenty-four hours, seven days a week phenomenon, and was 'a ravenous media which would eat you if you did not feed their ever-open maws' (ibid.). The stage was set for the spin doctors. Lloyd notes (p. 101) that the British media is more competitive than anywhere else in the world and Oborne (1999, pp 106–25) reminds us that New Labour's spin did not develop in isolation from changes in journalism: indeed it could not have flourished without what Oborne calls the rise of the Media Class in the period 1979–84.

Spin began with Labour in the mid-1980s, therefore, as a *defensive response* by the party to editorial hostility shown by the Murdoch British press (*The Times*, the *Sunday Times*, the *Sun*, the *News of the World*), the *Daily Mail* and *Daily Express* media groups between 1979 and 1994. After Blair's accession to the leadership in 1994, hostility from these sources turned to support or benevolent neutrality as New Labour accommodated itself to the core Thatcherite reforms of the 1980s. From that acceptance onwards, New Labour used the technique with enthusiasm for the *offensive promotion* of itself as government-in-waiting and then as government. That style of spinning reached its apogee under Campbell during his attack on the BBC during the Gilligan affair in 2003 after the start of the Iraqi war. Blick (2004, p. 312) observes that 'Campbell's partisanship verged on the obsessive.' His successor as Chief Press Secretary to the Prime Minister was David Hill, who was appointed Director of Communications to the Prime Minister in 2003 with responsibility for the political aspects of the Downing Street news management operation, as opposed to the civil service ones.[27] It became clear that Hill's style was much more discreet and understated than that of his predecessor.

Spin as propaganda

Political spin can be related to propaganda in the following way. It is one-sided, biased information put in the public domain by government or opposition parties with what Ellul (1962) identifies as one of the defining marks of propaganda: the intention to create a 'will to action' (p. x) among, in this case, voters so that they will support the propaganda sender. Spin is a weak or soft form of propaganda[28] where 'weak/soft' means that the activity happens in a democratic state; where the activity can be identified as information manipulation; where the information is more accurate than inaccurate; and where the purpose of the spin is known, i.e. to enhance the standing of the government or opposition party. UK governments and political parties have to communicate persuasively with their various publics if they want to maximise their seats in the House of Commons, the necessary condition for their holding or sharing in state power. Gaber (2000) has analysed spin as a process. Alongside it are other forms of government and political party persuasive communications (e.g. speeches in Parliament; party political broadcasts; electoral advertising; public information campaigns; and websites)[29] but spinning is, above all, associated with the persuasive management of journalists to secure favourable media coverage. Ministers do spin but most spinning is done by their agents.

Politicians who depend on periodic election for their jobs will always – and healthily so for a democracy – be concerned to present their policies and behaviour in a favourable light. It is this permanent need for self-presentation, for self-preservation, for party publicity, and for government promotion that makes spin the current version of the traditional habit of political news management. The propagandising imperative is a constant. The subsidiary question is whether ministers should do their own PR. Alas, the 'ever-open maws' of the 'ravenous' media (Lloyd above, p. 124) means that ministers need press aides to feed it with 'good' stories, and to limit the damage of 'negative' stories.[30] Hence the greater time spent by ministerial staff on media relations since the 1960s is a response to media growth. The propagandising imperative of politics no doubt made the extra allocation of time and effort away from policy deliberation easier to tolerate, as did the increase in the numbers of special advisers. Spinning also raises ethical questions of personal behaviour for politicians. Is it acceptable to badmouth colleagues behind their backs through spinning? (see p. 124). Is negative briefing against fellow ministers acceptable? It is not. Given the evidence, however, that this malicious gossiping happens, the presence of spin doctors makes it easier for it to be done. Ministers can use their spin doctors/special advisers to give 'negative briefings'; to promote what has been called the 'sneer and smear' culture.[31] When politicians behave disloyally against colleagues, the culture and conventions of politics should be such as to make it difficult for them to lay this task off onto a third party.[32]

Examining spin in terms of propaganda and of the culture of political civility does not exhaust the theoretical perspectives on offer.

Blumler and Gurevitch (1981) offer two conceptualisations of the government–media relationship, one in market terms and the other in military ones. They categorise relationships between government spin doctors (a term they did not know)[33] and journalists as *either* an exchange or a contest. Both relationships centre on the value of information, and of favourable publicity. Spin doctors are the actors on the government/party side of these two relationships. The exchange relationship can be characterised as a voluntary, informal contractual one because it mimics a market relationship in which information supplied by government is freely swapped for publicity supplied by journalists at the price where both sides gain equal satisfaction, namely where spin doctors and journalists estimate that the cost of what they gave to each other is equal to the benefit they get from each other.

The other, or contest, relationship, however, can be characterised as non-market, militaristic behaviour because government is not supplying information but is hiding it away from journalists. The latter have to discover and seize it from a camouflaging government, securing it for reasons other than those of the equal exchange mechanism of markets. That is, they seize it because of the disaffection, disloyalty, conflicting policy interests, party competitions, public interest instincts of politicians and civil servants. These militaristic contest relationships are usually associated with anonymous leaks, unattributable briefings and coded messages. The exchange relationship characterises government and media as traders; the contest relationship as opponents. The exchange relationship implies two equally satisfied parties while the contest one implies winners and losers. The role of the media as watchdogs is consistent with the contest model. Public relations people invariably favour the exchange relationship but are prepared and skilled for the contest one. That is another reason why journalists dislike them.

Corporate PR

Politicians are not the only spinners.[34] The term has entered everyday language to describe in a vernacular way any form of public relations; and, beyond that, any presentation to a layperson of a dubious proposition, the source or advantage of which is hidden. 'Spin' is the modern version of the older 'flannel' term (see p. 117). In a cultural sense, PR people should congratulate themselves that their project is so central to popular culture today that terms like 'spin' have been adopted to describe any persuasive transaction. Instead too many of them cringe at its popularity. Back inside PR territory, it is now businesses, public and voluntary bodies, interest and cause groups who also spin.[35] They do so, however, without that particular New Labour tone of aggression and manipulation. A rule of thumb has it that some 30 per cent of PR jobs in the UK are in corporate public relations (CPR), and with marketing public relations (MPR) (see Ch. 10) make up the industry's employment profile. Corporate public relations is also called 'public affairs', 'corporate affairs', 'governmental relations', and it is arguable whether CPR is the most common term. But in PR labelling terms, it is the most clarifying for it shows that PR is done for either marketing and commercial reasons or for government and stakeholder liaison reasons. The distinction is not about work relating to market and non-market activity, for in a capitalist market economy with a consumer culture there are few areas immune to market operations and attitudes.[36] CPR departments, therefore, do any or all of the following – lobbying; industry liaison; investor relations; corporate branding; community relations; employee communications; corporate advertising and small-scale corporate sponsorships.[37] Of these, lobbying governments at home or in Europe, influencing official regulators, and liaising with industry representative bodies is foundational work for CPR departments. If all these tasks are not done in-house, agencies are hired in for specific projects or for watching briefs, of which the most common and most mechanical is monitoring official documents.

The work was once puffed in an arch way as 'the thinking man's PR',[38] but that complacency has passed away under the dual realities of marketing thinking and feminism. CPR grew as a distinct field of work in the UK from the 1960s, and attracted notables such as Will Camp, who refused to call his work 'organised lying' because it was 'too strong' and preferred 'arranging the truth so that people will like you'.[39] There are various informal lunch and dining clubs where CPR people exchange professional gossip, but there is in the UK no discrete body for them alone to promote good practice. There is in the USA. It is the Arthur W. Page Society, which represents some 300 of the corporate PRs of the largest US businesses. Page was an influential PR man working for the American Telegraph and Telephone Company in the 1920s and 1930s, associated with the development of PR as listening communication,[40] and with its emergence as a business discipline. During the Second World War, he was sent to England in April 1944 to 'oversee indoctrination of the American invasionary force' (Griese 2001, p. 243). Now the group named after him promulgates six 'principles' of good practice (tell the truth; prove it with action; listen to the customer; manage for tomorrow; conduct public relations as if the whole company depends on it; remain calm, patient and good humoured).[41] There is no such organised schema of good practice promoted by British corporate PRs but a useful one is associated with Richard Reader, a corporate PR for the former nationalised British Gas. It relates stakeholder perceptions to organisational 'facts' and allocates a PR competence level to the four relationships.[42] To professional managers, these various operational learning and monitoring devices provide them with the rudiments of a management discipline. The most evaluated of these perceptions is those of government for lobbying is CPR's most important function, and relates it immediately to representative democracy. Because of these connections, corporate public relations for business attracts hostility and monitoring websites.[43] There has been a reaction from business to this attention and Deegan (2001) and John and Thomson (2003) describe the strategies and tactics of resistance by commerce. Business will wryly note that this attention comes because cause activists and trade unionists have copied their corporate campaigns. In his study of 200 such campaigns, Manheim (2001, p. 308) notes that this imitation is another example of 'the increasing reliance on techniques of strategic communication to shape political discourse, and, through it to shape the political system and the public policies that it produces'. Such a conclusion allows business and its opponents little discretion to ignore corporate PR.

Lobbying and campaigning

The case for and against PR as lobbying matches the anatomy of influence in a liberal democracy. In such a polity with individual rights of free expression and property ownership, approaching government to 'redress' wrongs and to 'petition' for change is constitutionally unimpeachable. Its traditional advocates usually trace its origins in the UK to the Magna Carta of 1215. Moreover, in the climate of accelerated pluralism that characterises organisation and group competition in the UK today, PR is unavoidable. It aids stronger, 'insider' groups (to use the distinction of Wyn Grant (1989, 1995, 2000)) to maintain public policy in their favour and this has been the principal use of lobbying in the UK (see Ch. 7). Schnattschneider was right in 1975 to say that pressure groups sing in an upper-class voice, though that is less true today. It is still correct, however, to say that in the UK it keeps a 'naughty but nice' image after the 'cash for questions' scandals of the early 1990s.[44]

But PR as lobbying (lobbying PR) is a technique with potential to add strength to weaker, 'outsider' (ibid.) groups that seek policy advantage. Technically, lobbying is an accessible set of low-cost techniques, not difficult to acquire, and revolves around a sense of collective interest, policy awareness and analysis, copy writing skills and organising ability. What militates against effective influence by 'outsider' groups is their lack of access to policy-makers. Compare their efforts to see a middle-ranking civil servant with the former and then largest British business, Imperial Chemical Industries (ICI), inviting all civil servant heads of Whitehall departments to the Royal Opera House, London. This was also the business that had six monthly, pre-diaried access to the permanent secretary of the Trade and Industry Ministry.[45] It remains true in the UK today that hiring lobbyists is expressive of the 'privileged but challenged and fractured position' of business in the political economy (Moloney 1996, p. 149). Against this structural power of big business, lobbying aids resource-poor, marginal groups in that it publicises their interests and so socialises the conflict which is to their advantage (Schnattschneider 1975) and at times business is ready to consult, if not negotiate, with them.[46] This is PR as a conduit for bringing in government and public opinion to rebalance the contest between interests of different power and influence.[47] If accelerated pluralism continues to grow and there is the introduction of subsidies for communicative equality (see Ch. 6), the predominance of powerful 'voices' will weaken, and PR as lobbying will be a means to more equitable representation in the competition of interests. This will be welcome in the light of business lobbying's ability to fix policy agendas through its powerful mobilisation of bias, a feature of Lukes's second dimension of power (see p. 93). Finer was right to end his early but seminal studies of British lobbying (1966, 2nd edn) with the call for 'light, more light', i.e. more transparency of decision-making. It is a modern call that connects back to Jeremy Bentham in 1843 and his argument that publicity is the 'fittest law' for securing public confidence in parliaments and national assemblies acting responsibly. PR messaging can be seen as raw material constituting parliamentary debate that combusts into the 'light' of publicity as legislation is scrutinised. It is, however, much more problematic to conclude that more PR messaging will generate more 'light' leading to more favourable policy outcomes for marginalised groups. To help rebalance policy influence in their favour, small reforms such as a register of public meetings between MPs, ministers and lobbyists could be introduced, and also the requirement that minutes of these meetings are kept.[48]

As an industry, lobbying in the UK grew in the decade from the early 1980s, with estimates of a doubling or trebling in turnover for lobbying businesses who hire themselves out.[49] It is, however, much harder to measure amounts of lobbying done in-house by the employees of organisations such as businesses, for the cost is rarely identified. Identification is even more an obstacle for the voluntary sector where 'campaigning' and 'information' work is the preferred term of public policy influence. Lobbying has also benefited from a new kind of pluralism – constitutional devolution. Lobbying always follows politics: lobbying firms have opened offices in Edinburgh, Cardiff and Belfast[50] as government has been devolved to these regional capitals. They also have a strong presence in Brussels as European supra-national government grows (see McGrath 2005).

Lobbying PR is a long game over time for influence. When to declare success turns on the balance of events and perceptions. Lobbyists for the food and drinks industry have 'For decades . . . sabotaged any attempt to instil a modern nutritional perspective on government thinking.'[51] In the UK, lobbyists against foxhunting with dogs hesitate to declare victory until a 2004 Act of Parliament has survived challenges in the highest British court, the House of Lords, and then the European Court of Human Rights. The balance of policy and commercial advantage on genetically modified (GM) food is unclear despite backing by Prime Minister Tony Blair in 1999.[52] Surrounding the immediate policy questions, he said then, were two 'broader issues': 'we need to be guided by good science, not scaremongering' and 'we should resist the tyranny of pressure groups'. These remarks illustrate the political pressure that can be generated by the PR of outsider groups: for 'scaremongering' read using media relations, organising petitions, designing news events to build public awareness and political pressure; and for 'tyranny' read combining these PR techniques into a sustained campaign that influenced government to modify its policy. By 2005 in the UK, it was clear that 'scaremongering' and 'tyranny' had delayed free markets for GM foods, pending scientific trials. The major British supermarkets had also banned them from sale in the face of an opposing public opinion.

This opposition demonstrates the power of PR by cause groups in the voluntary sector to generate political influence when it is done by a small central team of professionals and backed by volunteers around the country. West (1963, p. 127) makes this point in connection with a famous march by unemployed men in 1936 from Gateshead to London: 'The Jarrow march won more supporters than any handout.' He also notes, in a sardonic way, on his last page the connection with civil society:

> When people care so little for any cause that they leave the business or the argument to the experts, our society will be ripe for rule by an oligarchy of PROs and Professor Rollo Swavely will hold the chair of Image Building at MacMillan College, Oxford.

This generous compliment to PR done in civil society calls attention to public 'campaigning'.

Campaigns

PR people in both business and voluntary sectors talk a lot about 'campaigning'. One imagines that for business PRs this work is more attractive than the usual routines of answering media calls, planning for crisis communications, and meeting marketing managers. For PRs in charities and non-governmental organisations (NGOs), however, campaigning is more workaday, because they are employed to change the *status quo* in their area of concern; and campaigning is very conspicuous, public communications for change.[53] In the family of 'voice' metaphors, it is 'shouting' and at times 'slagging off'. Indeed, PR people in cause groups do not 'do' PR: they do 'campaign and information work'. Lubbers (2002) sets out how environmental groups do this in their campaigns against business 'greenwashing', their term for superficial shows of sustainability by government and business.

A PR campaign is a planned concentration of communication resources directed at the achievement of a pre-defined goal in a limited time, after a distinctive launch. It promotes a product, service or cause through press conferences, a flow of media stories, celebrity endorsement and stunts. It is the opposite of continuous, unchanged, conventional PR. It is professionally self-indulgent for its producers; it is one-way communication, with an edge of bossiness and of 'nanny knows best' certainty. It is used too frequently to be a very effective call for new thinking and behaviour. It has thus become the launch of a new car or fashion; another 'new' appeal for funds; more puffing of a marginal consumer service; more public information to engineer changes to our behaviour; and most oppressive of all, the communicative agitation of voters to push them into polling booths at general elections.

So why do the funders of PR support campaigns? They do so because they contribute to goals and causes that depend on public support. Public campaigns are often the 'megaphone' turned on after discreet, private lobbying fails or when it needs the visible support of demonstrations and media coverage. They are evidence of an axiom of communications planning, namely that attitudes and behaviours only change after many rounds of messaging. Anti-smoking campaigns started in the 1960s; safe driving ones are as old as the car; and it is hard to see an end to safe sex or anti-drugs ones. Sales campaigns for new products are a constant feature of profit-seeking producers in markets (witness the introduction of vegetarian and salad-rich fast food). Note that whole industries remind us that salt or GM food is 'safe'; and that to buy a pension is to secure a prosperous old age. Campaigns are periodic, communicative 'shouts' from interests and causes with long-term goals.

Stunts

Stunts, or in formal PR jargon 'event creation' and 'management', are a frequent component of campaigns by cause groups, NGOs and politicians, and an under-studied part of PR.[54] Examples are climbing cranes in central London in Batman gear for estranged fathers; burning fake £50 notes and flying plastic white elephants to stop regional government in northeast England.[55] Politics is a routine but tired setting for them – witness[56] a national party hiring a steam train with Pullman carriages to bring minor celebrities to Bournemouth for their conference. Study of stunts will enrich understanding of PR through tracing connections with popular culture, a linkage evident with the cultural jammers in the USA, such as the Adbusters (see p. 144). There is a US history of stunts in the persons of P.T. Barnum and less famously of Harry Reichenbach who performed in the 1920s.[57] Stunts should be seen principally as the work of PR press agents creating and managing public events, alongside street artists, for civic carnivals and marketing promotions; but not exclusively, for some are the creations of pressure groups, managing long-term economic and planning issues.[58] They are connected with what Levine (1993, p. xxiii) has called 'the grammar of direct public participation' and he shows how to think like a publicist. There is a StuntWatch website, and a related one that talks of 'The Art of the Publicity Stunt'.[59] Stunts open up PR production to more creativity, for they are founded on a carnivalesque, theatrical representation of events, themes and persons in the public domain. They remind PR professionals and campaigners that an eye-catching dimension to their work can be effective. Stunts can be made to work for human rights and for bringing the Olympic games to a city.[60]

Summary

After examining the generalised PR propaganda relationship with democracy in previous chapters, this one examines the balance of positive and negative PR effects on politics, the first of three institutions that deliver important public goods in a liberal democracy. (Markets and journalism are the others.) It is through these institutions that people judge whether PR is working for their interests, e.g. whether it delivers to them useful information about choices in markets and politics.

A merging of working styles and job contents between PR and modern politics is indicated by the media relations work of special advisers. Now half of them (40) are doing news management fully or partially. Such conflation blurs the boundary between policy and presentation, to the detriment of the former. Presentation does not bring peace, prosperity and justice: only right policy does. Another conflation is witnessed between the roles of information giving by civil servants and political promotion by special advisers, as indicated by the Jo Moore affair in the UK. It is likely that promotional culture will see more merging of PR and politics towards what has been called 'the public relations state' (Deacon and Golding 1994). Part of that assertive, self-advantaging culture is 'spin', aggressive news management devised by the Labour Party to secure better media coverage from the mid-1980s onwards. Labour 'spin doctors' were successful in their media campaigns, and the best known of them, Alastair Campbell, chief press secretary to the Prime Minister for six years, became the most influential PR person in British history. Spin, now a demotic word for any public relations presentation, remains weak propaganda when done by politicians and should be seen as the latest development in the long history of the political news management practised by UK governments.

Corporate PR managers are spinners in non-aggressive mode who promote good relations with government (the most powerful PR operation in a liberal democracy) and with non-marketing stakeholders. Their major task is lobbying, influencing public policy in favour of their principals. Lobbying has been – and still is – more effectively done by 'insider' organisations in private with government, than by 'outsider' ones through the media. Private lobbying makes policy-making in a democracy less open to scrutiny by elected representatives and the media. When it is the private mobilisation of bias by elites and powerful, unaccountable interests, Finer's (1958) call for more light on lobbying is fully justified.

Much lobbying is discreet but some of it is done concurrently with the 'shout' of public campaigning to mobilise broader support. Outside of politics and public policy-making, this concentration of PR resources into a short timetable with a single objective is much used by business and voluntary organisations to introduce novelty or to reinvigorate what is established. Campaigns are often enlivened by stunts, the nearest PR gets to the carnivalesque and public theatre. These concoctions often draw on popular culture and are a creative form of PR, mostly to be encouraged and to be integrated into the practice mainstream.

10 Markets, branding, reputation

It is hard to conceive of liberal democracy without markets. The rights to have property and to dispose of it ensure that. Markets, one of the oldest human institutions, distribute goods and services from suppliers to buyers via the two media of information and money. It is through information flows that public relations influences markets. The influence is beneficial for consumers and buyers in that PR sends high levels of one-sided, persuasive messages about goods and services onto the market. The messages come from entrepreneurs ready and able to produce PR material. These messages help buyers satisfy their needs. The first reaction of consumers, however, to this Niagara of weak propaganda should be to exercise the '*caveat emptor*' rule of 'buyer beware'.

This flood of PR marketing communications, however, gives rise to three concerns. They arise when people – in their role as consumers instead of citizens – conclude that an economy, which claims to provide value for money through a wide choice of safe products priced in unrigged markets, is exploiting them through flows of inaccurate, misleading or unsourced information. The first concern is the tension between acceptable market-place values promoted by PR, such as wide publicity, consumer awareness and good reputation for quality producers, and, on the other hand, the deceptive use of PR as 'education' and/or as 'objective' information. Weiss (2003, pp 168–9) notes similar defects with advertising.

The second concern centres on information flows into markets. It is whether all suppliers use PR equally in markets, and whether all potential consumers are reached by PR messages. In so far as the answer is no, PR in markets puts some consumers at a disadvantage *vis-à-vis* other consumers, and departs from the concept of competition set out in classical economics whereby product information as well as pricing information is evenly distributed throughout markets. In this way, marketing PR (MPR) creates a communicative deficit in markets. The third concern lies in the sheer volume of persuasive communications in our society today: the continuous pumping at citizens and consumers of promotional material – adverts, mail shots, telephone selling, logos, brands, sponsorships, press releases, competitions, exhibitions, road shows, stunts and T shirts with corporate messages. Plastic bags are branded and homepages vibrate with pop-ups. All marketing communications are one-sided and propagandistic, but not all communications into markets should be of the marketing kind (see p. 138, below).

A starting point for an analysis of PR effects on markets is to establish what PR people do in them. In his history of US PR, Cutlip (1995, pp. 174–81) notes that business was turning to advertising and to press agents, an early term for the modern PR person, in the 1870s in order to build up mass demand for mass-produced goods. He quotes the example of meat 'slaughtered weeks earlier and half a continent away' as in need of promotion. Bernays worked for Procter and Gamble for more than thirty years.[1] Large-scale involvement by PR, however, is a much more recent practice (Kitchen and Papasolomou 1997 and Harris 1991) and today MPR is the largest single source of work. One rule of thumb has it that 70 per cent of PR jobs are in MPR.[2]

MPR jobs are often gathered up inside the generic title of marketing communications that, besides PR, includes advertising, direct marketing and relationship marketing. All are ways of sending persuasive, one-sided messages about goods and services to consumers. PR work used to be categorised, in marketing jargon, as 'below the line' work in distinction to 'above the line' activity, such as advertising and personal selling, but that distinction is largely by the wayside now and is replaced by the idea of integrated marketing communications. One powerful reason for dropping this 'above' and 'below' distinction is that modern marketing propositions are more complex than previously and there are more of them. Put together PR and marketing disciplines and they are better able to handle multifaceted propositions. The rise of 'lifestyle' is an example. Fashion marketeers have 150 years' experience of persuading people to buy a suit with an advert alone; it is a complexity beyond a single medium's ability to persuade people to buy all the products of apparel, personal accessory, hi-tech gadgets, food, drink and domestic surroundings that comprise the 'lifestyle concept'. PR and marketing techniques together offer the marketeer a wide-ranging variety of expressive modes (words, photographs, visuals, sounds) and a multiplicity of message distribution channels (e.g. editorial, paid advertisements, logos, competitions) to communicate the complexity in a persuasive way.[3]

Writing is the major expression of marketing PR (MPR) for 'press release writing often forms the mainstay of the PR executive's role'.[4] Its importance is increasing as the word-based Internet makes language a reinvigorated medium of identity presentation (Morris 2000). To read home pages on a half-competently managed website today is to absorb the style of mid-market journalism electronically. Other PR product forms are exhibitions, roadshows and stunts. Over time, the PR product offered to marketing changes. In the 1970s when sponsorship was a relatively new and under-developed promotional activity, it was relegated to PR by the more powerful marketing departments; now large-scale product sponsorships are controlled by marketing departments, or they stand alone. PR today handles small-scale corporate sponsorships. The writing side of marketing PR is twofold: media releases (sent by post or email) about goods and services for the national, local and specialist press; and promotional copy for direct mail, brochures, leaflets, exhibitions, homepages and bulletin boards. The task is to create promotional statements (newsworthy enough to win space in the media or persuasive enough to get attention via non-media channels) that support goods or services on sale. There is also the related work of developing ideas with journalists and visual designers for take-up in feature articles, programmes, brochures, exhibitions and visuals; the organising ability to integrate these activities into campaigns; and the forensic skills to track and counter hostile web activists. Whatever the PR product or channel, the purpose is constant. A phrase has appeared in PR jargon that sums it up – the PR person must 'sell in' their story to the required outlet. The imperative is for the PR message to be published.

MPR and 'soft' selling

Another phrase associated with PR generally, but especially with PR for marketing, is 'soft sell'. Journalists are flown overseas to test drive new cars. The new models are associated with celebrities. 'Advertorials' about them appear in the local papers based on technical superiority and buyer advantage. Customers are invited to dealer showrooms on Sunday afternoon for wine and an inspection. The cars are on stands at summer shows.

Other common MPR techniques for creating newsworthy copy are through surveys that make a point in an 'independent, scientific' way favourable to the product; second, through association of 'celebrities' and colleagues[5] with products; third, through the creation of 'news events' or stunts (see p. 131); and, fourth, through the invention of front organisations, some of which are highly creative (see Kemp 1988, pp. 127–8, for the rise of the Budgerigar Information Council).[6] Indeed, MPR is the technical term for 'soft' sell.

Cause-related marketing, where a business, its goods and services are linked to a 'good' cause, is a contemporary, common form of 'soft sell'. It is in tune with the mood of business social responsibility and has benefits for a third party. The best-known British example is the scheme of the Tesco supermarket chain that supplied £92 million worth of computer equipment between 1992 and 2004 to schools.[7] The money was funded via coupons from customer purchases (Adkins 1999, p. 142). Business in the Community says cause-related marketing 'provides a win:win:win situation' where success relies on partnership, and when 'communicated in a compelling way and implemented efficiently, [it] offers a unique means of emotionally engaging the consumer'.[8] Business in the Community represents what government and part of the UK big business leadership see as 'best practice' and they have consistently promoted cause-related marketing as an expression of benign corporate citizenship. It talked of emotional engagement in 1997.[9] In 1998, it was a 'commercial activity' to 'market an image, product or service for mutual benefit. It is an additional tool for addressing social issues of the day.' It emphasises goals such as 'enhanced reputation', 'awareness, improved loyalty'.[10] Cause-related marketing lends itself to PR in two ways: it can be promoted via editorial and publishing channels with the aim of corporate and/or product differentiation, and most of its outcomes are those of PR, namely publicity, and more good reputation.[11] Business in the Community says that 'there are a variety of different tools that can be used to implement and leverage Cause Related Marketing programmes. These range from advertising, PR, direct mail and sales promotion.'[12] Adkins sets out benefits for marketing and causes, and when Tesco's Computers for Schools is the example they are substantial for both sides. She writes of mutual respect and balanced benefit (p. 118) as the ways to achieve them. The relationship, however, is at bottom an instrumental one of gain – either financial or affective – for all participants. The sub-title of Adkins book puts the distribution of benefits this way – 'Who Cares Wins'.

The phrase 'cause-related marketing' is a reminder of how integrated promotional methods have become. It is very improbable that a new version of Vance Packard's 1957 book *The Hidden Persuaders* would today focus on advertising. The integration, however, has a minor consequence in that it has put in question the boundary between PR and marketing. Five forms (domination, subordination, separation, equality and identity) have been attributed to the PR/marketing relationship,[13] and Hutton (2001, pp. 205–14) argues that PR is being marginalised within it. Such a conclusion of 'marketing imperialism' energises PR loyalists, and their representative bodies who want to police professional boundaries. Doole (2005, p. 290) ensures a bout of energetic defence from PR lobbyists who will see encroachment of their boundaries by 'mega marketing', which 'is where relationships must be sought with governments, legislators and influential individuals in order to make marketing effective on an operational level'.

Rather than defence, a better response to these boundaries disputes is to note that promotional modes are plastic in form (how different is writing for an advertisement and for a media release?), and that such malleability suits the multiple forms that PR takes.[14] What is clear over and above these conceptual and professional dog fights is that the marketing ideology unleashed by the neo-liberal reforms of the 1980s in the UK will encourage continuous experiment with new promotional forms to 'grow' markets, and that the adaptability of PR is an advantage. To take a long historical view, MPR is a successor to what was known as 'puffery', defined by Chonko (1995, p. 5) as 'sales representations that praise the product or service with subjective opinions, exaggerations, or vague and general statements with no specific facts'. The word is associated with R.B. Sheridan's Mr Puff in his play of 1779, *The Critic*.[15] To take a shorter view of history, MPR is at least 100 years old.[16] It first appeared as press agentry to attract audiences to watch the communication invention known as the 'movies' at the turn of the twentieth century. Today it has the 'digital age' to promote and it is well placed to be the narrative and stylistic platform on which that promotion will happen.

Promotional culture luxuriates in marketing and the effect on the language of marketing PR is lushness. The tone is that unnatural, unsubtle exaggeration, that ceaseless emotional brightness associated with forced enthusiasm for selling the product. Only a PR copywriter could write 'red hot loans'; 'invest with greater success'; 'glorious wood'; 'picture perfect entertainment'; or 'an entertaining advantage'.[17] PR copy is different from advertising copy because it is less compressed, more humourless, and is written in the belief that both banality and exaggeration will conceal its selling intentions. These two examples express its promotional tone. 'A French housewife wouldn't even hang out the washing without wearing a fragrance – in the UK, it's more, "I'm going out, where did I put it".'[18] A revamped Millennium Dome in London will 'provide international acts and sports teams with arena facilities of a standard currently unseen in Europe'.[19] Modern Mr Puff is alive and well and working in PR but his efforts usually fail to persuade for he seeks to narrate an impossibly perfect story (Surma 2005).

PR as marketplace information

There are two mass-mediated sources of communications into markets: MPR (as part of marketing communications), and market information from non-producer sources. The producers of goods and services are the source of marketing communications/MPR, for it is in their economic interest to disseminate data and opinion to consumers. Most communications into markets come from them. They are the originators of MPR for, in the language of marketing, MPR results in more 'informed' consumers who are thus more likely to buy. All these marketing communications by the producers of goods and services are persuasive. Self-interest ensures this.[20]

The second mass-mediated source of communications into markets is from market observers who do not produce goods or services. They are UK government departments, official regulators, consumer groups, market critics and commentators, and business data sources. These observers are either neutral or critical towards the producers of goods and services, but they are active communicators and they use public relations techniques such as press releases, brochures, briefing packs, exhibitions, conferences and lobbying. For example, the UK Treasury 'names and shames' pensions companies for mis-selling and for tardiness on paying compensation; the rail regulator rebukes rail companies for inadequate service; fair trade pressure groups tell supermarket customers about Third World labour practices; and business information services sell company news on the Internet. Information from them can be called *market communications* that are intended to monitor the selling or buying of goods and services, as opposed to *marketing communications* (including MPR) that are designed – with one exception – to aid selling. (The exception is product withdrawal communications, usually for safety reasons.)[21] Market and marketing communications combine to make up the category *mediated marketplace communications*, the sum of all communications in a market, except word of mouth.

Persuasive PR

Taken together, marketing communications and market communications add to the volume and source pluralism of communications flowing to consumers, and so provide data and opinion on which to make purchase choices. But identification of these two communications sources (market producers and market observers) raises the problem of whether all mediated marketplace communications are persuasive. Is the message issued by a UK car maker's press office recalling a model because of a mechanical fault persuasive?[22]

The argument here is 'yes', for marketplace communications of both sorts are part of a larger debate about communications. There is an extensive literature on persuasion in communication science. One of its conclusions is accepted here, namely that communications are of their nature persuasive, where persuasion is defined as a communicative process designed to influence others and is a quality embedded in messages for that purpose (Jowett and O'Donnell 1992). This conclusion is fully accepted with regard to PR. Acceptance does not deny that communications are designed for other intents (e.g. commanding, admonishing) held by the PR producer and which are separate from persuasion. Acceptance also allows for debates about the relationship between persuasion and reason in message construction and the ethical balance between them. It also keeps in contention the proposition that reason is persuasion in cognitive rather than affective form. Nor does acceptance rule out the view that persuasion, reason and emotion are all involved in PR messaging.

Debate on all these matters might amend, but would not deny, the general conclusion that all PR communications are persuasive in their intent because they seek advantage for their producers. Miller (1989, p. 47) puts the general point powerfully: 'that persuasion as a chief symbolic resource for exercising environmental control remains an indispensable and irrevocable dimension of human existence'. PR messages seek compliance from their receivers. The point is an important one for the argument in this book, namely that all PR is persuasive, including the fourth part of the Grunigian paradigm, symmetrical PR.

MPR as promotional excess

The argument so far about MPR has been in terms of its commercial effects on markets, principally retail. There is also a powerful aesthetic critique to be made in that MPR has become one of the most pervasive promotional forms aimed at UK citizens in their role as consumers. The overall effect on UK society of this search for more marketing opportunities is more and more 'walls of sound' around consumers. Moore uses that metaphor as a title in *An Introduction to Public Relations* (1996). This book opens instead with the metaphor of a PR Niagara falling on citizens and consumers. Both capture a sense of people being trapped in a rising quantity of communications, more often than not of the marketplace sort. Even street furniture is part of the PR Niagara now, with roundabouts sponsored by Chinese restaurants and by garages. Pay for a parking ticket in a public car park and the reverse side is a special offer for a 'McChicken sandwich and fries'. The public service bus is covered with company logos. Tesco supermarkets will give you a miniature loyalty card, complete with electronic chip, for fixing on to your car key ring. MPR is making a contribution to an excessive marketisation of public spaces in the UK. Pratkanis and Aronson (1992, p. 11) write about a 'message-dense environment', in which the average American will see or hear more than 7 million advertisements in a lifetime. The process is becoming more targeted and refined, and adding to what Gabriel and Lang (1995, p. 2) call 'the final stage of commodification, where all relations between people are finally reduced to usage and exploitation'. Spaces free of messaging for consumption become rarer: the small sponsorship sign on the roundabout is strategically placed just in the eye-line of the oncoming driver. The clifftop walker by the sea puts her fat-free chocolate wrapper in a bin sponsored by the local secondary school. Universities give away plastic pens with their logos on. In these small incremental ways, the citizen/consumer can find fewer and fewer physical or mental spaces where there is no MPR. Such density is evidence of promotional culture sweeping its Niagara of self-interested messages through every nook and cranny of cultural and material life. Indeed this avalanche of messaging suggests that there is a promotional phase being developed beyond commodification. It is one of 'personalisation' and it is exemplified in memorial plaques 'to commemorate your loved ones' that can be purchased for deckchairs on at least one seaside resort.[23]

Corporate branding

One promotional form that PR has taken from marketing with enthusiasm is branding. This is a difficult term to define and there are many verbal clusters proclaiming explanation but not offering clear meaning.[24] It is a term to which is ascribed very complicated social roles; Simmons (2004, p.

16) says, for example, that 'brands are a shorthand we use to make connection with others and to help define our own identities'. He writes about the product and corporate brand of Starbucks coffee. The brand, he claims (p. 175),

> starts with a commodity product – coffee beans – and invests them with extraordinary added value by creating an experience that transcends the simple act of drinking an unnecessary product. And this experience becomes an integral part of the daily lives of millions of people.

The definition of Armstrong and Kotler (2005, p. 234), however, has the virtue of clarity about an important term for PR people: 'A brand is a name, term, sign, symbol, or design or a combination of these, that identifies the maker or seller of a product or service.' They comment that 'building and managing brands is perhaps the marketer's most important task'.[25] Such an ascription would not be true of the PR person in relation to the branding of products where the marketing team would be in charge and would be 'buying in' PR services. Instead, branding comes into its own for PR when the 'building and managing' is for the corporate body, for the organisation or group being communicated about. This activity used to be known as 'corporate identity' work by PR people in the 1990s, and before that in the 1970s, when management was an activity without its own vocabulary, it was known as 'It's what we stand for'.[26] Such, however, is the influence of marketing as the ruling paradigm, even for thinking about non-commercial areas, that it is now referred to as 'corporate branding'. Balmer (2003, p. 300) says that 'a corporate brand may be a company's principal asset'. Schultz (2002) links brands with reputation via storytelling about *The Expressive Organisation* and thus sees organisations as symbolic entities. Constructing such entities amounts to the anthropomorphic exercise of giving to an organisation or group (e.g. to an engineering company, retail chain, school, university, trade union, protest group) human characteristics.[27] In this way, these collectivities become humanoid and the PR message is that they are typically some combination of the following vocabulary: 'modern'; 'caring'; 'quality'; 'friendly'; 'fun'; 'young'; 'sexy'; 'exclusive'; 'traditional'; 'cutting edge'; 'hi-tech'; 'best'; 'responsible'; 'excellent'; 'responsive'; 'fast-moving'; 'safe'; 'wealth-creating'; 'trustworthy'; and 'principled'. Indeed, Olins thinks the process included the sexual. He argues (2003, p. 7) that Virgin is a company which take branding so seriously that it is a 'classic seducer' wanting to 'win share of mind, then share of market'. The anthropomorphic connotation continues when branding is done a second time: 'Rebrands are designed to reinvigorate a marque.'[28] Saul (1993) also notes the PR propaganda advantage of choosing the fitting word. During twentieth-century ideological battles between democracies and totalitarian states, he says (p. 46) that 'The very act of getting the word "free" into the public domain on your side places the other side in a difficult position.' Jackall (1995, pp. 351–99) is one of the few academics who write about PR as work experience. He describes it as the persuasive manipulation of symbols (along with advertising and journalism) with a view to constructing the accounts of social reality wished for by its principals. 'Whether in a corporation or an agency, a public relations practitioner, in addition to meeting the normal bureaucratic fealty requirements of his station, must above all satisfy his clients' desires to construct the world in certain ways' (p. 362). From this follows a process of selective narration, and it is one that presents the PR with the ethics of relative truthfulness: 'In the world of public relations, there is no such thing as a notion of truth: there are only stories, perspectives and opinions. . . . Creating the impression of truth displaces the search for truth' (p. 365). Corporate branding is therefore the constructed presentation, by its dominant coalition, of the group or organisation to its stakeholders for immediate, favourable recognition. Its use is spreading to cities ('Bradford: a surprising place'; see Truman *et al.* 2004), towns, regions and whole countries. It is done through the media of words, phrases, visual design (logos, letterheads, signage), photographs, art, sound, architecture, uniforms and behaviour. Note the last medium for it is not on the list of instruments for product branding; but when the task is presentation of the organisation making the good or service offered, the role of people has to be accommodated. Corporate branding is a clear example of PR as 'self-presentation-for-attention-and-advantage'. It is 'the best foot forward' by the group or the organisation. It is usually associated with businesses but there is growing uptake by other entities. Think of New Labour as an exercise in corporate branding and you understand much about recent UK politics. Think of Friends of the Earth and the UNISON trade union, and you have insight into contemporary British civil society. Their brand is their compressed, self-regarding and comforting narrative about themselves. Its subject is themselves and it tells of betterment for significant others – the stakeholders – through association with them. It is a psychological conceit for the subject as well, in that it is consumed as 'corporate comfort food'[29] by the dominant coalition who put the story in place. If McAlpine (1997, p. xiii) is right about business as the 'most exciting and rewarding of all pursuits open to mankind', commemorative narratives will follow as surely as adventure stories follow war. But these tales are much less listened to by middle management and hardly at all by the shopfloor.

Corporate branding is a social construct to assuage, attract, make compliant shareholders, stakeholders, consumers, clients, employees, government and business regulators. Its 'character' is conceived by the corporate parents, the dominant coalition of the organisation or group, and the design work is passed to PR people. It is work that plays to their skills, for good PR writing is the narration of a story designed to attract attention. It is also related to concepts such as corporate personality, image, reputation and issues management, and when it comes into contact with the first two there is often confusion. At first glance, 'corporate personality' would appear to be the same as 'corporate brand' but it is used in some preceding sense of representing the corporate ideal, the perfect expression of what the organisation or group should be. The sense is that the observable expression of the 'corporate personality' is the 'corporate brand'. More confusion comes when these terms are used alongside 'image'. This latter term has two meanings. In vernacular English, it is used both to describe the corporate brand and perception of this brand by others. The confusion is avoided by not using 'image' in PR technical discussions, and by remembering that the construct 'corporate brand' is the subject that is perceived by others, namely stakeholders and general public. A corporate brand is the biography written about a corporate personality and read by others. It is a PR essay in popular corporate psychology. Corporate perception is what others think of the biography.

Is branding a corporate fashion item? A design accessory not to go without? The questions are answered by trying to think of organisations or groups that do not have a 'corporate brand' or 'identity'. It is a hallmark of military regiments (e.g. Napoleon's Imperial Guard); it has been traditionally cultivated by the better class of university (e.g. Harvard). One hesitates to say that it is part of the phenomenon of religion but think of Salvation Army singing, Buddhist orange, and Roman Catholic purple.[30] Indeed, there is more surety in turning the point around and noting that, historically, dominant institutions have published expressive culture about themselves and their interests[31] (e.g. the monarch's head on coinage; the cardinals' portraits, the queenly speech to soldiers before battle). In modern capitalist, market-orientated, liberal democracy, this expressive urge has become near universal – has been democratised. Businesses, trade unions, charities, cause and interest groups are all branded today. It is hard to imagine any corporate entity that is modest or altruistic enough to eschew the expense of branding. Without a brand, it fears that it would not be distinct enough to attract attention.

Human personality invariably generates both positive and negative reactions, and it is argued here that when businesses and groups anthropomorphise themselves, customers, clients and stakeholders will react in the same mixed way as they do in their personal relations with individuals. It is claimed that the 'caring' company attracts 'loyalty' from its customers: it can be argued that the feeling switches to 'anger' when the product fails. It is a new area of corporate development for the company to personalise itself and it risks the danger of inflating expectations. By giving itself an affective coating, the company is aligning itself with the changing emotional patterns of those in contact with it. Does this introduce another risk factor into business performance? Is it better to be supplied with goods and services by a company with a stable share price rather than by one with a 'refreshing new concept'?[32] The boundary between market economics and consumer psychology therefore needs careful patrolling by the PR person. Economics and branding are also in conflict when the relationship is focused on pricing goods and services in markets. Klein (2000) argues that marketing by human characteristic (branding) is a change from marketing by price, and is therefore the replacement of use value and exchange value pricing by experiential pricing. Such pricing is leveraged by non-economic factors, namely the emotions appropriated (e.g. 'caring', 'sexy'), store and product design, sponsorships, and community relations. Hannington (2004, p. 9) notes this point about emotional leverage on consumers when he quotes a 'Brand Advisor' to the effect that a brand is 'an entity that is loved so much that people are prepared to pay more for it than the material benefit obtained'. This emotionalisation of price weakens competition by price determined by use or exchange, and therefore the operation of efficient markets as classically defined, and is a strategy favouring oligopoly and monopoly. For consumers, it means paying more. Klein also notes that marketing by human characteristic is a threat to advertising as a prime promotional mode, and that it favours the narrative telling capacity of PR.

Brands, moreover, attract public attention in ways that are not always welcome to their constructors. Sometimes they are connected to popular culture in ironic, creative ways and are transformed into counter-cultural icons. Nike, McDonalds, Esso and Ratners are examples of brands given non-intended meanings. The US cultural jammers Adbusters who call themselves 'a maverick band of social marketers on a shoestring budget' are skilled at this. They invert the meaning of advertisements, mimic their copy and visuals, and publicly launch their creations. Thus they develop the 'black spot sneaker', which is an anti-Nike reference, and they say about the corporation that it has developed a 'bogus corporate cool'.[33] Adbusters also organise a named day with the most unwanted message business could wish on its customers – 'Buy Nothing Day'. They urge shoppers to take 'time to think consumer revolt'. The aim is to develop a popular culture of resistance to globalised companies (Klein 2000).[34] Snow (2003, pp. 151–2) lists cultural jamming, along with 'guerrilla marketing', joining protest groups, challenging the agenda of mainstream media, and reading outside 'your comfort zone', as antidotes to propaganda. The Adbusters also use the concepts of 'memes' in their campaigning. 'Memes' are the communicative version of genes and are described by Dawkins (1989, p. 192) as cultural replicators such as tunes, ideas, catch phrases, fashion that 'propagate themselves . . . by leaping from brain to brain via a process . . . which can be called imitation'. The Adbusters say that they are promoting a 'new lifestyle game . . . by spreading uncooling memes'.[35] This reference leads to the idea that PR can be seen as a distribution system for 'memes' that are propelled through social systems by PR's self-advantaging message system, and which are retained or rejected by the self-interest of the message receivers.[36] The more that they are retained, they have the quality of memorability that Gladwell (2000) called 'stickiness' in his thesis that the spread of some fashions, books, social trends in a society is analogous to the spread of viruses in an epidemic. This line of thinking opens up the possibility that PR is an active element, as a mode of persuasive communication, in cultural evolutionary psychology.

Other critiques of corporate brands are that the process may start with intentions to change not only the narrative and imagery of the organisation but also the behaviour of its employees or members. The latter is the most difficult to alter, and is the least likely area to succeed. Brands may seek to be multi-media expressions of the ideal corporate personality but they often reduce in practice to little more than a new logo and letterhead. Also the current PR paradigm of two-way symmetrical communications does not easily accommodate corporate branding in that the construction process is invariably asymmetrical and assumes acceptance by others. Sometimes this acceptance is not forthcoming and there follows public retractions. The £60 million redesign of the tailfins of British Airways airplanes with 'funky' ethnic art was publicly and famously scoffed at in 1997 by the then-former Prime Minister Mrs Thatcher.[37] The £2 million representation of Britain's Royal Mail as the Consignia brand was the source of much mocking humour and was followed by its withdrawal in 2002 after sixteen months.[38]

Corporate reputation

Corporate reputation has had a rising career over the last decade in British public relations as the master outcome sought by PR people. Coyle (2001) in her panegyric for neo-liberal capitalism has suggested a systemic reason: the new, less regulated 'weightless economy' of service industries needs good reputation as a marketing signal. Since September 1993, the then-Institute of Public Relations (IPR) has emphasised reputation in its definition as much as the traditional values of 'goodwill' and 'mutual understanding'. They were embraced at the foundation of the then-IPR in 1948. Now 'reputation management' has become a much more commonly voiced professional role than the achievement of those older and softer civic virtues. For the contemporary CIPR, 'A good reputation is key to organisational success. In today's competitive market, it can make the difference between success and failure.'[39] A few professionals own up to wanting to be 'perception managers' but while that has accuracy, it also has too much of the Orwellian about it for it to be a popular job description.

Corporate reputation is located in the 'other' (stakeholders, publics) and is the perception of an organisation or group by these other parties after their experiences of it. It is perception with judgement. The judgement may be a comparative, historical or an absolute one (e.g. about standards of customer service from banks, over time, against an ideal). It is a concept that has sources in many areas: stakeholding ideas of reciprocal treatment between self and other; in issues management (see p. 36); reaction to the human attributes embedded in the corporate brand (e.g. reactions by others to claims about modernity or technical efficiency); and in the historical record of an organisation (e.g. attitudes to apartheid in South Africa, and Nestlé and breast feeding). If you feel good about the characteristics claimed, and its behaviour towards issues important to you, you will empathise and judge reputation to be positive.

Corporate reputation is, therefore, like moral virtue and human affection (e.g. honesty and love) in that it is the consequence of other activities. It is, for example, the 'reward' for being a 'value for money' retailer with admired social responsibility programmes. It comes after these behaviours have been experienced by 'significant others'. It is bestowed and it cannot be called up on demand. Indeed, it is unlikely that it can be managed in any technical sense of input/output activity.[40] It is closely allied to trust, which is the strong expectation of others that they will be treated as benignly in the future as they have been in the past. Reputation is, so to speak, the connected-up trust of individuals across a public or a stakeholder group. It constitutes a non-specific, general opinion focused on one entity. It is a subjective phenomenon; it is what stakeholders (and publics) say it is and it changes over time. There are many examples of businesses (e.g. Barings Bank, Ratners) that have suffered disastrous reversals of reputation. The same experience afflicted British trade unions in the 1960s and 1970s. Reputation is also a plural phenomenon: a business may have high repute with City financiers but be held in contempt by employees and trade unions. An environmental group may be despised by farmers but admired by animal welfare people. In PR, the concept of corporate reputation has been very strongly associated with companies, as has corporate social responsibility. These associations are now broadening out to include other corporate entities such as cause and interest groups, and, with it, more scrutiny of their performance. The monitoring of these groups has its origins in the admission by Greenpeace that it published inaccurate information during the Brent Spar incident of 1996.

Corporate reputation, moreover, can be seen as the amount of prestige attached to an organisation or group by its stakeholders and by the general public. It is a positive, 'credit' in the 'bank' of opinion.[41] It is also a negative, a 'debit' in the 'bank'. In more affective terms, we can talk about amounts of low opinion or dislike in which an entity is held. It is indirectly measured through other indicators such as share price, balance sheet strength, surveys, membership, successful campaigns, positive media coverage, gossip, and opinion of influential persons and bodies (e.g. 'the great and the good', think tanks). The principal PR role in regard to reputation is media communications about behaviours and events which imply that reputation is positive and strong; and the publication of surveys and testimonials that proclaim the same. Ideally this witness is better coming from third parties: like all boasting, the corporate variety grates. Other PR work is the projection of corporate brand values, the selection of sponsor-ships and community relations that bolster them. These are written up in corporate brochures, explanatory sections of annual financial reports and accounts, and in triple-bottom-line audits of monetary, social and environ-mental performance. All these narratives are designed for the reader to think better of their source, to hold it in higher repute. Hannington (2004) sets out how to make these narratives into an operational plan, driven by the warning that reputation is 'the most important asset' of business (p. 3), a cliché to which is frequently added another – reputation is made over decades, and destroyed in minutes.

Beyond the clichés, the difficult questions about corporate reputation come when other organisational goals are laid alongside it. Is it the same as success and how does it rank against survival? Integrating, separating and ranking goals is a core task of dominant coalitions in organisations and groups. Official definitions of PR pragmatically avoid the philosoph-ical and political difficulties of a communications mode in its relationship with the purposes for which it is used. But PR people cannot help but note that they are asked to communicate about cross-purposes. Organisations and groups have to – may choose to – behave in ways that achieve other goals at the price of loss in reputation. Survival is the essential purpose of entities in the political economy and in civil society: survival may be at the price of reputation. In politics, it could be said that putting survival first is normal behaviour. Indeed, it could be offered as a definition of govern-ment. In the marketplace, the choice is a familiar one. Consciously or otherwise, suppliers of goods and services do trade off their reputations against other goals.[42] There is no organisational imperative for the reputa-tional goal to be always protected as conventional PR theorists imply. In 2004, organisational imperative worked against corporate reputation in the case of Shell, a global business that since the Brent Spar incident in 1996 had worked hard to improve relations with stakeholders towards open dialogue and human rights. Yet, Briggs (2004)[43] reveals that 'Shell managers' primary challenges were not concerned with Shell's reputation but with the more prosaic need to achieve short-term business targets' and it did so by over-estimating its oil reserves. For this, it was fined by the UK's finance regulator, the Financial Services Authority.

Looked at this way, PR people are naïve or disingenuous to make repu-tation their single, desired outcome for their employers and clients. In so doing, they are loading the gun and pointing it at their own professional feet. The then-IPR took this risk in 1993 when it added the second defini-tion of PR based on reputation. It is not wise for modern PR people to speak in mantra tones about 'reputation, reputation, reputation', and to make themselves the guardians of this important, social asset. They forget that reputation is a consequence of other goals. Their concentration places them at odds with these other goals of their principals and clients, and so puts their organisational role at odds with their declarations of professional purpose. Goals such as profitability, growth, downsizing, diversification, merger, campaigning for policy change often take precedence. Reputation therefore should be seen in a relative relationship with other corporate or group goals.[44] Resolving competition amongst goals is the work of dominant coalitions, and PR 'voices' their decisions.

Finally, it is important to discount any claims of functional imperialism made or implied by public relations and to correct a professional deformation that comes from it. Often in the speech of PR people there is an assumption that it is they, through their communications, who are the producers of reputation. Accountants, engineers, marketeers and reception staff produce reputation as much as PR people, and its production and projection is a state of mind and skills set that is widely accessible. This leads to the startling proposition that all organisational and group members are in public relations and that professional PR is but one way of achieving the goals set for it. PR is the producer of the communications wanted by its principals, and not the producer of the organisational goals of those principals. Public relations is one agency to achieve organisational goals, one of many. It is out of the work of these combined agencies that reputation comes.

Summary

PR has benefits and costs for its producers and its consumers in markets, politics and the media. This chapter reviews relationships connected with marketing and markets. The first is marketing PR (MPR), which spreads out promotional information to consumers, and so brings buyers and sellers together. But consumers should use MPR with caution under the *caveat emptor* rule of buyer beware. There is more MPR by volume than any other type; it is an adaptable PR form, and is an effective promoter of 'lifestyle'. It has higher credibility than advertising with consumers, especially when journalists uncritically publish its messages in their work. It is often called the 'soft sell' and it contributes to promoting the modern form of emotionally engaging customers, known as cause-related marketing. MPR and market PR by government, regulators and pressure groups together constitute the flow of mass-mediated marketplace communications outside of advertising. MPR creates communicative deficits if not all producers and consumers send and receive it. Its growth is leading to an aesthetic assault on public spaces that are now sites for promotional excess.

The idea of a corporate brand is a marketing form much taken up by PR people. Transferred from products, it is an anthropomorphic exercise to give human characteristics to organisations and groups. It is the construction of a favourable narrative about them. It is corporate biography produced by PR people and, like human biographies, produces negative reactions as well as positive ones. The negative feelings are exploited creatively by cultural jammers such as Adbusters and are turned into popular culture, often against big businesses. Branding is experiential pricing and weakens competition through creating emotional attraction to manufacturers and their products. It is imperfect competition by experience and emotion, and tends towards oligopoly and monopoly.

Corporate reputation is in part created by reaction to corporate branding, and has risen up the British PR agenda as a major professional output. It is perception tempered by judgement and defined most easily as amounts of 'credit' and 'debit' held in the 'bank' of opinion. It is bestowed by stakeholders and the public after experience of the organisation or group. Good reputation is the indirect consequence of other behaviours such as responsive customer care, sensitive issues management, large membership and effective campaigning. It is difficult to manage because it is a consequence of other behaviours. It presents therefore a professional problem for PR people because their principals set goals that run counter to good reputation, for example redundancies or foxhunting. Giving these examples is a reminder that reputation is plural and dynamic: different stakeholders award different reputations over time.

The next chapter looks at PR's relationship with journalism and why these two professions should behave in a more wary relationship.

11 Media matters

Since the 1980s, the UK public has had a mass media providing more information, entertainment and opinion than in any previous generation. Witness the exponential growth of radio and TV channels through entrepreneurship and digital technology. Witness more pagination in more newspapers with more specialist sections. E-media is now ubiquitous and it is hard to remember that in 1990 it was a rare sight on desktops, on ears and in hands. Now, it offers a personalised media to millions. Gillmor (2004) enthuses about the rise of the 'citizen journalist' who will publish their news via electronic media: 'The ability of anyone to make the news will give new voice to people who've felt voiceless' (p. xviii). The public respond to this great media mass with generous allocations of time. On average, the population watches twenty-eight hours of television a week and listens to twenty-four hours of radio. Nearly 35 million read a daily or Sunday newspaper, and 36.5 million a magazine. People accessing the Internet are 25 million (Lloyd 2004a).[1] This media expansion provides fertile ground for a corresponding PR expansion, because the media is the destination for most of the Niagara of PR (Ch. 1). Baistow (1985) notes PR's responsiveness to publishing opportunities and how in the past it benefited from developments in British print journalism with its penchant for 'action' and 'human interest stories'. Holtz (1998) judges that business PR will communicate via the Internet, both with its traditional audiences and a relatively new one made more powerful by cyberspace – activist groups.

The arrival of e-media is a reminder, however, to notice what is transient (technology, technique) and permanent in PR (sought outcomes). To read the 1906 (pp. 535–49) account by the 'muckraking' journalist Ray Stannard Baker about the PR campaign by US railway companies to stop Congress passing price-capping legislation is to see the distinction. The contemporary investigative journalist would see that the companies used the word 'campaign'; that their first target to influence was the media; that they hired a 'publicity bureau' with 'high-class clients, notably Harvard University'; that the agency took on extra staff and opened up five new offices; that the largest branch in Chicago had forty-three staff; that they did daily press clippings; that they visited editors and kept their profiles updated in a central file; that they changed their copy to interest local papers; that they evaluated the clippings, e.g. Nebraska was turned around in eleven weeks from 212 unfavourable references and two favourable to 202 favourable and four unfavourable; that they stirred up opinion formers against unfriendly editors; that the agency did not want publicity about its role; that they gave away tickets as 'freebies'; that they sent out media releases of favourable Congressional speeches; and that the railways' in-house PR departments were working in parallel with them, sending out briefings and copy, as well as an offer of paying for any extra printing costs. Change the date and today's investigative journalist would hardly know the difference.

The same contemporary journalist, if in the UK today, would, however, welcome some changes in PR propaganda practice. The first is the historical decline from the eighteenth century until the mid-Victorian age of government using working journalists as covert or open propaganda agents, usually paid. Grant (1994, pp. 10–54) traces the decline of this working journalist-as-government-publicist role, its temporary resurgence around the First World War and then its decline in the inter-war years. Journalists also lost out to advertising people and to civil servants as advisers to government on publicity. They were replaced by people such as Frank Pick and Stephen Tallents[2] who showed public relations talent, a talent in Grant's phrase (p. 249) for the 'sale of ideas'. But journalists still face the dangers of incorporation into PR. They are being colonised by it. There is a PR-isation of the media happening in the UK. This produces a growing identity in the attitudes, behaviours and personnel of journalism and PR. It produces a growing dependency of journalists on PR, leading to the disablement of their critical faculties. A similar process has been described in relation to the Australian and US media. Turner *et al.* (2000, p. 37) note in their study of Australian celebrity that 'Most of the publicists we talked to acknowledged that newspapers now have fewer staff and resources, despite operating within an increasingly competitive environment. Most recognised that these factors increased journalists' dependence upon the publicist.' The authors note dependence in entertainment and business news. Journalists also notice deal making about celebrity news and 'This is . . . where PRs are often able to exercise considerable power.'[3] Freelance journalists Blyskal and Blyskal (1985) identify in the USA the 'great bulk of stories that are the product of assembly-line factory journalism' (p. 35). It is the PR industry in the USA and UK that is supplying the prefabricated pieces. These relationships of dependency by journalists need to be reversed into independence. The more distance between journalists and PR people, the better for a liberal democracy. PR grows out of democracy, not democracy out of PR.

Citizens and consumers in market-orientated, liberal democracies need protection from the negative effects of PR propaganda. The first two lines of defence are wariness by individuals towards PR (a personal PR watch) and, then, a society-wide system of subsidy to make sure all interests have a PR 'voice'. In these ways, the messaging of all interests, dominant and subordinate, established and new, can be evaluated. The third line of defence is a mass media able to scrutinise PR messages. The media is most valuable to a democracy when it provides qualities that cannot be offered by PR. In Lloyd's words (2004a, p. 203), 'Media have the right – the necessity in a democracy – to maintain diversity, openness, to investigate, to attempt balance and objectivity.' There is doubt, certainly in the UK, whether modern journalism is doing diverse, objective, balanced scrutiny adequately. It is not surprising the issue arises for PR people spend more time dealing with the media and journalists than any other institution or group of professionals. If PRs did not get acceptable amounts of coverage for their media releases, story ideas and tips, most of them would be out of a job. The first public the great majority of PR people worry about therefore are journalists. One reason is the power of journalists to ruin PR reputations.[4] While that power is real in the case of individuals, there is the irony that PR as a set of attitudes and as editorial material is reducing the reputation of journalism by weakening its scrutiny role.

PR-isation of the media

If PR is unavoidable in a liberal democracy, and journalism is inevitable, how do the two practices relate to each other? Too many journalists accept colonisation by PR, the conditioning process that leads to 'PR-isation', the professional state where PR attitudes are incorporated into journalism's mind-set, and where PR-biased material is published without sourcing. They are content to accept 'newszak', news designed for a market and delivered in small bits for easy consumption, from their PR suppliers (Franklin 1997, p. 4). For journalism as public gossip and as entertainment, this colonisation is entrenched (see below). It is often active collaboration in the cases of celebrity news that spins off from reality TV; of lifestyle, consumer and real-life journalism, and may not be immediately damaging. PR colonisation, however, is immensely destructive of journalism as scrutiny. Political spin doctors, for example, have greatly grown in numbers in the UK (see pp. 123–5) since the 1970s and they use exclusives, bullying and complaints to editors to get compliance from journalists (see Jones 2002). For all journalists, scepticism up to polite hostility is the proper response of a media that calls itself 'free' and 'independent', both values which sit uneasily in the PR mind-set. Such a media should not be beholden to the suppliers of news, real or pseudo. Franklin (2004, p. 96–118), however, notes colonisation by local government, in that it, through its PR staff, is 'assuming an increasing importance in setting the local news agenda by providing resource-hungry local newspapers with what Gandy describes [1982] as "information subsidies"' (p. 96). Davis

(2002, p. 17) notes the same dependency. He concludes that 'what was once a "tug of war" between sources and journalists has been replaced by an increased media dependency on the "information subsidies" provided by PR'. He argues that PR has increased its influence, not because of spin doctors, but because journalists are 'increasingly stretched because of rising competition'. PR people notice this process. The then-president of the UK's CIPR wrote (2003)[5] that 'The burgeoning media environment . . . brings an insatiable requirement for content and copy. At the same time, pressures to follow a particular editorial line to maximise sales' change how journalists work. This PR-isation thesis overlaps to some extent with Bentele and Nothhaft's (2004) 'intereffication model' of PR/media relationships where 'PR and journalism – regardless of the question who controls whom – mutually enable each other'.[6] They note that journalism in liberal democracy is 'PR-reliant' (ibid.).

This reliance should be reversed and ended. Instead, an observable, critical distance between a wary media and a supplicant PR industry should replace it. Reliance on PR creates a dependency culture in journalists, taking out their critical edge of independent judgement, and substituting meretriciously the views of another for their own. This leads to the editorial deception of readers and audiences. Unhelpfully, this critical distance is shrinking over time. What is unsaid by most media commentators if they want to explain the dependency is that journalists are complicit in the intake of PR material.[7] But how does that complicity come about in the face of a culture, often trumpeted, of hostility by working journalists towards PR? Is dislike not enough to keep the two groups apart and stop any PR-isation, any colonisation? There are two related aspects about this contradictory mixture of declared hostility and complicity. The first is that journalists are too weak as a professional group to halt PR-isation. They are caught in markets in several ways. First, 'Media are mostly businesses' (Lloyd 2004b). Then, there is a structural process of marketisation operating on newsrooms, which is sucking in PR material to fill larger editorial spaces. Marketisation here is the process by which business values of searching for audience/readership increases, of cost-cutting and profit-seeking combine to weaken journalism as an independent process of investigation into public matters. Marketisation encourages PR-isation because this reduces the labour costs of media production. Attaway-Fink (2004) notes the rise of 'market-driven journalism' since the 1970s in her study of special sections of US newspapers: they are designed 'to meet reader interests, whether entertainment or local news' (p. 145). Her research suggests (p. 153) the appearance of 'a new model of the newspaper industry, one that includes business and marketing savvy blended with ethical journalistic standards'. This marketisation of journalism fosters media convergence, known also as multiple-platform publishing, where the work of a multi-skilled journalist is used across many outlets, thus increasing productivity. Quinn (2005, p. 37) notes that if convergence is introduced just to save money 'reporters could become too busy to verify the information they find and resort to publishing the material supplied by professional spin-doctors'. Moreover, at the individual level, journalists find that their labour market position is weakened. There is too much supply for too few jobs, undermining – through easy replacement – any principled stance against the process. In this environment, some journalists are hostile to PR, but they are too few. Their opposition, moreover, is undermined by the concept of 'the total newsroom', where the distinction between journalism and marketing is weakened by the co-ordination of the editorial, advertising, promotion and circulation aspects of a media outlet, such as noted by Attaway-Fink above. The position of regional and local journalists appears the weakest, with Harrison (1998, pp. 167–8) foreshadowing Franklin's later conclusion (2004 above) about the strength of PR professionalism. She argues that 'the professional local authority PRO, often a fully trained and experienced former reporter, is a more reliable source of news for the local authority than many local reporters acting on their own'.

Journalism's complicity

There is another factor at work in PR-isation that is usually unsaid: the most powerful news managers are working journalists. The process of 'manufacturing' events, people, words and visual images into news has been well researched (e.g. Glasgow University Media Group 1982; Cohen and Young 1973). These 'manufacturing' skills were noted earlier when Kisch (1964, pp. 95–6) wrote about well-known, by-line names writing for the PR campaigns of interest groups, an aspect of what he called 'new journalism'. Such 'manufacture' is also seen when editors do 'deals' with PR people to give publicity to stories and events that are known to be invented. In these ways, journalists have become entangled with PR because its ability to create news and celebrity eases a contemporary newsroom problem. It is not that there is too much news for too little space: there is too much space for too little news (Curran and Seaton 1997, p. 278). PR propaganda fills the gap. Gillmor (2004, pp. 184–7) provides evidence with the example of video press releases, condemning them as the 'media's lazy use of press releases as news' and as a 'stain' on both PR and journalism. They involve 'fake' reporters.[8] The former president of the CIPR, Professor Anne Gregory estimates (2003) that '80% of what appears in the business pages and up to 50% of general news has been generated or directly influenced by PR people'.[9]

Journalists are also complicit with PR in more internalised ways. Traditionally, most of them omitted PR material from their copy, challenged it or found alternatives. This was a common response because PR material was not so available in the 1960s.[10] Now they are more likely to accept it. Journalists have increased their reliance on secondary sources (including PR), especially when these sources produce copy in a pre-prepared, journalistic form. They have thus come to rely more on official and company spokespeople as primary definers of events. This reliance gives the sources the ability to co-operate or obstruct, depending on the favourableness of journalists' copy. Reliance is also a rejection of the most effective journalistic methodology – personal investigation. Furthermore, it means acceptance of professional help from PR as an information subsidy (Gandy 1982). This cedes some control over the news agenda, an advantage much sought by PR people. Davis (2003, p. 27) summarises this development in the UK: 'As news organisations have been forced to make cuts while simultaneously increasing output, so their dependency on PR "information subsidies" has grown.' He notes the 'new PR-saturated media environment' in Britain and how this helps 'resource-poor sources' gain more media access. Such a conclusion is an ironic one for this book, given that much of its argument is in favour of more media coverage for such sources. That argument, however, rests on an independent and critical media reporting the fullest range of PR 'voices', not on a subservient media republishing PR messages. Ultimately, a critical liberal democracy is a higher-order value for a civilised UK than a powerful PR controlling subservient media, even when that PR is from 'deserving causes'.

Reliance on PR has wider consequences beyond the individual journalist: a spiral of work consequences has set in that reinforces the PR-isation process and makes journalism as scrutiny more difficult to do. Newsroom budgets and numbers are cut as journalists move towards more passive reworking of PR material. More young, inexperienced and low-cost staff are taken on. Fewer tips needing follow-up are explored by news desks. They do not want the delay associated with investigation. They need new copy on short hourly cycles for morning/lunch/evening/night editions. In these ways, journalists reduce face-to-face contact with sources – which is when they transform scrutiny into journalism through observation, investigation, questioning, admission and indiscretion. Withdrawal into the newsroom moves journalism closer to cost-free, imaginative invention. Open letters to the Prime Minister or to the Governor of the Bank of England appear, for example, on the front page of regional evening pages. Once, and this is appropriate if the Prime Minister visits or if a factory closes. Twice, and it is a refuge from investigation.[11]

The dominance of marketing (and promotional culture) aids the PR-isation process. The culture of exchange for advantage is an operating environment to which PR easily adapts. Historically, public relations has been used mostly in favour of private interests, societal passivity, submission to elites, consumption and acquiescence: it has served these interests and entities more than public interests, social activism, popular creativity, abstention and critique. This balance in PR's production may not be harmful to journalism as public gossip or as entertainment, but it hinders journalism as scrutiny. Markets encourage endorsement and repetition.

They tend towards the conservative, the superficially new and that which produces more revenue. Journalism as scrutiny promotes critical engagement and rupture with the *status quo*. It wants the widest audience but is indifferent to revenue. There are today more critical PR 'voices' to be heard in the UK than forty years ago and journalism should pay more attention to them. 'Good causes' need as much scrutiny as established ones.

Journalists should always put more critical distance into their relationships with PR. If they do not, the gain invariably lies on the PR side as the history of the pseudo-event[12] shows. In Boorstin's account of its rise (1961), which he entitled 'From news gathering to news making', it is clear that journalists, politicians and PR people worked together on the *genre*'s development. Bernays needed the co-operation of the press to publicise his most famous pseudo-event, the 'Torches for Freedom' walk down New York's Broadway by women smoking in public at a time (1929) when it was a social taboo. He did not tell the media and they did not ask (Tye 1998, p. 54) that he was working for the American Tobacco Company; that his secretary was one of the walkers; and that she signed the invitation to thirty débutantes to come along which was also placed in the New York newspapers. Tye (pp. 169–71) also describes over-close relations between Bernays and US reporters who were covering the political difficulties the United Fruit Company (Bernay's client) was facing in the early 1950s from a reforming Guatemalan government. Baistow also notes this co-operation and calls (1985, p. 68) PR people the Fifth Estate as an ironic compliment to their influence and notes their role as 'creators of copy that is in effect subsidised with a commercial profit in view'. The most famous name associated with pseudo-events in contemporary Britain is Max Clifford and it is hard to judge where he or the *Sun* newspaper gained more from the headline 'Freddy Star ate my hamster' (13.3.1986). Such copy can only be 'manufactured' by co-operation between PR and journalists. It is arguable that such co-operation is still in the range of the conventional relationship between the two groups, namely love–hate, but sometimes it degrades to love–love (see Ch. 2) and this balance does not favour journalists. An example of the latter is the 'freebie' culture, where consumer and lifestyle goods are loaned or given to journalists; other 'freebies' are free travel, free holidays or car loans. The loans are sometimes declared by journalists who see that acceptance of them disadvantages readers if not stated. Other journalists worry that they are not working in enough 'plugs' to keep the PR people content. 'Freebies' are a black market of hidden favours traded at the expense of media audiences. Another 'freebie' area is personal finance journalism, where the connection between editorial endorsement and sales of a product is a tempting line to blur by favours.[13] Even PR people are sometimes shocked at its extent.

All these relationships are detrimental for journalists. More journalists should be more cautious, prudent and distant in their relationships with PR people than they are. PR-isation of the media has set in too far and journalists are too complicit with it. It is journalists who have travelled more to PR than *vice versa*. Indeed the Fourth Estate has watched passively as a Fifth Estate has settled on its boundaries, if not inside them, and has become an overweening neighbour.

Expansion into journalism

If journalists want help from PR people, there are many they can call on. Indeed, newspaper editors can hire PR agents to represent them.[14] It is estimated that there are nearly 50,000 people doing PR work in the UK, in jobs recognisable as such by job title and in otherwise titled posts where the work is PR.[15] They outnumber the 35,000 members of the National Union of Journalists.[16] Pilling (1998, pp. 193–4) notes that 'on most local papers fewer journalists are working harder and being far more selective in their coverage of local affairs than they were a generation ago', and that 'the "sweatshop journalists" are aided in their need to fill space by the press releases of resource-rich organisations'. This understaffing weakens the ability of local and regional journalists to resist PR-isation. Harrison (1998, p. 167) writes about them that they are 'in many cases hard-pressed, de-unionised, demoralised and poorly paid, are increasingly reliant on press releases and promotional material provided for them by vested interests'. But it is not only because of worsening work conditions that journalists are complicit with sources: professional submission is another. Cockett (1989, pp. 2–32) recounts how the UK national press were generally co-operative to the point of suspending judgement about the policy of appeasement towards fascist Italy and Germany followed by the Chamberlain government between 1937 and 1939. He writes (p. 2): 'Although one might despair at the level of control government was able to exert over the press during these years, it is nevertheless true that it could do so only with the willing connivance of journalists, editors and newspaper proprietors.' He quotes a young lobby journalist (p. 7) as saying that the over-close association with ministers led 'to an incestuous relationship between the government and the members of the lobby in which the journalists' intellectual independence was eroded and that the healthy "adversarial relationship" . . . was replaced with a relationship that was "too cosy and comfortable"'. Although their political masters in the two departments were antagonistic, the press offices of Downing Street and the Foreign Office both pursued policies of manipulating submissive journalists for departmental and political reasons.

Dowie in the introduction to Stauber and Rampton (1995) writes that there are 150,000 PR people in the USA as against 130,000 journalists. Some of the 'best' journalism schools send more than half their graduates into PR – 'an almost traitorous career choice to traditionalists like myself who instruct students how to handle PR executives and circumvent the barriers they erect between the truth and the story they want told about their clients' (p. 3). Dowie concludes (p. 4) that 'we' [journalists] have given an 'awesome power to an industry that gravitates to wealth, offers surplus power and influence to those who need it least, and operates largely beyond public view'. Journalists also collude with PR people by training them in various ways. They give interview training to senior business people; are compères and presenters for corporate videos; and chair business conferences. Journalist lecturers train PRs from the armed forces and they work with PR lecturers to demonstrate how journalists and PRs interview each other.[17] Salter (2005, p. 105) notes the danger of this co-operation for journalists: 'To be sure, public relations may benefit from journalism. But journalism does not benefit from public relations.' He argues that if the academy is 'to nurture democratic communications', journalists' understanding of the 'manipulative communications of public relations agents' should be prioritised over PRs' understanding of how to exploit journalists.

The British journalist Bryan Appleyard argues in a newspaper polemic (2003)[18] that PR manipulation has reached a level that threatens the integrity of many areas of journalism. He writes that 'aggressive PR' started in Hollywood with the promotion of cinema stars and passed through entertainment and sports reporting to reach UK politics with the appearance of New Labour spin. The consequence is that journalists have compromised their core professional proposition: 'the claim that the story they are telling is true or an honest attempt at the truth'. Something similar is happening in business journalism. Since market deregulation in the 1980s, UK financial journalists have been sought out by more PRs. Anthony Hilton, City editor of the *Evening Standard*, London, writes[19] about a 'constant barrage' of PR and that newspapers 'seem to be losing their independence of judgement'. The structural cause in the case of financial journalism is the evolution of the City of London away from long-term relationships in finance capital towards making deals. In PR operational terms, this change creates more opportunities with each potential and actual deal. For example, there are public announcements to make about a deal that is the 'optimum' solution; a deal that is 'better' than the alternatives; and a briefing that competitive deals are 'inferior'. Deals are also easy to personalise when business people are involved: there is a competition amongst opposing teams struggling with market forces, an easy representation for PRs and journalists to portray. Hilton concludes that 'the press has moved away from being an observer of the business scene to a participant in it', a view that mirrors a conclusion later reached by Davis (2002) about UK financial news in the 1980s. Davis writes (p. 82) that 'Because corporate PR is far more advantaged in the area of business and financial news, corporate communications came to play a much larger part in this news production process.' Hilton also writes that 'media manipulation has become a legitimate way for increasing shareholder value'. He notes that the media 'have been relatively starved of resources'; that talented journalists go on to be PRs; that 'more and more copy appears in newspapers as the PR people want it'; that finance houses are as much 'on message' as ministers; that the media lacks investigative journalists; and that critical journalism will be met with non-co-operation by news sources.

This analysis by the working journalist Hilton is reflected by the academic Franklin who adds other factors to account for the weakening of journalism. He notes (1997) that journalists are now dealing with collaborators and competitors who have communications skills similar to their own. Terms and conditions of service and pay have fallen for journalists; the National Union of Journalists has been weakened by the introduction of personal contracts. Vocational education has also played a part in the weakening. It has educated and trained large numbers of graduates in journalism and PR on courses where many skills, such as news sense, copy writing, layout on screen, Internet publishing and presentation, are interchangeable. It has not adequately emphasised the professional differences of attitude and motive between the two fields and sometimes uses the same lecturers on both sets of courses. These graduates leave to find researching, writing, editing and electronic publishing skills in both newsrooms and PR offices. Journalism graduates know that jobs are fewer than PR ones. New journalists are entering a labour market where there is over-supply, and wages are low.[20] A move into PR using transferable skills is tempting. There is already noticeable job traffic between PR and journalism: the freelance journalist who also does PR work for the local MP and runs a PR business as well; the former journalist who is now a PR manager. The *Sun* editor David Yelland left journalism and joined the London PR firm Weber Shandwick. He told the 2004 annual conference that, during his journalism training in the 1980s, he was advised that PR people are 'bad people' but 'Thankfully those perceptions have changed. Today, 75% of the names in an editor's contact book are those of PROs.' Another journalist travelling into PR was Phil Hall, a former editor of the *News of the World* who found a job with Max Clifford, and discovered that PR was 'fascinating'. He paid this compliment to his new employer: 'He [Clifford] has made PR fashionable when it was once scorned.'[21] The opposite flow of PR people into journalism is much smaller but is detectable: the PR graduate who does a radio journalism course, works for a local station, and then moves to be a Whitehall PR.[22] This interchange will grow with the media's increasing use of pre-prepared soft news – especially in business, lifestyle, fashion sections of the press, in magazines and in contract publishing – which originates from PR people. This material was significant in the 1970s.[23]

Tabloids and PR

The tabloidisation of the media is another example of the skills merger between journalism and PR. Peter Golding has characterised tabloidisation by four dimensions: more soft news; shorter stories and more pictures; change in mode of address – readers and writers are of the same status, a move away from the didactic to the diadic; market structure in which media are businesses, with the broadsheets trying to increase market share.[24] There has been a doubling (from a low base) of tabloid coverage of politics, suggesting a tentative, positive outcome of tabloidisation is that it makes politics more reader-friendly and encourages more coverage. A more negative outcome is that when the media see audiences as consumers, all topics, even politics, are treated in a personality-based, gossipy, unchallenging way in order to increase circulation. PR people note this, and also that journalists will 'fight tooth and nail to get one over the opposition and if that means playing ball with a media-savvy PR, then so be it'.[25] Yet, Harrabin (2000, p. 50) recounts the difficulty of getting the environmental theme of sustainable development onto the news agenda because it is not 'a story – it is an idea and what is more an idea which has already been expressed'.

These developments coalesce into the colonisation of journalism by PR. For concerned journalists and citizens, they contribute to what Langer (1998) has named 'the lament', a sense that the journalism necessary for citizens to contribute effectively to a liberal democracy is threatened by the expansion of soft news, human interest stories, and reality, tabloid TV. This expansion is aided by media managers seeing journalism as commodity creation to build bigger audiences and readerships. Indeed, PR people complain of too much choice with over twelve 'chat shows' on British terrestrial television.[26] The insertion of PR attitudes and material into creating this 'other' news is the colonisation of journalism by PR. Soft news and PR are synonymous.[27] Soft news is highly promotional about itself and often announces its arrival by a showy vanguard of presentational effects that strain for audience attention (see Humphrys 1999). It is the news category into which most media relations PR falls, for 'soft' is conventionally taken to mean that which is positive and pleasing about personalities, policies, events and organisations. Indeed, PR published in the media from a traceable source has a 'soft', uncritical, ingratiating quality, for PR cannot publicly criticise its own source and is loath to attack others for fear of retaliation. (Invisibly sourced PR has different qualities.) Further, the supply of soft news eases the process of marketisation of the media by turning editorial attitudes away from costly investigative, independently minded journalism that is created from uncertain beginnings with no guarantee of a successful conclusion.

For media market-makers, whether managers or journalists, the point of a readership or audience is to make it grow. This is done through soothing, entertaining editorial, constantly adjusted to attract the largest number of paying individuals in that market segment. Marketeers call it choice. This is not the voice of a thunderer, of an independent thinker, of a principled dissenter, of a critic. Marketeers call that negative thinking. This is not editorial persuasion on behalf of an opinion that may cost the persuader disadvantage: this is persuasion on behalf of an opinion constructed to increase advantage. Markets have a dynamic towards increased production, and media market-makers show that propensity in more pages and more air time. The soft news generated by PR is a cost-effective filler of space. It transfers the costs of its own production from the media market-maker to the PR source. It does not have to be sought out: it is offered freely – in superabundance, in binfuls. As consumer markets generate most PR and as the marginal media space is mostly devoted to consumer goods, services, entertainment, fashion and lifestyle, both the demand and supply from media market-makers and PR providers tends to rise. Journalists as market growers assume that their reader-, listener-, viewer-consumers want more and they respond in kind. Journalists as social critics know that they have to wait upon events.

There is an allied process of celebrity manufacture going on. Celebrity news is self-advantaging news about people and is therefore another strand in PR-isation. It is not new, for it was noticeable at the time of the rise of the film industry at the turn of the twentieth century, and there have always been press agents at work to fill the showbusiness columns of the tabloid press.[28] Celebrity manufacture, however, has greatly increased since the mid-1980s and Michie (1998, pp. 149–215) describes it from the PR perspective. It is now a staple component of tabloid, middle-market and broadsheet newspapers in the UK, their use of it distinguished only by amounts of column inches and bare flesh. Celebrities could not exist without PR production and media demand. A person who is known for well-knownness has to knowingly get known. This takes a careful self-presentation, a schedule of outings, entrées and partners to audiences. This is personality construction work, nice for those who can get it. It is a double market with supply and demand for what is produced; and then for the mechanics of production, for front-of-house perfection and backstage *faux pas*. It is a double market for readers wanting to know how it operates, and for PRs and journalists wanting to boast about how it is done.[29]

A separate media system

Journalism and PR should be operated as two distinct communications systems. A starting point for this separation is the reconceptualisation of PR as a media system in its own right, alongside those of journalism and advertising. Such a perspective befits the current status of PR as an industry and as a set of promotional attitudes. Historically, it developed principally as a service to journalism, often staffed by former journalists, offering pre-prepared copy to fill space. To a lesser extent, PR has roots in the advertising industry in that it was first often located in that industry's agencies. (See Tedlow 1979 for these historical relationships in the USA.) PR grew by the side, so to speak, of these older industries: now it stands alone, linked but separate. The literary flourish caught by Baistow (1985) in his 'Fifth Estate' phrase to describe PR reflects this new status.

Like journalism and advertising, PR constructs messages from data, opinions and values but in forms that have grown distinct from them (e.g. media releases, promotional videos, staged events, lobbyist briefings). It distributes these messages directly through its own distribution systems (community relations, corporate social responsibility programmes, campaigns, websites, e-newsletters, roadshows, sponsorships, contract publishing, conferences, exhibitions, direct mail) or indirectly and parasitically via other media systems (newspapers, broadcasts) to its stakeholders and publics. With these characteristics of distinct message forms, own and shared distribution channels, and separate aggregations of people that it seeks to persuade, it has the essentials of a media system in its own right. Moreover, PR is done by people, on both a paid and voluntary basis, who share identifiable skills and attitudes, and who can be found around the country in posts either explicitly or implicitly PR. Many of these skills are shared with journalists (researching, writing, presenting) but their professional motivations (advocacy for interests as opposed to scrutiny of interests) are antithetical. These PR skills and attitudes are not effective in the newsroom and only partially so in the advertising agency.

All media systems (Schlesinger and Tumber 1994, p. 4) impart a particular characteristic to the communications they transmit and the particular characteristic associated with PR is an intense instinct to persuade. PR is selective communication of the telling kind. It wants the listener to accept. This partisan characteristic marks it off from uncolonised journalism that transforms PR material by its scrutiny. Such journalism at its best is also persuasive in its assessment of the validity of interests but is not *a priori* committed to an interest. Where journalism is partisan to a media owner, political party or cause, it diminishes itself. More diminution comes when PR propaganda is hidden behind journalistic forms without declaration. This hidden sourcing and the related information subsidies to journalism cause public concern because they present a false identity: a form of journalism but a substance of PR. This falsity distorts access by UK citizens to an independent media (see pp. 154–7), and so indirectly distorts their views of a political system, claiming to be democratic and representative.

The separation thesis lets us see more clearly the case for the reform of PR/journalism relations. It is a conceptual foundation for separating out the two work practices. When journalists use PR material, they should rework it by scrutiny and scepticism.[30] If PR is mixed with journalism, the PR element should be identified. This visible sourcing of material is an important but not a new task. It was a minority and temporary practice in US journalism at the end of the nineteenth century (Stauber and Rampton 1995), and was the practice in the UK *Financial Times*, whereby technical press releases with their sources were grouped together on one page.[31] Journalists should stop training PR people and addressing their conferences. They should not take advice on professional behaviour from PR people, certainly not advice that 'We need to spend more time, not less, together.'[32] More separation comes by the PR media system developing its Internet presence and so messaging directly to its publics, avoiding media transformation of its material. The Internet can be seen as one component in the PR-controlled production chain of political communications, others being advertisements, posters, direct mail, stage events, stunts, party political broadcasts.[33] British political parties have increased their electronic presence since the 2001 general election, using information technology for internal party communications and for emailing electoral groups (Moloney and Colmer 2001, pp. 964–5). In the 2005 election, the Labour Party emailed supporters as much as three times a day. Business-critical groups campaign via websites and these pages are monitored by PR firms that have tactical responses (Holtz 1998, pp. 176–98). Gillmor (2004) offers ten rules for a PR 'pitch' using new media.

It is, however, possible that PR-isation has so weakened journalism that it – not PR – cannot exist as a separate media system, If so, the best defence for scrutiny journalism is to re-establish itself on a non-commercial basis. Gillmor (2004) argues for the 'citizen journalist'. Fallows (1996) argues for a 'public' or 'civic' journalism that is community-based in order to be 'journalism in the public spirit'. Such a non-profit journalism evokes the work of the seventeenth-, eighteenth- and early nineteenth-century politically radical printers and pamphleteers. E-media is the testing ground for its modern form.

Finally and ironically, separation from journalism is in the long-term and broader interests of public relations. PR-isation suits the interests of PR people on a specific campaign when their target media passively publishes their material, but it does not suit the longer-term interests of PR as an industry and professional practice. PR people want their material in the UK media because the latter has had a reputation for independence of view that conferred credibility on what it published. Publication is only a favourable testimonial when that independence is widely perceived to exist. PR-isation destroys that perception and so eventually dilutes the self-interest of PR producers.[34]

Summary

Media outlets increase at a time when journalism's independence from PR declines. The labour-market position of journalists has weakened since the 1980s, especially in the regional and local media, and fewer of them are doing more work in more insecure newsrooms. The marketisation of the media (its conduct as audience- and profit-seeking business rather than independent investigation into public matters) also weakens journalists, in that readers and audiences are seen by media managers as consumers to be satisfied and increased, rather than citizens to be informed and challenged.

PR 'soft' news is the major filler for growing spaces in an expanding media. These conditions together smooth the passage of PR material unhindered into print and broadcast. In these ways, PR has become a separate media system from journalism and advertising, and the most important supplier to a media that calls itself 'free' and 'independent'. They amount to a PR-isation of the media (its colonisation by PR attitudes) that weakens scrutiny journalism. Many journalists have been complicit in this process: they too often publish what they get with no or little amendment or declaration of its source; they are too reliant on 'soft' news; and they often train PR people. Journalists should treat PRs with scepticism, bordering on polite hostility. There should be no partnership between them. Instead, there should be an obligation of wariness, for, in a democracy, their work does not cohere. In the long term, the withdrawal of the PR colonists from journalism favours their self-interest – directly by increasing media credibility, and indirectly by strengthening adversarial and advocacy democracy. The next chapter looks at some consequences of PR propaganda.

12 The consequences of PR propaganda

Modern PR is competitive communication seeking advantage for its principals and using many promotional techniques, visible and invisible, outside of paid advertising. Defined thus, it is consistent with advocacy and adversarial types of communication (Barney and Black 1994). Since the last quarter of the nineteenth century, it has been political, commercial and social messaging for dominant interests and elected governments in maturing liberal democracies. In its early modern period (since the 1920s), its practice is associated with professionals such as Bernays, Elliot, Hill, Lee, Page and Tallents who used PR as a communications discipline to gain more control for the powerful business and ideological interests they represented. In its post-1960s period, modern PR has sought more influence for its principals in the climate of accelerating, competitive pluralism that marks out contemporary liberal democracy. These principals have increasingly included less powerful ones such as cause groups, charities and trade unions. But whether it is used by the very powerful or very weak, PR is weak propaganda. This is a conclusion that generates controversial consequences.

An unpopular conclusion

Amongst PR professionals, this conclusion will not be welcome, certainly not in the UK or USA. The connotation of the word 'propaganda' in the public life of these liberal democracies is unremittingly negative. No producer of PR publicly claims that they are sending out propaganda. Such a claim would bring public derision and commercial, political and cultural disadvantage. If the word is used at all, it is to revile the PR of competitors, opponents and enemies. It is sometimes, though, used privately and dismissively, to describe own output, but other professionals working alongside PR people use it more openly and easily.[1] It would be, in these circumstances, an act of professional demolition for a PR producer to describe their work as propaganda. There is, therefore, no realistic prospect that the term will be used in the foreseen future by them as a self-descriptor. Whether other academics will explicitly categorise PR as propaganda is an open question. For those inside the PR academy, it will be a difficult and in the beginning a self-isolating act of scholarly reallocation after the primacy of the Grunigian paradigm. For most academics outside, it will come only after more attention to PR effects.

There is a historical dimension to this semantic exclusion of propaganda. From the 1930s onwards, the word dropped out of public vocabulary as a term with positive connotations in the UK and USA. This was the period until 1989 of ideological and military struggles against fascism and communism. A large part of the Anglo-American (and Western) reply was – and is – to propagandise, first for capitalism, markets and personal freedoms, and latterly for democratic nation building. The propaganda involved covert sourcing, misinformation and psychological manipulation (Cull *et al.* 2003, Taylor 1999) and was in response to similar approaches by external enemies. In this pattern of reciprocal and mutually reinforcing usage by friend and foe, the word receded from comfortable public usage. Bernays (1927, p. 151) noted this process happening: 'Thanks to the war [the First World War], we have an idea that propaganda is the effort of some reprehensible person to poison our mind with lies.' The noted writer on pluralism, David Truman, also remarked in 1955 how the connotations of propaganda had become negative since that war but he nevertheless argued (pp. 222–3) that such negativity is 'of limited usefulness . . . because it prevents one from recognising that attempts to persuade large numbers of people constitute a basic process in our kind of society'. Truman based this defence on the need to control social attitudes in complex societies. Even if that is accepted, doing propaganda in liberal democracy still troubles its theorists and citizens because its official canon proclaims that such a form of communication is incompatible with government based on human rights, public debate and free elections.[2] Against this background, a semantic displacement process has excluded the word from comfortable, positive public discourse.[3] Propaganda has been, so to speak, exiled under a regime of vocabulary apartheid. Its banning, however, left a gap in the lexicon for words covering public and private communications of a persuasive, self-advantaging, often mass-mediated kind. The replacement phrase became 'public relations'. In the construction of its meaning, largely done under the Grunigian paradigm, it had to be free of the connotation of factual and emotional manipulation in the search for power; and to be re-clothed with softer, civic qualities such as goodwill, mutual understanding, adaptability and trust, all qualities compatible with liberal democracy.

In the PR academy, the conception of PR as weak propaganda is an unconventional, if not isolated, one. For example, Banks (1995, p. 19) favours PR as altruistic, mediating and translating activity in the communications of a society. He joins Kruckeberg and Starck (1988) in developing a communitarian view of PR, one concerned with its social consequences because it is constitutive of communities of interest. There is a strain in

European PR thinking that also emphasises it as the communicative aspects of social cohesion. L'Etang (1996a, pp. 30–1) reviews the mostly US claims to PR as lobbying having a non-governmental 'diplomatic' status: one claim talks of PR 'as the lubricant which makes the segments of an order work together with the minimum friction and misunderstanding'. Above all, however, the idea of PR as weak propaganda rejects the widely accepted, normative, Grunigian view that PR should aim to be (or is) a practice of symmetrical communication between mutually respectful message negotiators, amending their meanings to achieve a balance of advantages.

Instead, PR propaganda is theorised here as a mixture of the other categories in the Grunigian paradigm, namely the press agent, public information and the two-way asymmetrical. This theory of PR as competitive communication for its principal's advantage is reached after reviews of US and British literature; the observation of current PR practice in UK politics, markets and the media; the reaction of PR consumers in the USA and UK; and an interpretation of how 'spin', the demotic shorthand for PR, is used in popular culture. It is important to note, however, that the Grunigians do not deny that most PR is the promotional search for persuasive, communicative advantage. Indeed, the founding academics, Grunig and Hunt (1984, p. 26) write about the popularity of self-advantaging PR for they note: 'We estimate that about 15% of all organisations today use the two-way symmetric model.' These minority users are mostly big businesses regulated by government and they face the most powerful institution in a liberal democracy (elected government) and have little choice but to adopt a respectful, negotiating PR form. But the Grunigians can be read as though they regret the popularity of asymmetrical PR, it being an under-developed form. Regret, however, is not a consequence of the PR and propaganda identity. That identity is the natural outcome of PR practice in its drive for communicative self-advantage, and it is an outcome that is sought after.

Self-interest and PR

PR propaganda is the one-sided presentation of data, belief, an idea, behaviour, policy, a good or service in order to gain attention and advantage for the message sender. It seeks attention and advantage through attitudinal change and then through behavioural compliance. It intends to persuade through the use of selective facts and emotions in its message construction. Merton indicates how the factual and emotional elements can be combined in the least manipulative, if not non-manipulative, way. He writes (1995, p. 271) that 'mass persuasion is not manipulative when it provides access to the pertinent facts. It is manipulative when the appeal to sentiment is used to the exclusion of pertinent information.' The place for emotion is a precise one: 'Appeals to sentiment within the context of relevant information and knowledge are basically different from appeals to sentiment which blur and obscure this knowledge' (ibid.). But PR practice is not an academic, scientific or judicial activity, founded on the search for the even-handed, the fully validated and the just. It is a promotional activity built on favourable, partial and self-selected data, and has been – and is – much used by the resource rich. Anti-capitalists and aesthetes do not like these two features but they cannot wish PR away: it is built into the social fabric of liberal democracy. On the other hand, it has happened that the Grunigians have unwittingly become associated with PR as a communicative idealism. PR teachers and students glide over the state-ment that three parts of the Grunigian typology are pathologies of the fourth and not much practised part (two-way symmetrical). By dint of exposure and repetition, the 'ought' of the fourth has become the 'is' of the other three. There is an implied judgement that PR has become two-way respectful dialogue with others – or that it soon will.

It has not, and will not. PR propaganda is not a practice in search of an altruism or moral ideal. It is rooted in the pluralist, self-advantaging promotional culture associated with liberal democracy and free markets. Above all, it is communication designed to further the interests of its prin-cipals. They would not invest resources in PR if it was otherwise. It is competitive messaging with both public good and private advantage as outcomes. That is seen most clearly in marketing PR in all its forms, from product press releases to celebrity endorsements. It is seen in corporate branding (organisational story-telling) where businesses, charities, public services, trade unions present their most appealing features to their stake-holders, actual and potential. These self-advantaging, self-interested activities, however, have limits: tactically they are moderated when the balance of circumstances facing an organisation or group obliges it to reduce its interests by extent, intensity or time. This changes the category of self-interest from the 'immediate' into the category of the 'enlightened' or deferred. Business executives instruct their PR producers to amend their messaging from a higher profit forecast to a lower one; the religious PRs serving confessional leaders send messages on homosexuality that maximises internal unity; trade union leaders lower their pay claims after the first bout of negotiations, and political news managers more downplay taxation increases nearer to elections. Such behaviour is the 'trimming' and 'fudging' of competitive entities when the uncertainty of the external envi-ronment moderates the calculus of self-interest. PR messages are amended to reflect the calculus, and if they express respect, dialogue or symmetry, it is in these enforced ways of manœuvring for more lasting advantage.

However intense the search for advantage, PR propaganda communi-cating values, untruths or behaviours that are unethical or outside the law or which hurt others cannot be condoned. PR producers are not relieved of the ethical imperative for all citizens to speak and behave within the law and without hurt to others when they communicate for-attention-and-advantage. Jensen's (1997) telling phrase that PR people are 'hemispheric communicators' is accurate, but they should tell the truth, behave lawfully and charitably from that position. It is clear, however, that many do not so act from that position. What, therefore, guards a liberal democracy from the political, economic, social consequences of their lies and hurtful behaviours? What protects buyers from rent-seeking entrepreneurs who distort markets by making false claims for goods and services?

First, by way of personal practice, and by way of first step in civic resistance to promotional culture, all consumers of all PR should apply the *caveat emptor* rule of 'buyer beware'. This is the first rule of PR literacy to counter negative effects. Not all – even most – PR consumers will apply it, even if they know of it. This differential application, often along the lines of class and education, makes the case for PR literacy to be a component of media education at schools and colleges. However widespread *caveat emptor* behaviour is, it remains a defensive reaction by individuals. Another defence – more systemic and societal – against negative PR effects is provided by the competition for advantage in a pluralist society. PR is the 'voice' of these interests in this marketplace of claim and counter-claim over material, ideological or reputational advantage. At the end of this sequence of 'inter-voicing' – observed through personal experience or the mass media – the receivers of PR messages can judge which 'voice' has the more validity. But these two devices to counter negative PR effects do not overcome the problem that PR capacity is differentially spread across the pluralism of interests in a liberal democracy: resource-poor causes and interests are often not heard. It is at this point that the concept of equalising PR resources through public and private subsidy is pertinent. The aim of such an intervention in the communicative economy of PR is to produce the state of PR resource equality. This is defined as the state where causes and interests in society that want to be heard have the capacity to so be, up to the threshold level of effectiveness. This can be seen as a normative theory of PR. Its achievement depends on a subsidy, a transfer of PR productive resources from the resource rich to the resource poor. There is only very limited evidence of this resource transfer in the UK. When she draws a comparison with lawyers and PR people, Parsons (2004, p. 111) observes that the legal system is established but that 'No such system exists in the arena of public communication.' A principal aim of this book is to argue for a PR system based on this idea of communicative equality, and for a funded, practical system of subsidy to ensure it. In this way, a public system of communication would exist alongside a public system of justice, both predicated on ideas of fair and equal treatment. Communicative equality sets a minimum threshold for PR 'voice', not a maximum. It does not limit free speech; it is a device to offer it to those not heard.

One response to this normative theory is the reply that it mirrors the idealism of two-way symmetrical PR. There is, indeed, hope in it – if not idealism – for equality in diverse, competitive social circumstances is always an elusive goal. The equality sought here depends on the intervention of extra resources into PR message production, and as such depends on multiple decisions – by public and private subsidisers – to intervene. In this way, the desired outcome is incremental in that it depends on many others who are external to the deprived condition of unequal PR resources distribution, and who have a will to make a change. In this dependence on many unrelated social actors, it is a modest idealism to aim at, and its core mechanism of subsidy is already part of the legislation governing UK referenda, and part also of the practice of a few providers through their *pro bono* work (see pp. 81–2). Hence the normative theory of PR communicative equality via PR resource subsidy for all those who want to have 'voice' in the political economy and civil society is achieved (as opposed to conceptualised) inductively. The theory, moreover, is not posited on PR as an ideal activity. Rather, it rests on the need to regulate the quality and quantity of public knowledge and debate in a future liberal democracy in the interests of equal participation. It is not a correction in the interests of equal outcomes: it is indifferent to outcomes. It is a correction to the historically observed PR condition of unequal distribution of communicative resources amongst interests in actual liberal democracy. The correction is sought because of the essential contribution to the democratic good of more equal public debate; and given this status, the monitoring of progress is essential. A possible monitoring precedent is the American Institute of Propaganda Analysis set up in 1937 and disbanded after the Pearl Harbor attack in December 1941.[4] The more powerful monitor, however, of PR 'voices' whether of dominant or marginalised interests, is a media that rejects the PR-isation process by which journalism incorporates the attitudes and material of public relations, and so loses its scrutiny role. The media monitor is also one that publishes a broader range of competing editorial views. What is not clear yet is whether the Internet will further develop a PR scrutiny role through counter-cultural websites, blogging and through a daily published electronic citizens' press.

It is this concept of communicative equality via PR resource subsidy, allied to the belief that more truthful statements follow from democratic debate amongst wary individuals and amongst competing media, that differentiates the thesis here from Bernays's PR propaganda model in *Propaganda* (1928). There is another difference as well. Bernays welcomed propaganda as unavoidable. He wrote (p. 159) that 'Propaganda will never die out.' He thought that 'The instruments by which public opinion is organised and focused may be misused. But such organisation and focusing are necessary to orderly life' (p. 12). Bernays was correct about permanent propaganda in a democracy. He was also correct to nominate PR as the new propaganda. He was, however, too optimistic about its consequences in a democracy, for he saw PR as scientific propaganda, based on the emerging discipline of social psychology. Whatever science (or art) constitutes it, a better judgement, after 130 years of PR practice, is that scepticism is much more warranted than optimism about its relationship with democracy. PR is weak propaganda. It can have some socially positive uses and effects (e.g. ironically, promotion of democracy; the 'voice for interests'; public information campaigns; creation of attention-catching messages, their speedy circulation); but negative uses and effects exist too (disproportionate messaging from dominant interests and elites; undisclosed lobbying, gross factual distortions and negative emotional appeals). These negative consequences have to be countered by equalised, competitive public messaging, and by the scrutiny of individuals and competing media. It is a scrutiny that should operate inside a culture for public debate with distinct features: no party to the debate has the final say; no party has the authority to stop debate (Cummingham 2002, pp. 192–6). It is scrutiny with all these features that is the necessary corrective to PR's selectivity of fact, opinion and presentation. It is this apparatus and culture of scrutiny that the Bernays model lacks.

Celebrity and employee communications

This view of a future, reformed PR both includes and excludes the modern phenomenon of celebrity. The inclusion flows from public relations theorised as a communicative consequence of business, interest and cause group activity. Celebrities are often supporting role players for organisations and groups, offering testimonials of support by association. In this way they can be seen as human resources available to the PR production of businesses and cause groups, and as being effective because of the links to popular culture and the phenomenon of fame. Sports people, actors, entertainers and authors are often sponsors of mass-marketing businesses and cause groups, and there is then a transference effect of 'being famous' to their corporate brands. Such celebrities can be viewed as the human component of corporate brands. Others, however, are the human component of product brands, and so can be seen as mass-mediated, personal sales agents for goods and services, such as clothes and fashion accessories. This is the distinction between a member of the British royal family being a patron of charitable 'good causes', and a comedian promoting a credit card.[5] The latter association is better understood through the social psychology of personality traits, and marketing theories of product endorsement and customer relationship,[6] and is thus a non-PR activity.

Internal communications is another PR activity that fits only partially within a definition of PR as competitive communication for advantage. Examples of inclusion are internal communications about work contracts, terms and conditions of employment, reward systems, staff motivation and attitudes. These examples involve two interests – an employer and staff, with a trade union or a staff association representing the latter. These two 'sides' negotiate over the price of the productive labour of staff and the contractual terms on which that price is supplied. Seen from this competitive stance, the PR of employee relations is an internal market inside organisations about asset use and asset mix. The market exchange aspects of this are manifest when pay is the subject being negotiated, but are less so when job description and evaluation, job grading and pay progression are the matters in contention. They are, however, all technical components in the supply of and demand for staff labour. Other examples of employee communications being consistent with PR as weak propaganda are staff newsletters, brochures and email messages from chair people and chief executives, videos, and 'awaydays'. These are communications devices that build the cultural values, motivations, attitudes, work goals and behaviours sought by the dominant coalition in workplaces and which encourage employees to speak positively to other stakeholders (see Dawkins 2004, pp. 116–18). Indeed the phrase 'culture change' is a common one since the privatisations, restructurings and redundancies of the neo-liberal market reforms of the 1980s. The connection of employee communications with organisational culture is organic in that the PR messaging strategy and tactics will be determined by the culture of the workplace, i.e. whether there is an integrated culture set by the dominant coalition; a differentiated one where there is challenge; or a fragmented one where there is a series of sub-cultures based on staff groups (Martin 1992). Where the work culture is integrated, PR messaging will be downward from the dominant coalition; where it is differentiated or fragmented, messaging will be competitive with the staff sending messages as well. Trade unions and staff associations are PR active as well with employees who are members, and they use PR propaganda for recruitment of non-members. In all these circumstances, it is communications with employees that count as competitive PR messaging. Excluded from PR propaganda are the internal communications of technical and personnel arrangements (e.g. announcing new computer and telecommunications systems; car parking and security arrangements; timings of institutional opening and closure; refectory services; new staff arrivals). PR people often advise on the writing and presentational aspects of these tasks but they are peripheral to PR propaganda. Instead, they are technical and personnel messaging. However, the increased focus on marketing by businesses and public sector bodies sometimes gives non-technical, affective connotations of narrative to employee communications. Then the messaging tone is personalised and relational, if not evangelical, and is expressed in phrases such as 'staff are our best ambassadors', 'staff are our most valued asset', and 'Right-thinking organisations keep their need for effective internal communication under continual review' (Dorward 1997, p. 128). The marketised approach to staff reaches an apogee with phrases such as 'your Internal, or Employee Marketing' and 'Your people now are your brand' and 'Engaging staff and reaping the rewards'.[7]

Trust

PR as weak propaganda attenuates any role for public relations as a harmonising influence in society, as communication to create trust between citizens. PR, at the very least, puts organisations and groups in contact with each other. But trust is a fragile, human feeling, sensitive to its nurturing circumstances.[8] It is connected with the idea of social capital (networks of supportive people, Putnam 2000) and it is the strong expectation that others will treat one supportively in future because they have done so in the past. Trust is an expression of social cohesion, centring people around commonalities rather than separating them with particularities. It stabilises social relations in times of accelerating pluralism. It is the gift of another, the receiver of PR messages. It is not in the gift of PR message producers. Behaviour earns trust, not messages. PR producers are agents of communications for their principals whose behaviour they 'voice' (and 'whisper' in private lobbying). They message in the competitive social environment of accelerated pluralism for marginal gains of more material, ideological, policy or reputational resources. This communicative 'argy-bargy' flows from the foundational nature of group intermediation in liberal democracy. This condition has many societal costs (e.g. the reduction of government to policy auctions, the externalisation of one group's costs to another group), and one is what Tannen (1998) has called an 'argument culture'. She draws a distinction between the positive of *making an argument* in public for a point of view and the negative of *having an argument*. She writes about US society, but the argumentative tone is echoed elsewhere as a 'grumble culture' (see pp. 85–6). This culture of having an argument is usually assertive in either a defensive or offensive way, often to a combative point. These behaviours do not incubate trust. Instead the arguing 'voices' intensify the cacophony of public pleading and preening by interests in liberal democracy. Such an outcome enfolds an unwelcome contradiction: such democracies hear much PR 'voice' but witness trusting relationships struggling to prosper.

Moreover, there is another dimension to this culture that takes it further away from trust. Sometimes PR is a 'shout', a megaphone and, indeed, Susskind and Field (1996) explicitly blame PR for its loud contribution to what they call an 'angry public'. Theirs is a characterisation related to the argument culture, in that anger is a common and powerful cause of public debate. Theirs is also a characterisation that distances public relations from trust (see pp. 85–6). In front of this communicative chaos of argument and anger, it is naïve to the point of perverseness to expect trust from PR message receivers, be they organisations, groups or individuals. The chaos negates the creation of trust. A trusting receiver of PR messages is likely to see others as kindred and co-operative, and gives trust in turn. Instead, PR producers see others as competitors for scarce resources; as consumers of goods and services, as publics to be told, or as influentials to be persuaded.

There is, however, a case for PR messages making an indirect contribution to trust. What alleviates the social competition between interests and causes is that most reach agreement with their competitors and opponents after bouts of intense argument. They know that in a democracy (a state that rejects violence for policy-making), their competitors, opponents and enemies will still be there after all the 'voicing', 'shouting', 'argument' and 'grumble', and that in the last resort compromise is inevitable (in most cases). The self-interest of democrats encourages reciprocal restraint. Otherwise, it is civil war. Conflict between business, trade unions, pressure, interest and cause groups, and between all of these and government, gives way to temporary settlement as the players exhaust their resources, and assess the new political settlement. The PR 'voice' goes through its sequence of strident assertion in the conflict phase, and is silent or soothing in the periods of quiescence. These periods last until groups judge that their interests are being threatened in a serious way, and they then turn up the PR 'voice' for defence or advantage. We note that Truman (1951) pictured society as a self-balancing set of interests, and the pluralists as a level playing field, even though Isaiah Berlin mused about the incommensurability of values, behaviours and interests in a liberal democracy. Before them, the Victorian democratic theorist John Stuart Mill argued that truth is what is left after public debate. In these periods of settlement or quiescence amongst interests, trust-creating conditions of mutual tolerance and understanding *may* appear because of the observed behaviour of the one-to-be-trusted. After a global company buys a national company, the PR message receivers will wait for cost reductions or more investment. Which action they observe will decide whether they give trust. They will assess their interests: if shareholders they will applaud cost reduction; if employees they will welcome job security. If they do give trust, the causal link with PR is indirect and tenuous. It cannot be more direct if it is accepted that PR is a communicative agent of its principals. Public relations and trust, therefore, are distanced both by PR's agency status, and by the competitive search for advantage and survival of the organisations and groups on whose behalf it communicates. PR and trust are not an excluded combination, but any connection between them depends on the behaviour encoded in public relations messages.

Finally, if this argument of distance between PR and trust is accepted, it has implications for the corporate branding of professional bodies representing public relations (either as individuals or as businesses). Conventionally in the UK and the USA, the definitional connotations have resonated values of social harmony, such as that PR helps organisations and publics 'adapt mutually', and maintain 'mutual understanding'. This discourse of public harmony is at odds with the discourse of social competition underpinning an attenuated PR/trust relationship. Such asymmetries are not uncommon when representative bodies are publicly describing the work of their members. These bodies make dignified claims about contribution to society that are to be expected in public rhetoric. They create, however, a problem of corporate branding between themselves and the general public when the gap between claim and performance is perceived by the public to be so wide as to weaken credibility. The width of that gap has now reached the point of incredulity, for the observable, efficient role of PR in the political economy and civil society is to give 'voice' to competing interests. Publics and stakeholders see much of the efficiency of PR but little of its 'dignity'. It is now timely for PR's representative bodies to 'rebrand' themselves for professionals whose role is communicative advocacy and defence rather than social harmonisation.[9]

Permanent PR

PR propaganda is not going to disappear from liberal democracies or from market economies such as the UK and USA, where it first developed. Nor will it wither in what was known as the Western world. Emerging market economies and democracies in Asia, Africa and South America already have it and are developing their own forms (Sriramesh and Vercic 2003). PR is a mind-set, a set of techniques and an industry that will expand in developing economies, and in new democracies, around the world. Constitutionally, it is a consequence of the rights to property ownership, to freedom of expression and to petitioning government; sociologically, it is a consequence of a pluralism of values and behaviours; commercially, it creates markets in promotional messaging; and politically, it is the 'voice' of competitive group intermediation and of government news management. As a mode of public communication, PR is in an increasingly favourable position to compete with paid advertising for the messaging resources of its principals; and it has strengthened its hand *vis-à-vis* journalism for direct access to publics and stakeholders. As the mainstream journalism of press and broadcasting is weakened by incorporation into business conglomerates, and journalism in this way becomes 'PR-ised', the balance of advantage in reaching publics and stakeholders with chosen messages, meanings and values falls more towards PR. For both thoughtful PR person and citizen, this is a serious concern, affecting both the quantity and quality of public debate in a liberal democracy. The concern also links the PR reform agenda with questions over the diversity of opinion in the media, and is another reason for more critical academic attention. There is thus a rich asymmetry of connections when more positive effects of PR in a democracy depend on rigorous scrutiny of its messages by a more competitive and diverse media.

PR is promotional 'voice'. Historically in the UK and USA, the PR industry has mostly worked for the dominant interests of finance capitalism and big business to stop or limit state intervention and to build markets. It has been in the past too expensive for trade unions, welfare groups and liberal civil society to employ themselves or to hire in. Generally, the industry has been at the service of the classes and elites, which have a disproportionate share of wealth, influence and power in these two liberal democracies, and others like them around the world. The use of PR does not cause elite and capitalist wealth and power: it is a consequential communicative expression of those existing assets, and is used repeatedly to reinforce their dominance. In this way, the PR industry has been an effective 'voice' sustaining asymmetrical relationships of power and wealth in liberal democracy, especially in the forms of lobbying PR and ideological transmission PR.

Anti-capitalists will applaud this critique and some will then draw an excessively negative conclusion: that PR can only advance capitalist and elite interests. In a historical sense, the PR industry has been paid by those interests mostly. But since the 1960s in the UK, an accelerating pluralism has seen the low-cost, moderately difficult to master, accessible messaging techniques of PR working for greater numbers of less wealthy and less powerful interests, causes, organisations and groups. This pluralism is not using a 'virtuous' PR that is categorically separate from a 'reprobate' PR. There is no 'PR' in capital letters that is reprobate, and a 'pr' in lower case that is virtuous. PR cannot be separated into the perverse category of 'propaganda and manipulation' and the laudatory one of 'information and campaigning'. PR techniques do not have integral to them moral values.[10] They are communicative modes. They are used by principals who have moralities, ethics and benign interests in a democracy and in markets – or not. Thus PR propaganda is 'voice' for children's charities as much as for tobacco manufacturers; for disaster relief charities as much as for animal liberation lawbreakers; and for hospitals as much as for arms manufacturers. PR propaganda will not disappear from the agenda of any organisation or group that seeks advantage in the marketplace of goods, services, beliefs, ideas, reputation or behaviours. Nor will it disappear from the practice of elected governments and political parties who historically have been the other major users of PR alongside big business, and who have much used it to get elected and to govern.

Instead, PR will spread more widely through the civil societies and the political economies of liberal democracies. We cannot wish PR away.[11] As citizens and consumers, we will support, reject and question its 'voices' as suits our interests. And after reform, with all 'voices' who want to speak audible to all who want to listen, and that listening done in a sceptical way in person or via a diverse media, liberal democracies and markets will have more varied and informed public debates. In this way, the positive effects of PR will outweigh the negative ones – just.

Notes

1 A great Niagara of PR

1 Source is CIPR survey reported in PRWeek, 11.11.05, p. 1, 'CIPR study: PR industry is worth £6.5 bn.'

2 Max Clifford reports that young women phone his office asking about the media scandal value of footballers. Source: 'What's the damage?' *Financial Times* magazine, 2.10.04, p. 22.

3 The author was once upbraided by Prof. Sam Black for saying 'PR' and so spreading negative perceptions, particularly when 'public relations' was becoming a subject taught in higher education. Source is author's memory of a conversation at Bournemouth in 1989.

4 See obituary of Prof. Janet Kear, the *Guardian*, 6.12.04, p. 21.

5 The Grunigian school has a penchant for 'Excellent PR' and has researched its features. See J. Grunig (ed.) (1992b) *Excellence in Public Relations and Communications Management*, London: Lawrence Erlbaum.

6 See Moloney (2000b) *Rethinking PR*, p. 2

7 'Public domain' means in this book the areas of public life associated with the political economy and civil society. It is the areas of public life out of which arise public relations communications. It therefore excludes family, private sexual, religious, aesthetic and artistic communications. It covers the areas of public life associated with the institutions of the public, commercial and voluntary sectors. It is not the same as the Habermasian 'public sphere' because it includes commercial communications and self-interested communications. It is different from Marquand's 'public domain' in *Decline of the Public* (2004) because it includes communications from markets. See his p. 135 for the features of a contemporary post-Habermasian 'public sphere'.

8 The definition of PR offered by the Chartered Institute of Public Relations (IPR) in the UK has become more layered and nuanced since the early 1990s. The following is offered (2004):

> Public relations is about reputation – the result of what you do, what you say and what others say about you. Public relations is the discipline which looks after reputation, with the aim of earning understanding and support and influencing opinion and behaviour. It is the planned and sustained effort to establish and maintain goodwill and mutual understanding between an organisation and its publics.

See www.ipr.org.uk/looking/index.htm. Accessed 6.10.04. The IPR became a chartered body in February 2005 and its title changed to 'Chartered Institute of Public Relations'. See www.ipr.org.uk/charterspecial/release _ 170205.htm.

9 There are connotations of Social Darwinism in references to 'struggle for

advantage'. Prime Minister Tony Blair may share them. He is reported as saying to a Labour Party conference in 2004: 'We have not won yet. Life is a perpetual struggle. This is the fate of humankind.' He was talking about pride in national achievements under his Labour governments since 1997. Source: 'Brown's public service pledge', the *Guardian*, 13.3.04, p. 2.

10 The author has noted that when talking to colleagues with a communication studies background, there are multiple references to one- and two-way communications, and negotiations; when talking to those with a political studies background, much less so, and more references to power, and resources.

11 PR people invariably use the word 'education' in a manipulative way, e.g. the CEO of a large agency described sending out a booklet about how to consume a product via an interest group as 'something of a Trojan horse, sneaking in to influence'. Source is a guest lecture, Bournemouth University, 2004.

12 See Seitel (1995, p. 6) for how American PR leaders counted that number in 1975. Experienced PR people more or less ignore conversations about definitions.

13 This is a reference to the case of Tony Martin that caused a controversy over the amount of physical force to be used by a resident when confronting a burglar. See 'Read all about it', the *Guardian* G2 section, 4.10.1999, p. 16.

14 Neo-pluralism is associated with the later writings of Dahl (1982, 1989), and the work of Lindblom (1997). It is a development of classical pluralism in that it singles out business from among all the interests in liberal democracy as the most powerful influencing public policy. Neo-Marxism is that variant of Marxism which emphasises the mediating role of the state amongst competing interests and classes (see Barrow 1993), and which explores Gramscian ideas of building cultural hegemony through ideology in a formally free society (see McLellan 1979). Classical pluralism is associated with Bentley (1908) and Truman (1951), and has at its core the idea that all interests have the possibility of competing equally for influence on policy.

15 If detectives were once vicars, they can now be middle-aged PR women. See Agatha Raisin, the creation of M.C. Beaton, who sold her London agency to retire to the Cotswolds.

16 The author first worked in PR for a large manufacturing company in 1969. He was frequently told by his boss that there would be PR directors in most UK boardrooms before long, and that PR would rival marketing in corporate favour. It has not happened.

17 The definition of PR by Herman (1992, p. 168) in his 'doublespeak dictionary'.

18 The first four are, following medieval political economy, the Crown and Nobles, the Church, the Commons, and, following Macaulay, the press.

19 Examples of moderate appeals to positive emotion are given in *Encyclopaedia of Public Relations* (Heath 2005, pp 614–5) in the Persuasion Theory entry: appealing to compassion in fundraising for hungry children; arousing guilt in drivers who drink; arousing fear to sell house security alarms; and focusing on romance to sell diamonds.

20 While the PR function is an agency one in organisations and groups, individual PR people may be members of the dominant coalition of an organisation or group, and so act as controllers of that function and its staff.

21 The term 'big business' is used for that category of private and publicly quoted companies that are transnational, national or regional in their operations and have significant market shares for their goods and services. It is used in contradistinction to micro, small and medium-sized companies.

22 Those who turn 'corporate power against itself by co-opting, hacking, mocking and re-conceptualizing meaning'. See p. 1 of http://depts.washington.edu/ccce/polcommcampaigns/peretti.html. Accessed 22.3.05.

2 PR from top to bottom

1 *PRWeek*, 3.7.98, p. 28.
2 See www.catholic-ew.org.uk/nav/newsandevents.htm for Catholics in England and Wales; and www.bedfordgurdwara.org.uk/pix.htm for Sikhs. Accessed 24.3.05.
3 The *Guardian* education section, 1.6.04, p. 8.
4 The *Observer* notes ('Adults teach hatred as Sarah is mourned', 13.8.00, p. 5) that a leader of a group on the Paulsgrove council estate, Portsmouth 'will only talk in the presence of the self-appointed press officer'.
5 The everyday tale of super-cynical, lobbying folk from the consultancy of Prentice and McCabe.
6 Edition of 30.4.04, p. 20.
7 Edition of 25.6.04, p. 5. Another instance of university involvement with PR is the search by Hertfordshire University for an agency to improve its relations with the local community on a £100,000 two-year contract. Source: 'Herts uni to boost community ties', *PRWeek*, 6.8.04, p. 10.
8 The head of Imperial College calls Luton University 'third rate' in March 2004, and, in October, the head of the university gives a paper on 'reputation management' at the Effective Marketing in Higher Education conference, reporting increases in staff morale, admissions and national profile. The Luton head revealed a good PR tactic when under attack: appear puzzled rather than angry. See 'Insult transforms Luton's fortunes', *The Times Higher Education Supplement*, 29.10.04, p. 1.
9 Edition of 13.3.86.
10 By A. Davis (2004) from Palgrave Macmillan of Basingstoke.
11 By Paul Richards (1998) from Take That Ltd of Harrogate.
12 By E. Yaverbaum and R. Bly (2001), California: IDG Books Worldwide.
13 Jasper Gerard, 'The Dorchester chronicles present us with the regal Bridget Jones', *The Times*, 9.4.01, p. 16.
14 Edition of 10.1.98, p. 8.
15 Foreword, November 2003. See www.ipr.org.uk/unlockpr/Unlocking_Potential_Report.pdf. Accessed 23.3.05.
16 Source is David Michie (1998), p. 12. Calculated by adding the PR companies' and the in-house departments' sub-totals.
17 Source of the £3 billion figure is head of public affairs, CIPR, in an email to the author of 29.4.04. Turnover and employment figures, however, should be treated with caution, e.g. in 1993, *Public Relations: Journal of the IPR* 11(3), p. 3, gave employment at 48,000 with the comment working 'in some way' in PR.
18 Prof. Anne Gregory at www.anti-spin.com/index.cfm?TERTIARY_ID=O&PRIMARY_ID=21&SECOND/. Accessed on 25.9.03.
19 Website, 30.5.04.
20 Reported by the CIPR on 29.4.04 in an email to the author.
21 Source is 'A post-Blair generation?' *The Times Higher Education Supplement*, 6.8.04, p. 2.
22 Source is 'Career Opportunities', the *Evening Standard*, London, 23.9.04, p. 59.
23 Topics include corporate social responsibility and small businesses; lobbying in Italy; e-communications by MPs; and corporate branding by multinational mobile phone companies competing in the UK.
24 Source is CIPR map on back page of *Behind the Spin* 9, February 2005. There are also eleven postgraduate degrees approved and six postgraduate diplomas.
25 See the brochure *IPR Excellence Awards 2005*, p. 2, from the CIPR.
26 See www.ipr.org.uk/charterspecial/release_170205.htm.
27 *PRWeek*, 23.1.04, p. 1, and IPR annual review (2003), p. 3.

28 Alison Clark's letter to the *Financial Times*, 26.8.02, p. 8, 'No place in PR for manipulation'.
29 See www.ipr.org.uk/Careers/what/definition.htm. Accessed 25.2.05.
30 March/April 2001. See *The Times*, 9.4.01, pp. 1, 4, 5, 16 for a summary.
31 Managing perceptions extends from seeking mundane commercial advantage to avoiding moral guilt. Doreen Lawrence, the mother of the murdered black teenager Stephen Lawrence, rejected the admissions of racism in the London police by their Commissioner Sir Paul Condon as 'That is a PR job', (the *Guardian*, 2.10.98, p. 1).
32 The *Independent* magazine section, 26.10.96, p. 30.
33 Stephen Farish in the commemorative publication *Managing Communication in a Changing World*, London: IPR in 1998, p. 58.
34 It was awarded chartered status in 2005.
35 *PRWeek*, 23.2.96.
36 *PRWeek* supplement, 26.4.96.
37 *PRWeek*, 7.6.98, p. 7.
38 *PRWeek*, 25.6.04, p. 21.
39 As *The New Machiavelli* (1997).
40 By Phil Harris and Andrew Lock (1996).
41 For a review of hired lobbyists, see Moloney (1996).
42 By White and Mazur (1995) and Oliver (ed.) (2004).
43 A survey carried out by the author in spring 1998. The numbers are small because the PR Educators' Forum then had forty-three correspondents in sixteen universities and colleges.
44 Webster (1995, p. 101): argued in relation to the public sphere concept.
45 *Viewing the Century* – Noam Chomsky, BBC Radio 3, 21.6.98
46 The second edition, published by Penguin, 1981, has some updating.
47 McQuail (1987, p. 293) says about PR and advertising that the 'relevant mode is mainly that of "display-attention"'.
48 Source is a CEO of such an agency visiting Bournemouth University, winter 2004.
49 Edition of 8.6.00, p. 8.
50 Source: *TBI Yearbook* (2004), London: Informa Media Group.
51 Source: *World Radio TV Handbook* (2004), Oxford: WRTH Publications.
52 Matthew Parris in 'Milburn a communicator? No, he's just his master's voice', *The Times*, 11.9.04, p. 26.
53 The effect on journalists of more media space to fill was described in an article by Brian MacArthur (*The Times*, 11.9.98, p. 40) and it is an effect that favours the PR person.

> A journalist quickly learns sharp lessons about the modern media industry when he becomes poacher (journalist) turned gamekeeper (PR person). . . . One of these lessons, now that there are so many local and national radio and TV stations and newspapers have grown so big, is the insatiable appetite of modern news editors. They need to fill all those hours with talk or all those empty editorial pages with new articles.

54 The phrase is the title of *The Media and the PR Industry: A Partnership or a Marriage of Convenience?* (1991), London: Two-Ten Communications.
55 *Journalist* magazine, October 2004, p. 29. 'PRs "proud to be pants"' reported a survey showing that British PRs were the 'worst in the world', and UK journalists the 'most corruptible'. It was produced by a PR firm. More on 'love–hate' relationships in 'Don't call me a spin doctor' by Colin Bryne, CEO of Weber Shandwick, a London PR agency, in the *Independent* media weekly, 28.3.05, p. 19.

56 See p. 137 for origin.
57 *Financial Times* weekend section, 29–30.11.97, p. iv.

3 A future with PR

1 See Moloney and Harrison (2004).
2 The three were West (1963), Baistow (1985), Carty (1992).
3 Miller goes further in *RedPepper*, June 2003, p.3 with:

> Indeed PR is the very lifeblood of the global capitalist economy. It can only flourish as a profession and an industry in a society run on market principles, and the neo-liberal turn has been accomplished in no small measure with the aid of PR.

 See www.redpepper.org.uk/June2003/x-June2003-globalpr.html. Accessed 6.12.03.
4 Source: the *Guardian*, 6.8.04, p. 7, 'Football scandal'; p. 34, 'End of the affair is just the start of embarrassment for the FA'.
5 Lynn Barber, 'Barbergate', the *Observer Life*, 8.11.98, pp. 16–23:

> Any magazine that relies on having a big star on the cover every month and whose news stand sales depend to some extent on the appeal of that star, have already sold the pass to PRs. . . . But nowadays PRs are terrifyingly efficient. They have taught all celebs never to give interviews except when they are plugging something.

 The Schiffer interview was in the *Financial Times* creative business section, 27.7.04, p. 8, 'Claudia's new business model'. The journalist refused to submit her copy to the PR agency.
6 See *The Times*, 25.9.04, p. 1 for background. Paul Bigly, the brother of the hostage, talked of a 'campaign' on *Today*, BBC Radio 4, on 27.9.04.
7 Edmund Burke, *Reflections on the Revolution in France*, first published in 1790. See 1969 Penguin edition, p. 135.
8 Berger says (p. 355) that the US philosopher Horace Kallen coined the work 'pluralism' in the 1920s.
9 Source: www.cbdresearch.com/DBA.htm. Accessed on 6.4.05.
10 The literature on voluntary groups is replete with distinctions between interest, sectional, pressure, cause and promotional groups. As Alderman (1984) has pointed out, making these distinctions has turned into an academic speciality all of its own. The main emphasis in this text is on interest and cause groups. The terms 'sectional' and 'promotional' groups are not used. The distinction hoped for is that between a business group or a trade union (interest groups) on the one hand, and an environmental or racial equality group (cause groups) on the other. Both categories apply pressure on policy-makers when it suits. They will be called 'pressure groups' when that aspect of their work is being primarily expressed.
11 The increase in pressure group activity has been criticised (e.g. Brittan (1995), Olson (1982)) on the grounds that it unduly influences public policy when government controls a large proportion of national income, leading to ills such as pluralist stagnation, pork barrel politics and making the UK 'ungovernable'. In so far as PR strengthens group activity, these authors, often from a public choice theory stance, will disapprove of it.
12 Stonier quotes Prof. Sydney Gross on the women's movement to the effect that 'Public relations can have a thoughtful and eminent role in translating the slowly-gathering waves of . . . revolution as they crash against the shores of established settings'.

13 Changes in personal behaviour and in group development are a well-recorded historical phenomenon, and in no way unique to the period discussed here. For example, wealthy women in the eighteenth century asserted 'rights' modern women would acclaim today and, in religion, Unitarians held ideas about the workings of the universe closely associated with the 'laws' of modern science. Voluntary associations have a long history in the UK; in the modern period they date back to the political clubs of the late eighteenth century and to Chartism in the early nineteenth century. They continued throughout the Victorian period with the growth of the trade unions, co-operative and hobby/leisure movements. They also used techniques that we today would label as PR. See Wring (1998) for insights into the use of PR by the political left in the 1930s. He details the public relations strategy of Herbert Morrison, the 1930s Labour leader of the London County Council, and support for it from the unions and from professional PR people at County Hall. Black (1973) writes of the major involvement of the National Union of Local Government Officers in the 1948 foundation of the UK's Institute of Public Relations.

14 See Grant (1995) and Ch. 1 for a discussion of the connection of social movements to voluntary groups and their proliferation. See p. 2 for business represented by over 1,800 trade associations.

15 Source is email from the National Council for Voluntary Organisations, 16.8.04.

16 Maybe found in the churches, the theatre, and occasionally in the universities. Even if the practice of the public sphere concept is minimal, the concept is an important intellectual reference point. In their review of how the British press represents the EU, Anderson and Weymouth (1999) note the current predominance of the view that knowledge is socially constructed and how, in the press, that construction has a commercial bias. They say (p. 16): 'This alleged manipulation of information in the public sphere has been given an additional impetus by the development of the corporate art of public relations.'

17 The marketplace of ideas is an extension to the marketplace of goods and services, and is a theory of truth whereby truth arises from competition amongst ideas (and by extension amongst datum claimed to be fact). The modern source of the concept is Justice Oliver Wendell Holmes in the US Supreme Court case Abrams v. US (1919) in a dissenting opinion that included

> when men have realised that time has upset many fighting faiths, they may come to believe even more than they believe the very foundations of their own conduct that the ultimate good desired is better reached by free trade in ideas . . . that the best test of truth is the power of the thought to get itself accepted in the competition of the market.

18 Business supporters are well aware of activists' groups who have mastered the media. See Deegan (2001); John and Thomson (2003). Halfon (1998, p. 3) argues that some of these groups have ideas such as corporate responsibility that are 'fundamentally at odds' with the capitalist system.

19 The post of press officer is associated with all sorts of good, indifferent and evil causes. Hitler had one. Heinz Lorentz was the Führer's press liaison officer says a letter to *The Times* from R.W. Leon who interrogated him as he tried to escape from Berlin, posing as a Luxembourg journalist. See 'Hitler's cruel fight to twist history', *The Times*, 2.10.2000, p. 17.

20 A headline in a leaflet about Christchurch Older People's Forum, Dorset, June 2004.

21 See Jordan and Maloney (1997), p. 173, note 13, for an example.

22 PorterNovelli, a multinational PR agency, had a Latvian branch in October 2004 with clients in banking, telecommunications and insurance. Source is

private email to the author from a former corporate communications student at Bournemouth University.

23 This global spread of PR is reflected in the sixteen country profiles found in Sriramesh and Vercic (2003).

24 The Foreword is by Robert S. Lynd.

25 The author remembers that the Labour government's 1964 national plan was distributed publicly in booklet form.

26 The CIPR says PR 'can also give those a voice who wouldn't otherwise be heard and put issues on the agenda that wouldn't normally make it'. Accessed at www.ipr.org.uk/conference/index.htm on 20.10.04. Also the CIPR gives 'public relations a voice at the highest levels'.

27 The view of Jon White, one of the first UK academics specialising in PR, in a 1989 conversation with the author.

28 Dr Steve Mackey of Deakin University, Australia, reported to a Bournemouth University seminar (22.11.04) the start of such a speculation among leading US PR academics at the National Communication Association Convention, Chicago, 11–14 November.

29 Source: *Documents in Early American History* at http://courses.smsu.edu/ ftm922f/10.htm. Accessed on 26.7.04.

30 The phrase 'public wrangling' borrows from the work of the US rhetoric scholar Kenneth Burke who wrote (1945, p. 23) about the marketplace of ideas as follows: it is the 'Scramble, the Wrangle of the Marketplace, the flurries and flare-ups of the Human Barnyard, Give and Take, the wavering line of pressure and counter-pressure, the Logomachy, the onus of ownership, the War of Nerves, the War.' See Heath (1992, p. 20) for this quotation and commentary on it.

31 See Crossley and Roberts (2004), p. 21, for four conditions set by Mill in *On Liberty*.

4 PR and propaganda

1 'Principal' here means the most important usage of PR material, i.e. getting compliance from PR consumers, and is not a volume indicator. As regards volume of PR produced, marketing public relations is probably the most voluminous.

2 Bernays (1947) wrote, to the dismay of his colleagues, about the 'Engineering of consent'. It lacked, in their view, the discretion of knowing when to say less. He is not an author much referred to by contemporary UK academics.

3 None known to this author since he first published this thesis in 2000.

4 The present author reached a similar conclusion to Lambert before he had read the latter in July 2001. Lambert was not referenced in *Rethinking PR*. Lambert went on to define some of the features of a 'certain stage' of liberal capitalist democracy: big businesses; competition; democratic government.

5 The huckster origins of PR can be traced to the US circus owner P.T. Barnum and other contemporaries at the end of the nineteenth century. It was said of these publicists by a contemporary journalist that they were 'the only group of men proud of being called liars'. The source of this reference is a review by S. Rampton of Ewen's (1996) book *PR! A Social History of Spin*, published on the Internet by the Centre for Media and Democracy, which describes itself as a 'nonprofit, public interest organisation dedicated to investigative reporting on the public relations industry'. Continuing with sobriquets about PR, Goldman (1948, endnote 2) notes twenty-eight entries in the *American Thesaurus of Slang*. They include 'advertisementor', 'aide-de-press', 'flesh peddler', 'pufflicity man', 'space grabber' and 'tooter'. For a sympathetic biography of Barnum but one which acknowledges that he 'made a profit, and that was because of his

publicity techniques' (p. 22), and that he 'had early learned the art of pleasing editors' (p. 52), see Harris (1973).

6 Schnattschneider (1975, p. 31) noted the 'pro-business or upper-class bias' of the US pressure group system.

7 Quoted on p. 131 of Ewen, as cited in Beale (1936), p. 546, and Cochran and Miller (1942), p. 333.

8 The Government Accountability Office was called in to investigate three alleged cases. See www.npr.org/templates/story/story.php?storyId=4493856. Accessed 21.2.2005.

9 It is ironic that US government got bigger under the conservative Republican administration 2000–4. Neo-conservative US political thinking argues for 'small' government.

10 Tye (1998, p. 169) notes in his biography of Bernays that '"Propaganda" was a word Bernays seldom used in a pejorative sense.'

11 See the interview in Olasky (1987, p. 81): 'We cannot have chaos . . . and that is where public relations counsellors can prove their effectiveness, by making the public believe that human gods are watching over us for our own benefit.'

12 See Tye's (1998) biography of Bernays.

13 Lee was an expert on railway affairs and wrote technical articles about their pricing. His expertise outside of PR was one of his attractions to his industrial clients. After working for Rockefeller, he became knowledgeable about what we would now call welfare capitalism. He lectured at the LSE, London, on that subject and on railways (see Hiebert 1966, p. 59). See Tye (1998) for the breadth of Bernays's written output.

14 See Stauber and Rampton (1995), pp. 21–4.

15 Concepts are renamed over time: note that the sociobiology of the 1970s has become the evolutionary psychology of the millennium. See 'Human nature totally explained', *The Times Higher Education Supplement*, 12.3.99, p. 18, for a statement of this argument.

16 Habermas's translator notes, in his introduction, that the German word *Offentlichkeit* can be rendered in three ways: (the) public, public sphere, publicity.

17 See McCarthy (1996), p. 382.

18 In Communication World, Feb/Mar 1999, pp. 13–21. It is the newsletter of the International Business Communicators' Association.

19 See PRWeek, 1.3.2002, p.12, 'Talking Change' for an interview with the then director of communications at the Department of Health.

20 Unlike Bernays and Lee, Grunig is not an operational PR man, but a teacher and researcher.

21 But it has a strong competitor in the rhetorical and critical contextual approaches to PR. In particular, see the work of Robert Heath and Elizabeth Toth.

22 'Persuasion is not a dirty word, although it is often confused with its "black sheep" cousin, propaganda'.(Encyclopedia of Public Relations (2005, p. 614).

23 This Utrecht lecture is the shortest and clearest statement by Grunig of his and Hunt's typology.

24 He uses the phrase 'promotional philanthropy' (pp. 67–9) and associates it with cause-related marketing that is not controversial or negatively perceived.

5 PR propaganda in the UK

1 Also see pp. 402–5 of Simmons and Biddle (1999) for publicity and public relations by railways in Britain.

2 L'Etang has nominated among others the documentary film-maker John Grierson; Sir Charles Higham, an enthusiast for managing public opinion; Alan Campbell-Johnson, Lord Mountbatten's Press Secretary in India, 1947–8, and

President of the IPR in 1956–7; J.H. Brebner who worked for the Post Office, for the Ministry of Information and for the nationalised transport industries, and who wrote the first UK book on PR; S.C. Leslie, a PR man at the Gas, Light and Coke Co. in the 1930s, who later became a civil servant and who called for a Ministry of Public Enlightenment; Sir Stephen Tallents, secretary of the Empire Marketing Board; A.P. Ryan who managed the 'Mr Therm' campaign and was later Assistant Controller of Public Relations at the BBC in the 1930s. See L'Etang's 1999 paper on Grierson's influence on PR. Gillman (1978) lists many other names, perhaps not so prominent in the main. In this author's experience, there was a middle-class provenance to many PR managers in the 1960s. An example is the life of Major Harry Witheridge who had a distinguished Second World War military record; set up the Brunswick Boys' Club, Fulham, London in 1949; and joined the overseas branch of the Midland Bank as 'their first public relations officer'. See the *Daily Telegraph*, Obituaries, 10.12.02.

3 See L'Etang's article in *Public Relations Review* (1998) for the sensitivity about associating PR with propaganda: she starts with an apologia for so doing.
4 Grant (1994) in her review of domestic publicity by government in the period 1918–39 uses the terms interchangeably.
5 They used the phrase (p. 4) to describe rising government spending on advertising and the then Government Communication and Information Service.
6 It became a chartered body in February 2005.
7 Source is video with Tim Traverse-Healy, June 2004, produced at Bournemouth University, and available at www.bournemouth.ac.uk/media2/on-linelectures.
8 *Preparing for Emergencies: What You Need to Know*, published by HM Government. An earlier example of active persuasion by PR was the 1999 DTI leaflet inserted in newspapers entitled *Killed in Her Bed*, about carbon monoxide poisoning by domestic heating systems. In the period of most public utility privatisations from 1987/8 to 1992/3, there was a decline in government advertising expenditure from £90.5 million to £47 million, as the number of sell-offs declined. Expenditure rose under the impact of New Labour welfare policies from £69.4 million in 1996/7 to £105 million in 1998/9. Figures supplied by the COI on 30.9.99 for a majority of government departments but not all.
9 See the *Financial Times* weekend section, 25. 9. 04, p. 1, for the case against breast screening.
10 Source is 'Blair in row as Whitehall adverts soar by 157%', the *Guardian*, 26.4.01, p. 13.
11 This frequency was pointed out by David Blunkett, then Secretary of State for Education and Employment, on the BBC Radio 4 *Today* news programme on 16.9.98. When asked whether this was propaganda, he replied 'no' and noted that these soap operas often used their storylines for passing on publicly useful information.
12 Source is Lord Carrington who worked in MAFF in the 1950s, *The Food Programme*, BBC Radio 4, 30.9.01.
13 Regulations were introduced by the Political Parties, Elections and Referendums Act (2000), which gives the Electoral Commission a statutory right to assess the question posed in any referendum; to register political parties, bodies and individuals wanting to spend more than £10,000; and to allocate public money to bodies representing outcomes to the referendum question. See www.electoralcommission.gov.uk. Accessed 1.12.04.
14 Grant (1994) gives this example and notes that 'prestige advertising' was the term used for it. Bernays used it in the USA: he promoted the lorry manufacturer Mack by promoting the development of an inter-state highway system.
15 Simmons defines PR as means that companies/political parties 'may adopt to put themselves on continuously satisfactory terms with the public' (p. 253). He

concludes (p. 269), however, that such efforts did the companies little good, for by 1900 'the general public did not love them, and left them with alacrity when better and cheaper means of transport were afforded' by trams and buses. The successors to these Victorians are the contemporary train-operating companies.

16 See his obituary in the *Guardian*, 5.9.2000, p. 22.

17 The source of attribution of PR people to individual organisations is from either L'Etang or Gillman. The latter was an IPR president and BOAC public relations chief. He notes, *inter alia*, that in 1809 the Treasury, which was *porte-parole* for foreign policy, asked the War, Foreign Affairs and Admiralty departments to read the papers each morning and send on a summary or 'a hint of the line which it wished should be taken'.

18 Williams's count of propagandists and PR people in January 1944 was: Ministry of Information in the UK, 2,719; civil ministries, 661, and armed forces ministries, 1,016.

19 Interviewed in 'Jolly champions need to embrace change', *PRWeek*, 12.07.02, p. 24.

20 There is some interesting happenstance here. Basil Clarke was a journalist turned PR man who worked for the British Health Ministry. Earlier he worked in Dublin explaining British government policy at the time of the Irish War of Independence when de Valera was a leading figure in the revolutionary party Sinn Fein. See Gillman (1978) for the short reference to Clarke.

21 Other developments in the new Irish state of 1922 illustrate something of relations between government and media in revolutionary circumstances. The new government soon had a press adviser, Sean Lester, a former news editor, who was later its director of publicity. In the civil war of 1922–3, the government and opposing republican forces used persuasion and intimidation to control media content and editorial style. Type composition at gunpoint and the smashing of presses with sledgehammers happened. The government was insistent that the rebels were never reported as holding a rank and were never to be called 'forces', 'troops' or 'army', or worst of all 'Republican'. See Horgan 2001, pp. 5–27.

22 See the catalogue of the GPO film unit from 1935–9, with titles such as *The Post Office in the Thirties; Providing a Service*. Available from the National Film Archive, London, and Consignia Film Collection, Sittingbourne, Kent.

23 'As advertising falters, PR can take its chance', edition of 15.6.01, p. 11.

24 He concludes, however, on a congratulatory note. His last paragraph includes the following: 'the vast majority of PR activity has always been innocuous and at best a force for enlightenment'.

25 Source is the *Guardian*, 30.9.2000, p. 4.

26 McNair in L'Etang and Pieczka (1996), p. 36.

27 Tedlow concludes about US academics (1974, p. 205) that 'The public relations of public relations among intellectuals has deteriorated steadily since the days of the watchdog activities of the Institute for Propaganda Analysis [est. 1937].' Tye (1998, p. 297) still notes coyness by academics in front of PR: Harvard gave him a grant for his biography of Bernays 'while most academic institutions and foundations shied away from a book in public relations'.

28 Tim Traverse-Healy (1988) *Public Relations and Propaganda – Values Compared*, p. 5.

29 The UK exceptions are L'Etang and the author.

30 See *Encyclopedia of Public Relations* (Heath 2005), the entry about Betsy Plank, p. 624.

31 Jowett and O'Donnell (1992) say in their introduction (p. ix) that they do not cover advertising 'although presented as the most prevalent form of propaganda in the US'. On p. 266, they write: 'The economy dictates the flow of propaganda relative to the sale and consumption of goods.' This could be read as an implicit reference to PR for marketing purposes.

32 O'Shaughnessy notes (1999) that 'while all propaganda is necessarily biased, much bias is not all propagandist'.

33 Apart from Americans, Grant quotes (1994, p. 12) the following, *inter alia*, as concerned about gullibility of the masses: J.S. Mill, L.T. Hobhouse, Jose Ortega y Gasset.

34 Taylor (1999, p. 115) notes that when UK Bomber Command did leaflet drops over Nazi-occupied Europe, the crews called them 'bullshit bombs'.

35 Traverse-Healy (1988), p. 10, is quoting D'Artillac Brill of the Netherlands.

6 Can PR and democracy co-exist?

1 See Moloney (2004) in *Journal of Communication Management* 9(1). pp. 89–92 for another earlier attempt to synthesise PR, propaganda and democracy.

2 See 'Salt: time to slug it out', *The Times* body and soul section, 18.9.04, p. 2.

3 Source: BBC Radio 4, *Today* programme, 21.9.04.

4 The sequence is: SMA media release on funding new research, 4.10.04; FSA on rejection of complaint against it by advertising regulator, 12.10.04; SMA deny rejection by regulator, 18.10.04; SMA case study also on 18.10.04. Accessed on 27.10.04 at www.Saltsense.co.ukUK/releases/re1006.htm and www.food.gov.uk/news/pressreleases. Accessed again on 2.12.04, the SMA site showed two earlier releases – 15.11.04 on 'weak science', and 22.11.04 on a second case study. Five months earlier, there had been another 'inter-voicing' when Kevin Hawkins of the Retail Consortium defended on BBC Radio 4 *Farming Today*, 19.6.04, the gradual reduction of salt in processed food over four years, after the Health Minister had criticised the industry for slow progress. The SMA website was accessed again on 6.4.05 to reveal the 2005 media releases dated as of 26.1.05 and 16.3.05. The full set of 2004 FSA releases is available at www.food.gov.uk/news/?year=2004.

5 See 'Blair refuses to apologise for Iraq war', the *Guardian*, 14.9.04, p 2, and 'TUC conference', p. 13. The Prime Minister visited the conference at Brighton on the 14th. See www.labour.org.uk/tbtuco4 for his speech.

6 The National Association of Mortgage Victims has appeared after distress among people who have borrowed from high-interest lenders. See '1,000 stung by loan broker want him out of business', *The Times*, 30.10.04, p. 8.

7 See 'New breed of dinosaurs bares its teeth', the *Observer* business section. 19.9.04, p. 3.

8 See www.babymilkaction.org/boycott/prmachine.html. Accessed 4.10.04. Baby Milk Action is part of a larger international campaign.

9 Accessed 17.9.04 at http://search.abc.net.au/search/cache.cgi?collection=abconline&doc=http/www.abc.net.au.

10 See Jon White, 'Acting in the public good', the *Independent*, 19.7.89, op. ed. page.

11 Kymlicka writes (2002, p. 79) that 'inequalities due to circumstances beyond people's control, such as their natural talents . . . should be remedied or compensated'. His other categories for compensation are class and race. These are ascribed roles based on material circumstances and social constructs, and can be redefined. But how can, say, a lack of musical ability be compensated for by the state? Can education implant a talent? Does education develop what is latent?

12 Trade unions, for whatever defensible or indefensible reasons, sometimes fail to give 'voice' to the unemployed. The author was secretary of the Council for Academic Freedom and Academic Standards (CAFAS), a support group for academics in conflict with and/or dismissed by their organisations, and often heard that academic unions were patchy in their support. The two principal reasons offered were lack of staff resources and negative judgements about particular cases.

13 See Moloney, *Rethinking PR* (2000b), pp. 38–9.

14 The Council organises occasional 'masterclasses' in PR. Source: email to the author of 28.9.04.

15 Source is www.mediatrust.org. Accessed 29.9.04. Two PR firms involved were Weber Shandwick through *pro bono* consultancy advice, and Tangerine PR with 'PR coaching'.

16 These benefits have been stated by Cutlip *et al.* (2000, 8th edn) in their supplementary pack of teaching material (electronic transparencies) for their *Effective Public Relations*. The five 'Social Positives of Public Relations' are summarised here as:

  1 it improves professional practice by codifying and enforcing conduct and standards of performance;
  2 it improves the conduct of organisations by stressing the need for public approval;
  3 it serves the public interest by making all points of view articulate in the public forum;
  4 it serves 'our segmented society by using communication and mediation to replace misinformation with information, discord with rapport';
  5 it fulfils its social responsibility to promote human welfare by helping social systems adapt to changing needs and environments.

17 '[So]me communications services' is a reference to new media. Source is www.ncc.org.uk/communications/index.htm. Accessed 27.9.04.

18 Accessed 22.9.04 at www.asa.ogr.uk/index.asp.

19 A more unlikely body for regulation would be a legislation-backed Office for PR Regulation, OfPR. This is conceivable only after the adjunct solutions had been tried and found wanting.

20 See www.electoralcommission.gov.uk and scroll to fact sheet 06–04. Accessed 24.9.04. Public monies were dispersed to two designated organisations, totalling £200,000, during the 2004 campaign for the regional referendum in the northeast of England on the question of devolved government. Source is conversation with Electoral Commission on 5.4.05.

21 See www.ofcom.org.uk/about _ ofcom. Accessed 24.9.04.

22 One can already hear the phrase 'granny's PR state'.

23 Public subsidy for resource-poor groups was tried in the 1980s by the Greater London Council (GLC) under the leadership of Ken Livingston, though communication was not much singled out, if ever. The practice drew the ire of the then-Conservative government, and became part of the indictment against the GLC.

24 In the anti-vivisection area, there are SHAC (Stop Huntingdon Animal Crusade); SPEAK (who forced out the contractor Montpellier from building an £18 million private research laboratory in Oxford); PCRM (Physicians' Committee for Responsible Medicine); PETA (People for the Ethical Treatment of Animals). These groups are monitored by the Centre for Consumer Freedom. Source is 'Kill scientists, says animal rights chief', the *Observer*, 25.7.04, p. 2. Other interested groups are the National Association of Pension Funds who initially put up £25 million reward money for information leading to the conviction of animal rights extremists. The Research Defence Society wants legal protection for scientists against extremism. Source is '£24m bounty to combat animal rights terrorists', *The Times*, 24.7.04, p. 1; and 'Animal activists turn fury on Oxford', p. 4.

25 See *Dad's Army: The Men Who Stormed the Palace*, Channel 4 television, 11.10.04, 9 p.m., for a portrait of their media relations strategy and their planning of stunts. The price of this PR 'voicing' and 'stunting' is that the chief judge of the UK High Court's family court will not meet with the group. They also have a double-decker bus with a loudhailer outside her Devon farmhouse. She does,

however, meet their more moderate competitors, Families Need Fathers. See 'The Guardian profile: Elizabeth Butler-Sloss', the *Guardian*, 12.11.04, p. 12.

26 Christian Voice put on their website the names, addresses and telephone numbers of BBC staff involved with the broadcast of *Jerry Springer: The Opera* (8.1.05) on BBC2 TV. There were threats made against these staff. Christian Voice said later 'We regret that there have been threats.' See the *Guardian* media section, 11.1.05, p. 8.

27 Two examples from August 2004 illustrating what Graham may call 'fragmentation', and others pluralist variety.

   1   Pharmaceutical companies and pro-vivisection groups representing doctors argue that campaigning by animal rights activists is leading to firms relocating overseas to escape high levels of welfare regulation and to have lower costs. Rebutted by the RSPCA, which argues that animals suffer in vivisection, regulation levels are not excessive, and that the industry periodically threatens to leave the UK (source: BBC Radio 4, *Today* programme, 27.8.04).

   2   The gay pressure group Outrage! complains that the BBC should not broadcast homophobic songs at the Music of Black Origin (Mobo) awards ceremony in the Royal Albert Hall. Mobo said it condemned homophobia, had not nominated one allegedly homophobic artist, and left nominations to its panel of music promoters and DJs (source: 'Gay rights group urges boycott of Mobo awards', the *Independent*, 25.8.04, p. 7.

28 Some animal welfare and animal liberation groups in the UK are alleged to use violence against property and people. 'Kill scientists, says animal rights chief', the *Observer*, 25.7.04, p.2, reports Jerry Vlasak, a prominent figure in the anti-vivisection movement, as saying 'I think violence is part of the struggle against oppression. It is inevitable that violence will be used in the struggle and that it will be effective.'

29 Sport is an important zone of civil society and a site of much PR activity. Sometimes, football supporters came up against powerful interests wanting to buy their clubs, as in the Glazer bid for Manchester United PLC in 2004. Mark Borkowski, the London-based press agent, called the supporters' public objections to the bid a 'homespun PR campaign' and added 'It will . . . signal to all the multinational giants that the power of PR is falling into the hands of the people.' See 'Power to the people', the *Guardian* media section, 18.10.04, p. 11.

30 The obstacles listed are 'the ethnocentrism or simple unreliability of assumptions about associations and their effects, and a failure to account for the impact of globalisation, economic re-structuring, political corruption and power relations of different kinds'.

31 See www.ipr.org.uk/charterspecial/release_ 170205.htm. Accessed on 18.02.05.

32 See Bates (2004) for an account, in particular pp. 125–41.

7 Is PR damaging democracy?

1 The last two negative effects were taken from the 'Social Negatives of Public Relations' transparency, part of the learning resources package connected with *Effective Public Relations* (2000, 8th edn) by Cutlip *et al*.

2 See Henwood (1997) for an analysis of the US financial system that (p. 3) 'performs dismally at its advertised task, that of efficiently directing society's savings towards their optimal investment pursuits'. The system's main beneficiaries are the creditor/rentier class.

3 These authors write that the elite tries to deny this widening gap for reasons of 'fear and self-interest' (p. ix), and that it wants to eliminate the word 'class' from respectable debate.

4 It was the Pennsylvania Railroad that employed Ivy Lee to reform its poor reputation with the press about giving information after crashes. Also see Piasecki
   (2000) for more on the PR of the early US railroads.

5 An insight into market attitudes is given by Gary Mulgrew, one of three British
   bankers being extradited to the USA on fraud charges: 'You get absorbed by
   greed. . . . The desire to get the next cheque is all-embracing.' See 'Extradition
   entreaty', *Financial Times* magazine, 18.12.04, pp. 16–22.

6 David Miller writes in the anti-capitalist magazine *Red Pepper*, June 2003,
   on p. 6 of the website text that 'It has taken years, but the tobacco industry
   is on the run (in the US and UK anyway) and other industries engaged in
   environmental destruction or human rights abuses can go the same way.' See
   www.redpepper.org.uk/June2003/x-June2003-globalpr.html. Accessed on
   6.13.03.

7 Anecdotes may be evidence of larger trends: one walks on a Dorset headland;
   one is approached by a middle-aged, middle-class man bearing a leaflet; one is
   urged to come to a protest meeting in the church hall about fencing off part of
   the headland; one notes that the pamphlet gives – without instruction about
   what to do with it – the telephone number of a local radio station.

8 They are: economic resources to fund a PR operation; good standing with the
   media; talented human resources; empathy with news producers; PR expertise.

9 Is lobbying a PR activity? Many professional lobbyists, especially in consultancies, would say 'no'. One such threatened the author with legal action if he was
   written about as being in PR. Some lobbyists say that their work is allied to PR.
   Nearly all PR people claim to have lobbying in their discipline, and usually call
   it 'public affairs' or 'government relations'. PR degrees in the UK teach
   lobbying as a PR activity.

10 A journalistic statement of the thesis is *The Dirty Race for the White House*,
   Channel 4, 1.11.04, 8 p.m.

11 But lobbying has a history. Alderman (1984) shows that at the height of railway
   development in Victorian Britain in 1868, railway companies had 125 directors
   who were also MPs.

12 HMSO Dd. 8389342. Shortly afterwards, UK lobbyists set up the Association
   of Professional Political Consultants (APPC) to establish standards of conduct.

13 It is even hard to establish whether lobbying takes place. The *Guardian*,
   27.10.04, p. 1 reports 'Tobacco firm gained secret access to Blair'. The
   Guardian later carried a letter (4.11.04, p. 27) from the Downing Street press
   office saying that 'The prime minister has met no one representing the gaming
   industry from the US, this country or anywhere else on the gambling bill.'

14 His book can in part be read as an instruction manual on how to influence
   public policy: see p. 15 for writing opinion columns in the press; appearing on
   talk radio; making public service announcements; doing mass mailings, and
   holding rallies.

15 She also describes the involvement of leading UK public relations people.

16 A MORI/FT poll, June 2003, gave out that 11 per cent of the general public
   trusted 'directors of large companies' to tell the truth; 80 per cent did not. In a
   February 2003 poll, business leaders came sixteenth out of nineteen in a list of
   people to be trusted to tell the truth. The figures were given by Stewart Lewis,
   MORI director, on 20.2.04, at the 'Trust in the Age of Suspicion' conference,
   Miramar Hotel, Bournemouth, organised by the Centre for Public
   Communications Research, Bournemouth University.

17 Pearson quotes Smythe (1981) and Galbraith (1983) as supporting references.

18 An example is the credit union movement in the UK, which provides loans at
   below market interest rates and which is poor in PR and marketing resources. It

competes against banks that are promotionally resource rich. Credit unions find it difficult to 'get their message heard'.

19 The phrase was used by President Andrew Jackson in his Farewell Address of 4 March 1837. Source is *The Dictionary of Quotations*, edited by Bergan Evans, 1968. Similar phrases with the same sense are, however, attributed to others. The earliest attribution is to John Philpot Curran, in a speech before the Privy Council on 10 July 1790.

20 An example of 'inter-voicing' of PR messages (one message replies to another) is the call for the closure of level crossings on UK railways by the RMT trade union, followed in less than twelve hours by its rejection in a message from the Rail Safety and Standards Board. See 'Union call to close crossings rejected', the *Guardian*, 8.11.04, p. 8. Also the p. 1 box 'Rail union is accused of scaremongering over level crossing dangers'. Another example is between Associated British Ports (ABP) and Dibden Bay Residents' Association over the building of a new container port on the western, New Forest side of Southampton Water. A central point of contention was the number of shipping movements needing container facilities. ABP publicly said 55,000 movements a year. The residents said two container ship movements a day were relevant and not the 38,000 ferry movements included in the 55,000 figure. Source is a note to the author from Paul Vickers, secretary of the residents' association, 6.12.04.

21 They are name calling; card stacking; bandwagonning; testimonial; 'plain folk' association; transfer of emotion via symbols; and 'glittering' generalities. See Snow 2003, p. 113.

22 Whether they are different or not, they are studying a popular subject. Max Clifford says 'PR has become very glamorous, and it is now one of the most popular degree courses.' See the *Guardian* media section, 13.12.04, p. 28.

23 See 'Faking it', the *Observer* magazine, 31.11.04, p. 61, and note the phrase 'PR fig-leaf' to describe corporate social responsibility by big business.

24 A well-known PR person in the UK, Julia Hobsbawm, uses the 'gatekeeper' analogy, saying that it is 'hardly practical' for a CEO to handle his or her own calls 'during a busy period of media interest'. See the *Guardian*, 17.11.03, p. 8.

25 See Anthony Hilton, City editor of the *London Evening Standard*, on manipulation of financial journalists in *Management Today*, January 1999, pp. 29–32.

26 An exceptional event was the Spin and Corporate Power conference at Strathclyde University, 18–20 November 2004.

27 In the UK style of these things, it could be named OfPR – Office for PR regulation.

28 L'Etang (2004b) has reviewed the history of the Institute's disciplinary committee.

8 Ethics, social responsibility, stakeholders

1 L'Etang (2004b, p. 169) notes an editorial of 1961 in the IPR Journal *Public Relations*: 'There are still too many in . . . public relations who think that Ethics is a county in the South of England.' This is a word play on 'Essex', the county east of London.

2 Tim Traverse-Healy says that what distinguishes 'good' propaganda from 'bad' propaganda is the nature of the subject to be propandised. See http://media3.bournemouth.ac.uk/cgi-bin/lecturesonline/playlecture.pl?id=22. Lecture recorded July 2004, with the author as introducer.

3 Cutlip (1995) titles Chapter 3 of his history of public relations as 'Greatest public relations work ever done' and starts with the sentence 'The power of propaganda to mobilize public opinion was relied on heavily in the history-

making campaign to ratify the United States Constitution in 1778–9.' He ends the chapter with 'But truly, winning ratification of the United States Constitution was "the greatest public relations work ever done".'

4 In a *Financial Times* weekend section, 9.10.04, p.4, interview with entrepreneur Sir Alan Sugar, the reporter writes 'Then he [Sugar] recited once more the stunning list of individual applications' of a new emailing device.

5 To promote new ways of eating Stilton cheese, a PR campaign aimed to give the product a 'sultry and sophisticated new image' and gave to journalists a box that looked like a pornographic film with the title 'Stilton Dreams, An Adult Fantasy'. Source is 'Salad with chocolate', *Financial Times* weekend, 11.12.04, pp. 1–2.

6 The NUJ introduced their code in summer 2004 for members working in PR and information services. See 'NUJ launches PR guidelines', *Journalist*, October 2004, p. 11.

7 Also see McElreath (1997) and Harrison (1994).

8 Author's experience at Bournemouth and at other universities teaching PR.

9 The situation described is loosely based on the closure of three businesses in the AA group of companies, as reported in '900 jobs to be axed as AA shuts repair shops', the *Guardian*, 9.10.04, p. 31.

10 Prof. Anne Gregory, President of the IPR, 2004–5, writes of these torments, She says in the Foreword to Parsons (2004), p. xiii:

> Although they [PR people] want to tell the truth, sometimes their understanding of the truth is imperfect for a variety of reasons. Making consistent ethical decisions in a diverse world where cultures and values clash is not easy. Being loyal to employers while living with a conscience can bring conflict.

11 See www.bitc.org.uk/resources/research/statbank/bottom _ line _ benefit/index. html. Accessed 16.12.04.

12 See Cerin (2002, p. 46) for 'Some critics claim environmental reports are merely an exercise in public relations.' The phrase 'air cover' is also used.

13 Executive summary of *Behind the Mask: The Real Face of Corporate Social Responsibility*, published by Christian Aid, 21.1.04. Accessed at www.christian-aid.org.uk on 27.7.04.

14 Day and Woodward (2004) found that out of 400 required disclosures, there was a 44 per cent rate of substantive non-disclosure.

15 See *PRWeek* of 1.10.04, p.17, 'CSR trails ethical route to market?' by Tom Williams for a review of whether consumers pay attention to corporate social responsibility (CSR) behaviour by companies when purchases are made, and reports of views on the effects of CSR on sales.

16 Private conversations with guest lecturers from business who speak at Bournemouth University.

17 There is little academic work about CSR and small and micro-businesses. See Jenkins (2004).

18 Civil associations are often very local: the Humanist Association in Dorset meets in a private house.

19 See pp. 223–30 of White and Mazur (1995).

20 It is a widely held position. See *Behind The Spin*, PR magazine from St Mark and St John College, Plymouth, issue 8, October 2004, p. 11, for research into forty-one PR people in the northeast of England. While 47 per cent 'agree, strongly' that 'ethics is good business', 49 per cent 'agree' and 2 per cent 'disagree'. See also Cerin (1994, p. 52) for Electrolux managers reporting that green products return higher revenue than others.

21 See the HSBC bank's CSR report for 2003, issued by Group Corporate Affairs. Readers are invited to write to 'HSBC in the Community'.

22 Nigel Griffiths MP, UK minister for corporate social responsibility, is reported as saying that CSR should not be a public relations 'tool'. Source is www.bitc.org.uk/news/news _ directory/mori _ rep.html. Accessed 16.12.04.

23 Some critics see 'window dressing' at present but with hope for genuine communications in future. See 'A worthwhile policy or simply propaganda', the *Guardian* jobs section, 11.7.04, p. 23, for a TUC spokesperson saying 'A lot of people feel that CSR reports are more a PR exercise' but the author, Nic Paton, ends with 'it may be – just may be – that CSR will begin to become a more credible workplace issue'.

24 Defined here as the substitution of words in the place of intention or action. It is the most common and severest criticism of PR: presentation but no performance.

25 See Department of Trade and Industry news release, 5 July 2004, ref. P/2004/248.

26 Dick Hubbard is owner of a New Zealand cereals company, who works shifts in his own factory, manufactures in a labour intensive way, thinks advertising is unethical, and shares 10 per cent of profits with employees. Source is 'The cereal socialist', the *Independent Review*, 28.08.02, pp. 6–7.

27 Businesses and charities may give as acts of philanthropy to those who have no influence over them, e.g. to the destitute, the young and old. Examples are firms and charities giving away excess food and surplus clothes to soup kitchens and hostels for the homeless.

28 An example of co-operation by competing pressure groups is collaboration between Mothers Against Guns and the British Association For Shooting and Conservation to hold a joint conference against gun crime. Reported BBC Radio 4 *Today*, 7.7.04.

29 See *Encyclopedia of Public Relations* (Heath 2005), p. 809, for identification difficulties.

30 See Kathy Cutts, Bournemouth University, and her PhD work-in-progress on small firms and CSR.

31 Cornelissen (2004, p. 109) has a term for these trespassers – 'dangerous stakeholders' are 'those who have power and urgent claims but lack legitimacy. They are seen as dangerous as they may resort to coercion and even violence.'

32 See Vercic and Grunig (2000, p. 38) for 'Stakeholders have a relationship with a firm but it is not brought to the level of consciousness yet.'

33 Grunig's situational theory of publics is more sensitive on this point: segmented publics become distinct on the basis of their perceptions of a relationship with an organisation. See Grunig *et al.* (2002), p. 324.

34 For a fuller account of situational theory on publics see Grunig (1997).

35 Hamlet cigars carried the message 'Smokers die younger' in the UK in 2004.

36 'Fast-food giants join war on fat', the *Observer*, 5.12.04, p. 6, reports that these companies are financing a trust titled Healthy Eating Active Living (HEAL) to produce advertisements on healthy eating and exercise.

37 Or 'air cover' as an alternative description for camouflage by organisations of the true position. Witness 'Tory hopeful Clarke "must cut tobacco tie"', the *Observer*, 21.8.05, p. 5. This reports an internal paper of the BAT tobacco company in 2000 as saying: 'The process [of CSR] will not only help BAT achieve a position of recognised responsibility but also provide "air cover" from criticism while improvements are being made.'

9 Politics, corporate PR, campaigning

1 For example, Dr A. MacDonald of the SDLP in Northern Ireland said about the IRA's expulsion of three of its members after the murder of a man in Short

Strand, Belfast, that it was 'a PR exercise . . . to make it look good'. Source: BBC Radio 4 *Today* programme, 26.2.05.

2 The UK government sent to all 25 million households in June 2004 a leaflet about action to take in a terrorist attack. An interview with a villager at Ridge, Hertfordshire, said about the distribution; 'It's propaganda. It makes them feel that they are doing the right thing.' Source BBC Radio 4 *Today*, 26.7.04.

3 See *Oxford Dictionary of English* (2003, 2nd edn). The word's usage is described as 'Brit. informal'. See also *Brewer's Dictionary of Phrase and Fable* (1999, 16th edn) p. 448, 'Evasive or flattering talk; "soft soap"'. Another phrase with propagandistic connotations is 'bringing people with them' as in the following example. The Archbishop of Perth, Australia, said on BBC Radio 4 *Today* programme, 25.2.05, that Anglican bishops 'must bring their people with them' over the row about homosexuality.

4 The consumer as: chooser; communicator; explorer; identity-seeker; hedonist; artist; rebel; activist; citizen.

5 Blick is one of the few academics writing about government to refer to government 'public relations' consistently. Most avoid the term and use 'information'.

6 Those doing media relations full time were apparently eight in mid-2002. See Blick 2004, p. 266. There were thirty-one special advisers in 1974. See Blick, p. 315. An early 'spin doctor' before the term was known was John Harris who worked for Roy Jenkins in the late 1960s. See Blick, pp. 110–17.

7 These examples are provided by Conor MacGrath. Peter Luff: researcher to Conservative MPs Peter Walker and Edward Heath in late 1970s/early 1980s; then lobbyist at Good Relations and Lowe Bell in late 1980s/early 1990s; then Tory MP since 1992. Charles Hendry: special adviser to Conservative MPs John Moore and Tony Newton; then public affairs counsellor at Burson-Marsteller; then Tory MP since 1992. Damien Green: special adviser in 10 Downing Street Policy Unit, 1992–4; then self-employed public affairs consultant, 1995–7; then Tory MP for Ashford. David Miliband: parliamentary officer, National Council for Voluntary Organisations, 1987–8; head of policy unit for Labour leader and Prime Minister Tony Blair, 1994–2001; MP for South Shields since 2001. Hilary Benn: head of policy and communications for MSF trade union; then special adviser to MP David Blunkett; MP for Leeds Central since 1999. Charles Clarke: chief of staff to Labour leader Kinnock, 1983–92; chief executive Quality Public Affairs, 1992–7; MP for Norwich South from 1997.

8 See *Labour Today*, summer 2004, p. 9. It is a magazine for members. The words are attributed to Tony Blair.

9 Peter Mandelson was Director of Communications for the party between 1985 and 1992; Alastair Campbell was party press officer for Tony Blair MP from 1994, and then Chief Press Secretary to him as Prime Minister, 1997–2003; Charlie Whelan was special adviser and press officer, 1997–9, for Gordon Brown MP, Chancellor of the Exchequer.

10 See http://news.bbc.co.uk/1/hi/uk_politics/3466005.stm for an account of the dossier's construction. P. 2 reports that 'Downing Street media chief Alastair Campbell tells JIC chairman John Scarlett (intelligence officer) that the "may" in the main text wording of (45 minutes warning of a missile attack) claim is "weaker than the summary".' A day later 'Mr Scarlett tells Mr Campbell the language on the claim in the main text has been "tightened".'

11 See p. 3 of http://news.bbc.co.uk/1/hi/uk_politics/3466005.stm. Inquiry member Field Marshall Lord Inge is quoted to this effect.

12 The Government Communications Network (GCN) came into existence in February 2005 and replaced the Government Information and Communication Service (GICS).

13 Franklin reports (2004, p. 6) that between 1997–9, the New Labour govern-

ment issued 20,000 press releases, 'an 80 per cent increase on the output of the Major government'. See also Cohen (1999).

14 The official giving the information was Mike Granatt, Head of Profession of the then-Government Information and Communication Service, now the Government Communications Network. The quotation is his.

15 Jo Moore was special adviser to Stephen Byers MP, Secretary of State for Transport, in 2001. Very soon after the Twin Tower terrorist attacks on September 11, she sent an email to the Head of Information in the department saying 'It's now a very good day to get out anything we want to bury.' She later resigned.

16 See Boorstin (1961), *The Image, or, What Happened to the American Dream*, Ch. 1, for their origins: he involves journalists and politicians in their development as well as PR people.

17 One title for this skills transfer into politics is 'Machiavellian Marketing', a movement tracked by Harris and Lock (1996). See also Harris *et al.* (1999).

18 Disraeli extended the franchise in Great Britain in 1868 to middle-class householders and skilled working men.

19 That Harold Wilson found PR 'degrading' is in a letter of Malcolm Muggeridge to *The Times* of 27.6.61. In the letter, Muggeridge refers to his own definition of PR as organised lying. From West (1963, p. 97).

20 Foreman notes that the 1784 Westminster election (pp. 136–59) was important to the Whigs and to Fox in particular in their fight against Pitt and King George III. The salacious and the political is not a new, modern taste. The Pittite *Morning Post* (p. 150) associated her frequently with sex: 'she was either "granting favours", caressing "her favourite member", looking for the "right handle in politics", or grasping the "fox's tail"'.

21 Derek Draper (1997, p. 210), former research assistant to Peter Mandelson and later a lobbyist for hire, writes that spinning is not new in politics and can be news management at its best.

22 Sir Nicholas Lloyd, former *Daily Express* editor and later PR consultant, said in a guest lecture at Bournemouth University, 20.2.02, that Alastair Campbell arrived at Downing Street in 1997 saying to the government communication service 'What are tomorrow's headlines? – we write them.'

23 Alastair Campbell was reported in February 2005 to have sent an email to a BBC reporter containing two swear words when the latter enquired about two controversial posters. He said that he had mis-routed the email. See www.dowseworld.com for 7.2.05.

24 See also 'Blair's blackest art', the *Observer*, 2.7.00, p. 29. In it, allowing negative briefing to happen is one of the charges made by Ken Follet against Prime Minister Blair. The opposite to negative briefing by a third party against colleagues is what Follet calls 'manly' behaviour – saying the criticism to the face of the person. His wife is Barbara Follet, Labour MP for Stevenage. She is reported by the *Guardian* to have attacked the 'sneer and smear' culture ('MP Follet backs husband on "sneer and smear"', 7.7.00, p. 15). Another feature of the spin culture is that it encourages linguistic invention. Ken Follet called (ibid.) spin doctors the 'rent boys of politics'.

25 The 'spin machine' was different apparently in the Major government years, 1990–7. Kenneth Clarke's special adviser was Tessa Keswick and she describes her media work as

> what we call 'good news items'. . . . In consultation with the press office you would decide which day this announcement would go out and you would look at the press release and make sure the good information was up at the top. It was just rather a minor sort of public relations we would play there.

See Blick 2004, p. 231.

Notes

26 Both Simpson and Hattersley are cited in 'Blair's fallen star', the *Times* 2, 5.5.00, pp.3–5.
27 See www.number-10.gov.uk/output/page4404.asp. Accessed 28.2.05.
28 To sense the intensity of spin/propaganda in the UK, imagine it alongside that of Goebbels, Stalin and Senator McCarthy. The imaging of propaganda as soft/ hard is a powerful one: it brings to mind the imaging of pornography; and so leads to the proposition that all propaganda lies on a scale of harmful/obscene in a democracy.
29 Nigel Jackson, of Bournemouth University, estimates that the number of MPs with websites has 'only marginally increased' to 450 (out of a total 650) by early 2005 from 412 in June 2002. See his paper 'Integrated communications: campaigning communication in context' to the Political Marketing Conference, PSA, 24–5 February 2005 at Grange Holborn Hotel, London.
30 In a study of Australian 'media advisers' Richard Phillipps of the University of Sydney, Nepean, noted that media advising 'has gradually evolved as a separate role from that of policy adviser', p. 32, of his unpublished PhD thesis 'Communicating politics' (2000).
31 See 'Blair's blackest art', the *Observer*, 2.7.00, p. 29.
32 That politicians gossip maliciously against each other with or without spin doctors is evidenced by Trevor Lloyd-Jones, himself the chief spin doctor to Prime Minister Harold Wilson, 1964–70. See Lloyd-Jones's letter, *The Times*, 5.7.00, p. 19. For a witness to Wilson's malicious gossip about colleagues read Anthony Howard in the same edition of *The Times*, Times 2 media section, p. 9.
33 They also remind the reader that language is a fashion in these matters: they do not write of 'soundbites'; rather 'golden phrases' (p. 478). The spin metaphor lends itself to phrase making. 'Spin nurse', 'spin patrol' and 'spin pathology' have been spotted in the UK press.
34 Note how Bates (2004, p. 171) describes the news management of the Church of England in the public row over homosexual priests. As a distraction to take media interest into other stories, an official – 'the nearest Lambeth Palace had to a spin doctor' – suggested 'alternative attractive stories' such as the new Archbishop of Canterbury Rowan Williams reading his own poems; making a high-profile intervention in the House of Lords; or announcing a new theological prize. The tactic was that the issue of homosexuality '"had to be managed in media terms by seeking to take the sting out of it and displacing it in the public mind"'. None of these was apparently taken up.
35 Remember that spin is a form of news management, and that the latter can be simple and direct. The chairman of Starbucks was asked whether he was aware that some experts argued that coffee is unhealthy. He replied 'no' and closed the discussion. Source is 'Full of beans', the *Guardian*, 16.10.04, p. 32.
36 Inside higher education, it is now common to hear and read the words 'business model', 'marketing' and 'marketisation'.
37 In the early part of the 1980s, when sponsorship was a new publicity technique, its schemes were generally small scale, and could be attached to either PR or advertising departments. As sponsorship schemes grew into mainstream promotions, they have migrated to their own departments when they have multi-million pound sterling budgets, or are part of large marketing departments.
38 Richard Lambert (1940) who worked for the BBC as editor of its weekly magazine the *Listener* in the 1930s in its 'Public Relations Division'. He saw the rise of corporate PR and rather grand it was in those first days: the early PR 'has access to all the archives and information of the concern which he represents. . . . He can employ countless different methods . . . through public speaking and service on public committees, to the emission of books . . . he must be a supremely clever handler of men' (p. 178).

39 See his obituary, the *Guardian*, 29.1.02, p.18.
40 To extend the 'voice' metaphor of PR, Page could be said to have given PR 'ears'.
41 See www.awpagesociety.com.
42 1 facts = good, perceptions = good, PR status: competence; 2 facts = bad, perceptions = bad, PR status: honesty; 3 facts = bad, perceptions = good, PR status: manipulation; 4 facts = good, perceptions = bad, PR status: incompetence. Richard Reader was a part-time lecturer at Bournemouth University.
43 In the case of British corporate PR, www.spinwatch.org was set up in autumn 2004.
44 See 'Turning around lobbying's reputation', *PRWeek*, 3.9.04, p. 20.
45 Source is private information to the author while researching his PhD in 1994–6. Note that he was told it 'confidentially'.
46 See an article by the chairman of BP entitled 'Time to engage with pressure groups' in the *Financial Times*, 2.4.01, p. 2.
47 Many UK trade unions use lobbying firms in London. Connect Public Affairs is one such firm. In 1999, the Transport and General Workers' Union used the lobbying firm APCO to publicise their 'Don't fly Lufthansa' campaign after 270 workers were sacked by the airline. Source is *PRWeek*, 23.7.99, p.4, public sector column.
48 Publishing diaries of meetings with lobbyists was proposed by Moloney (2000b, p. 163); that and keeping minutes by Lord Neill, chairman of the Parliamentary Committee of Standards in Public Life, to the British House of Commons public administration committee in 2000. See 'Neill attacks bill's lobbying inquiry curbs', the *Guardian*, 8.6.00, p. 14.
49 See Moloney 1996.
50 Spasmodically in the case of Northern Ireland, where devolved government has been suspended since 2003.
51 See 'Exploiting our sweet tooth with fatal consequences', *The Times Higher Education Supplement*, 24.12.04, pp. 18–19. The authors are Philip James, chair, and Neville Rigby, director of policy and public affairs, of the International Obesity Task Force. Note the 'public affairs' title.
52 See 'GM foods: we stand firm' by Tony Blair, the *Daily Telegraph*, 20.2.99, p.22.
53 Occasionally, it is communication for no change. Think of Forrest, the pressure group for the right to smoke, and the Countryside Alliance, for foxhunting.
54 One of the few books on stunts is Fuhrman (1989).
55 Source is 'Personal view', the *Daily Telegraph*, 15.11.04, p. 36.
56 See 'Tories seek the magic right stuff', the *Observer*, 10.10.04, p. 12.
57 See his 1932 assisted biography *Phantom Fame: The Anatomy of Ballyhoo*.
58 See how the Dibden Bay Residents' Association fought off a plan to build a container port opposite the existing western docks at Southampton. Before the start of a planning enquiry in 2003, they put up two kilometres of barrage balloons, rising 33 metres above water level, to indicate the amount of environmental disfigurement that would result from building a port there. See their website at http://members.aol.com/dibdenbay. Accessed on 18.4.05.
59 See www.borkowski.co.uk/stuntwatch. Accessed 4.1.05. An associated site is 'Improperganda – The Art of the Publicity Stunt', also from the Mark Borkowski Press and PR agency. See as well 'It's a sad day for capitalism when a man can't fly a midget on a kite over Central Park', the *Guardian* media section, 5.6.00, pp. 6–7. Then look at 'Smirnoff hires "rocketman" for relaunch', *PRWeek*, 16.6.04, p. 30, for an example of a contemporary stunt. The rocket man rose to 152 ft and entered the *Guinness Book of World Records*.
60 A worldwide campaign against torture employs a press agent. Confidential information given to the author. Mark Borkowski writes that London should

employ 'the showman's approach to publicity' in order to be chosen as the site for the 2012 Olympic Games. Source is 'Just taking part is not good enough', the *Guardian* media section, 26.1.04, p. 9.

10 Markets, branding, reputation

1 Also for American Tobacco; New Jersey Telephone; Dodge Brothers Automobile; and Filene's department store. Source is Internet Museum of Public Relations at www.prmuseum.com/bernays/bernays _ 1931.html. Accessed 4.1.05.

2 Based on Bournemouth University's twelve years of placing PR students in year-long work placements. The other 30 per cent are in corporate PR/public affairs work.

3 A good example of the complexity of modern lifestyle PR messaging and advertising is the 'How to Spend It' supplement of the *Financial Times*.

4 Source is the CIPR brochure *IPR Training Spring and Summer 2005*, p. 3.

5 A record company is reported to use schoolchildren to sell music to their friends in a 'peer group selling initiative'. See 'Lessons in hard sell', the *Guardian* media section, 20.12.04, pp. 2–3.

6 This organisation was

> born out of one of the most inspired public relations briefs, or, more precisely, one of the most inspired marketing briefs. . . . It was the Petfoods division of Mars that initiated the Council at a time when the birdseed market had come to an apparent standstill.

The market was saturated and the solution was 'to expand the budgerigar market'. 'There were endless budgerigar clubs and shows, pamphlets, articles, press conferences, books – a real orchestration of activity designed to start a budgerigar craze. It worked.'

7 See Brassington and Pettitt (2003), p. 827. Figures available at www.tesco.com/everylittlehelps/socialdetail.htm. Accessed 24.2.05.

8 Accessed at www.bitc.org.ik/resources/research/research _ publication/game _ plan.htm on 16.12.04.

9 Quoted from *The Game Plan: Cause Related Marketing Qualitative Consumer Research* (1997), published by Business in the Community, London.

10 Quoted from the *Cause Related Marketing Guidelines* (1998), published by Business in the Community, London.

11 Cause-related marketing has a constant, direct outcome that PR has not: it raises funds for causes. PR has an indirect relationship with revenue creation.

12 Quoted from the *The Game Plan* (1997), referenced at Note 9 above.

13 See Heywood (1990, pp. 156–7); Harris (1991, p. 35), Fill (1999, pp. 6, 414) and Kitchen and Papasolomou (1997, pp. 239–71).

14 See p. 1 of this book for multiple forms.

15 See *Brewer's Dictionary* (1999, 16th edn, p. 952).

16 See Moloney (1999) for the view that PR in the service of selling to consumers is as old as PR itself, a conclusion corroborated by a look at the cinema in the early twentieth century.

17 A selection compiled by the author from UK newspapers in autumn 2004.

18 Source is 'Perfume got personal', the *Financial Times* weekend section, 27–8.11.04, p. 1.

19 Source is 'That was then, this is now', the *Observer* review section, 5.12.04, p. 41.

20 Kotler in Harris (1991, introduction) writes about the need to 'win' the consumers' hearts, minds and money. Bell (1991, p. 24) says 'if you are a PR consultant you're in the persuasion business'. Thorson and Moore (1996, p. 1)

write of 'integrated marketing communication' that 'its aim is to optimise the impact of persuasive communication on both consumer and non-consumer'.

21 An example is an advertisement in the *Guardian*, 2.4.05, p.13, 'Product recall'. It said that a 'foreign object' had contaminated one carton of orange juice and, as a precaution, a whole batch up to a date code was recalled. The next day, the *Observer*, 3.4.05, p. 4, carried a story headlined 'Police probe factory as a syringe is found in Sainbury's fruit juice'.

22 These press releases are carefully crafted to meet minimum requirements set by the Department of Trade and Industry, and to protect the reputation of the brand. Source is guest lecturers at Bournemouth University.

23 Noted in the newspaper of Bournemouth Borough Council, *Bournemouth Journal*, August/September 2004, p. 2. The price is £10.

24 Jeff Bozos of Amazon offers some clarity about what is a brand: 'It's what people say about you when you are not in the room.' Source is 'And the brand played on', the *Observer* business section, 20.6.04, p. 5.

25 Some business people have a different ranking. For example, Tony Froggatt, CEO of Scottish and Newcastle breweries, said that

> Even though, I come from a marketing background, I view brands as vehicles for driving growth and value. . . . We can talk about the beauties of brands and all that sort of stuff, but at the end of the day investors just want to know what they are going to get in terms of returns.

Reported in 'The beer necessities', the *Guardian*, 26.1.05, p. 30.

26 Organisational culture, out of which corporate identity grows, was known as 'It's what we are'.

27 After product and corporate branding comes the branding of people. They are called 'celebrities'.

28 See 'Surviving change', *PRWeek*, 11.2.05, p. 29.

29 The author's metaphor.

30 Clergy today debate the difference between marketing and evangelising, the Chaplaincy at Bournemouth University tell the author. The separation of metaphysical and lifestyle aspects of religion are discussed.

31 In the Channel 4 television programme *Who Wrote the Bible?* on the origins of the Christian gospels (25.12.04, 8.30 p.m.), it was noticeable how the presenter, theologian Robert Beckford, and expert witnesses referred to 'spin' and 'propaganda' as they explored different views on the sources and meanings of the documents.

32 See *Financial Times* property section, 11.12.04, p. 16, and the advertisement headline 'Introducing a refreshing new concept in the pied-a-terre. You don't actually pay when you're not "a terre"'.

33 Accessed at http://adbusters.org/metas/corpo/backspotsneaker/kickass.html on 8.12.04.

34 It has been well noted that the publisher of Klein's book, Flamingo Harper Collins, is a global company.

35 See 'Communique 12: Reclaiming Public Space', 8.3.05, from jammers <\\>@>lists.adbusters.org.

36 Blackmore (1999) writes that ideas which spread widely through populations do so because they are copyable, capable of imitation. Are PR people the spotters and then the transmitters of such ideas? The reference to memes by the Adbusters on 8.3.05 is the first time that this author has seen the 'meme' term used in a PR operational way. Its use, and the provenance of the term in the biology of genes, raises questions about the sources of the PR paradigm described in this book in Social Darwinism.

37 She famously covered up one of the funky designs with a handkerchief

from her handbag. See http://news.bbc.co.uk/1/hi/uk/1335127.stm. Accessed 21.12.04.
38 See pp. 831–2 of Brassington and Pettitt (2003) for a case study.
39 See the CIPR brochure *Managing Reputation*, p. 2, for its conference on 11.4.05 at Copthorne Tara Hotel, London.
40 Patrick Kerr, head of communications at Unilever UK, said at the MORI reputation conference, London, on 28.10.04 that 'you cannot manage reputation; rather it is like beauty in the eye of the beholder'. Reported on www.bitc.org.uk/news/news_directory/mori_rep.html and accessed on 16.12.04.
41 Like most terms in PR, there are many definitions for each entity. Reputation is 'the totality of emotional and intellectual disposition towards an organisation' in the opinion of Stewart Lewis, head of corporate communications research at MORI at their reputation conference, London, 28.10.04. Accessed at www.bitc.org.uk/news/news_directory/mori_rep.html on 16.12.04.
42 For example, Southwest Trains in the UK lowered its reputation with travellers in 1998 when it cancelled services because of the cost reduction policy of sacking drivers. Alstom, the train maintenance company, also reduced its reputation in the town of Eastleigh, UK, when it announced the loss of 540 jobs with the closure of its depot there in the week before Christmas, 2004. Source is 'Alstom cut 540 jobs at Southampton as orders stall', the *Guardian*, 18.12.04, p. 24.
43 See 'Can Shell survive reserves affair?' *PRWeek*, 3.9.04, p. 15. Paddy Briggs retired from Shell in 2002, after thirty-seven years.
44 Lex the columnist is right. Writing about a struggling engineering company quoted on the London Stock Exchange, 'It is worth risking your reputation as long as the rewards are healthy.' Source is 'Jarvis', the *Financial Times*, 11.10.03, p. 18.

11 Media matters

1 All the preceding readership and audience figures are from Lloyd 2004a, p. 9.
2 Grant notes (1994, pp. 33–4) that Pick was a solicitor and statistician, and got his job in charge of publicity for London transport only because he complained about its quality; and that Tallents, one of the most influential British PR people of the inter-war years, was a career civil servant with no experience of PR.
3 The view of Roy Greenslade, former assistant editor of the *Sun*, written in 'When dirty deals backfire', the *Guardian* media section, 9.8.04, p. 4. He adds that PR/journalist deals are 'common' and 'in many ways, do not comprise either side'.
4 An example is Colin Gibson, PR of the English Football Association (FA), who was reported in 2004 to have briefed against the English national team's coach in order to preserve the anonymity of the chief executive of the FA, as regards alleged involvement in a sex scandal. The *Guardian* ('Fleet Street veteran who fell for a tabloid turnover', 3.8.04, p. 4) reported that Mr Gibson was taped offering to give details for publication about the manager in return for anonymity for the chief executive. The PR was a former tabloid journalist himself.
5 See Prof. Anne Gregory's 'The press, public relations and the implications for democracy' at www.anti-spin.com/index.cfm?TERTIARY_ID=0&PRIMARY +21&SECOND/. Accessed on 25.9.03.
6 The quotations are taken from the summary of the paper by Bentele and Nothhaft to the 'Public Relations and the Public Sphere' conference at Leipzig, Germany, 23–6 September 2004.

7 Bryan Appleyard of the *Sunday Times* is an exception, as is Anthony Hilton of the *Evening Standard*.

8 This author has never seen an event condemned as a 'stain' on both PR and journalism. Gillmor reports that the first G.W. Bush administration in the USA used video press releases during the passage of the drugs-benefits bill through Congress in 2003/4. Another allegation of 'fake journalists' is by David Miller of *SpinWatch* on 15.3.05. The allegation is that BBC Scotland did not explain that a reporter in Iraq was employed by a Ministry of Defence agency, rather than a body independent of government. See http://spinwatch.srver101.com/ modules.php?name=Content&pa=showpapge&pid=342. Accessed 15.30.5. Miller later reported that the BBC had replied that the situation 'was not ideal' and 'will not happen again'. Reported to the author in an email of 23.3.05 from owner-edu-pr-net<\\>@>deakin.edu.ac on behalf of David Miller.

9 See p. 2 of Prof. Anne Gregory at www.anti-spin.com/index.cfm? TERTIARY _ ID=O&PRIMARY _ ID=21&SECOND/. Accessed on 25.9.03.

10 The author's experience as a journalist in the UK regions in the 1960s.

11 Thanks to Philip MacGregor for these observations on current working practices in UK journalism.

12 PR people do not talk about 'pseudo-events' or 'stunts', though the latter is used privately. The professional discourse is about 'event management'.

13 See 'Put the brakes on freebies', the *Guardian*, 10.7.99, p. 20, and 'Freebies and the personal finance sector shouldn't mix', *PRWeek*, 13.8.99, p. 6.

14 The *Guardian* reports ('Diary', 17.8.04, p. 14) that the secretary of the editor of the *Daily Express* told its reporter to phone the editor's PR agent to discuss a matter.

15 CIPR estimate of 2005.

16 See www.nuj.uk. Accessed on 11.2.05.

17 Private knowledge of the author.

18 See 'Don't believe a word they say about them', the *Sunday Times*, 18.5.03, p. 3.

19 See *Management Today*, January 1999, pp. 29–32.

20 See the case of a journalist on a £18,000 salary who is twenty-eight, has a first-class honours degree, and four years' experience. Her salary is £6,000 less than the then-national average UK salary. She resigned to become a local government officer. See 'Going for broke', the *Guardian* media section, 31.1.05, p. 11.

21 See 'I wanna sell you a story', the *Guardian* media section, 3.7.00, pp. 2–3.

22 These examples are from the author's experience.

23 The memory of Valerie Cowley, who was a national newspaper journalist at the time. Also the memory of the author who observed the appearance and rise of lifestyle journalism in the regional press.

24 His research shows that in the periods 1952 to 1992 word counts in *The Times* stories have decreased but *Mirror* counts have increased; in the same period, entertainment stories (animals and celebrities) have increased in the tabloids from 6 per cent to 17 per cent. The tabloid coverage of politics has increased from 3 per cent to 6 per cent of content, and 10 per cent of broadsheets are entertainment. This account is based on the session by Prof. Peter Golding at the Media and Democracy seminar, Loughborough University, 6.1.98.

25 The opinion of PR man Richard Harvey at www.kentonline.co.uk/business/ features/featarue _ 100.asp. Accessed on 21.11.04.

26 The complaint of Mark Borkowski in 'The politics of chat', the *Guardian* media section, 25.10.4, p. 5.

27 But they are not coterminous, for political PR deals with the workings of liberal democracy.

28 See Moloney (1999) for more background on film press agentry.

29 The personality construction work has been well described by Ekow Eshun:

There is among the public today a greater awareness of the process of manufacture involved in creating a star. We know that they are not simply born. Instead . . . they must seize their moment and spin it and spin it until the result is newspaper headlines, TV appearances and lucrative product endorsements. Thanks to the media's own obsession with spin, we are all less naïve about the collusion between event organisers, agents, paparazzi and stars that helps create a tabloid sensation.

See 'Celebrity nobodies', the *Guardian*, 23.6.98, p. 18.
30 Rodney Tiffen, associate professor in government and international relations at the University of Sydney, Australia. See 'Under (spin) doctor's orders', *The Age*, Melbourne, 21.11.04, p. 15.
31 The author supplied the *Financial Times* with such releases in the 1970s.
32 The words of Julia Hobsbawm, a London PR agent, in 'Why journalism needs PR', the *Guardian* media section, 17.11.03, p. 8.
33 See Moloney *et al.* (2003) 'Mapping the production of political communications'.
34 Former CIPR president Anne Gregory notes that for the media, PR people and society generally 'It is not good that the media regurgitates uncritical, trivial pap.' See p. 3 of Prof. Anne Gregory at www.anti-spin.com/index.cfm?TERTIARY_ ID=O&PRIMARY_ ID=21&SECOND/. Accessed on 25.9.03.

12 The consequences of PR propaganda

1 This view is based on the author's experience of doing and witnessing PR over a career.
2 The Shadow Chancellor of the Exchequer, Oliver Letwin, said on the BBC Radio 4 *Today* programme, 9.2.05, that the Freedom of Information Act was a 'propaganda act' used by the government to control the release of official papers on Britain's withdrawal from the European Exchange Rate Mechanism in 1993.
3 For a US experience of this displacement see Jackall. He reports (1995, pp. 223–4, footnote) that the American Institute for Propaganda Analysis was set up in 1937 'to detect and to analyse propaganda' and that its work included looking at 'various corporate campaigns'. He notes that it 'suspended operations' after Pearl Harbor in 1941 and Bolinger (1980, preface) connects the decision to close it down with the fact that 'the country was too busy generating propaganda to spend much time analysing it'.
4 See note 3 above.
5 The UK comedian Jennifer Saunders, who writes and appears in the *Absolutely Fabulous* satire of London consultancy PR, was the 'celebrity face' of the promotion for the credit card Barclaycard in spring 2005. See 'Friends' parting', the *Guardian*, 20.1.05, p. 20.
6 'How to manage and leverage celebrity relationship' and 'Developing a celebrity sub-brand as part of your communications strategy' are two themes in the celebrity section of the Public Relations and Corporate Communications Summit 2005 conference, 8–9.2.05, Café Royal, London.
7 See the brochure of the 'Brand Building through Employees' conference on 25.4.02, at the Natural History Museum, London, organised by the Centre for Marketing Excellence, for the first two quotations. The third quotation is from the brochure for the Internal Communications Conference of the CIPR, 28.6.04, at the Copthorne Tara Hotel, London.
8 The Edelman Trust Barometer 2005 reports that 'For the second straight year . . . opinion leaders are significantly less likely to trust individual US-based global corporations operating in Europe and Canada.' It suggests that

this trust discount 'is tied to opinion leaders' perceptions of US culture, values and government'. See http://www.edelman.com/news/ShowOne.asp?ID=57. Accessed 9.3.05.

9　During 2004, it was noticeable that the CIPR was making reference to the 'voice' metaphor about PR on its website. By 2005, the metaphor had developed to include the CIPR itself as being 'the eyes, ears and voice of the public relations industry'. See the Institute's brochure *Managing Reputation* for a conference at the Copthorne Tara Hotel, London, on 11.4.05.

10　The difficult case is lobbying PR. Lobbying does not have to be limited to powerful, 'insider' interests, or done in private, and without prior diary notification or minutes afterwards. Political decisions can reform those features. See p. 129.

11　See 'And the brand played on', *FTmagazine*, 5.2.05, pp. 34–6, for a lamentation about, but acceptance of, PR in the classical music industry. It says, in part: 'A necessary evil? The American culture of hard sell sits uncomfortably with music's wordless purity – but with no PR, classical music's voice in the modern world would be muted.'

Bibliography

Abercrombie, N., Hill, S. and Turner, B. (1980) *The Dominant Ideology Thesis*, London: George Allen & Unwin.

Adkins, S. (1999) *Cause Related Marketing: Who Cares Wins*, London: Butterworth Heinemann.

Adonis, A. and Pollard, S. (1997) *A Class Act*, London: Hamish Hamilton.

Albig, W. (1939) *Public Opinion*, New York: McGraw Hill.

Alderman, G. (1984) *Pressure Groups and Government in Great Britain*, London: Longman.

Anderson. P. and Weymouth, A. (1999) *Insulting the Public: The British Press and the European Union*, London: Longman.

Andriof, J., Husted, B., Ruhman, S. and Waddock S. (eds.) (2003) *Unfolding Stakeholder Thinking*, vol. 2, Sheffield: Greenleaf Pubishing, pp. 9–12.

Armstrong, G. and Kotler, P. (2005) *Marketing: An Introduction*, 7th edn, New Jersey: Pearson Education International.

Aronoff, C. and Baskin, O. (1983) *Public Relations: The Profession and the Practice*, St Paul, MN: West Publishing.

Atkinson, S. (2004) 'Ethics and the corporate communicator', in S. Oliver (ed.) *Handbook of Corporate Communications and Public Relations*, London: Routledge, pp. 427–35.

Attaway-Fink, B. (2004) 'Market-driven journalism: creating special sections to meet readers interests', *Journal of Communication Management* 9(2), pp. 145–54.

Austin. E. and Pinkleton, B. (2001) *Strategic Public Relations Management*, New Jersey: Lawrence Erlbaum Associates.

Baistow, T. (1985) *Fourth-Rate Estate: Anatomy of Fleet Street*, London: Comedia.

Baker, R.S. (1906) 'Railroads on trial', *McClure's Magazine*, 26 March, pp. 535–49.

Balmer, J. (2003) 'Corporate brand management', in J. Balmer and S. Greyser (eds) *Revealing the Corporation: Perspectives on Identity, Image, Reputation, Corporate Branding and Corporate-Level Marketing*, London: Routledge, pp. 299–316.

Banks, S. (1995) *Multicultural Public Relations*, London: Sage.

Barney, R. and Black, J. (1994) 'Ethics and professional persuasive communications', *Public Relations Review* 20(3), pp. 233–48.

Barrow, C. (1993) *Critical Theories of the State: Marxist, Neo-Marxist, Post-Marxist*, Wisconsin: The University of Wisconsin Press.

Bates, S. (2004) *A Church at War: Anglicans and Homosexuality*, London: IB Tauris.

BDO Stoy Hayward (1994) *The Public Relations Sector*, London: Department of Trade and Industry.

Beale, H. (1936) *Are American Teachers Free?* New York: Octagon Books.

Beaton, M.C. (2001) *Death of a Dustman*, New York, Mysterious Press.

Bell, Q. (1991) *The PR Business*, London: Kogan Page.

Bentele, G. and Nothhaft, H. (2004) 'The intereffication model: a review of the theoretical discussion and the empirical research', Public Relations and the Public Sphere conference, Leipzig, 23–6 September.

Bentham, J. (1843) 'An essay in political tactics', ed. J. Bowring, *The Works of Jeremy Bentham*, vol. 22, Edinburgh: William Tait, pp. 299–373.

Bentley, A. (1908) *The Process of Government*, Chicago: University of Chicago Press.

Berger. P. (1998) *The Limits of Social Cohesion: Conflict and Mediation in Pluralist Societies*, Oxford: Westview Press.

Bernays, E. (1923) *Crystallizing Public Opinion*, New York: Boni and Liveright.

—(1927) *The Minority Rules*, New York: Bookman, pp. 150–5.

—(1928) *Propaganda*, New York: Liveright.

—(1947) 'Engineering of consent', *Annals of the American Academy of Political and Social Science* 250, March, pp. 113–20.

—(1965) *Biography of an Idea: Memoirs of Public Relations Counsel Edward L. Bernays*, New York: Simon & Schuster.

Black, S. (1962) *Practical Public Relations*, 1st edn, London: Pitman.

—(1973) *The Institute of Public Relations 1948–73: The First Twenty Five Years*, London: The IPR.

—(1989) *Introduction to Public Relations*, London: Mondino Press.

Blackmore, S. (1999) *Meme Machine*, Oxford: Oxford University Press.

Blick, A. (2004) *People Who Live in the Dark*, London: Politico's.

Blumler, J. and Gurevitch, M. (1981) 'Politicians and the press: an essay in role relationships', in D. Nimmo and K. Sanders (eds) *Handbook of Political Communication*, London: Sage.

Blyskal, J. and Blyskal, M. (1985) *PR: How the Public Relations Industry Writes the News*, New York: William Morrow.

Bolinger, D. (1980) *Language: The Loaded Weapon*, Harlow, UK: Longman.

Boorstin, D. (1961) *The Image, or, What Happened to the American Dream*, London: Weidenfeld & Nicolson.

Brady, R. (1943) *Business as a System of Power*, New York: Columbia University Press.

Brassington, F. and Pettitt, S. (2003) *Principles of Marketing*, 3rd edn, London: FT Prentice Hall.

Brebner, J. (1949) *Public Relations and Publicity*, London: National Council of Social Science.

Brewer's Dictionary of Phrase and Fable (1999) 16th edn, London: Cassell.

Brittan, S. (1995) *Capitalism with a Human Face*, London: Edward Elgar.

Bryant, B. (1996) *Twyford Down*, London: E & FN Spon.

Bullock, A. (1967) *Life and Times of Earnest Bevin: Minister of Labour 1940–1945*, London: Heinemann.

Burke, K. (1969) *A Grammar of Motives*, Berkeley: University of California Press [original edition published 1945].

Butler Report (2004) *Review of Intelligence on Weapons of Mass Destruction*, London: Stationery Office. HC 898.

Carey, A. (1995) *Taking the Risk out of Democracy*, ed. A. Lowrey, Sydney: UNSW Press.

Carty, F. (1992) *Farewell to Hype*, Dublin: Able Press.

Cassidy, S. (1992) 'The environment and the media: two strategies for challenging hegemony', in J. Wasko and V. Mosco (eds) *Democratic Communications in the Information Age*, Toronto: Garamond Press, pp. 159–74.

Cerin, P. (2002) 'Communication in corporate environmental reports', *Corporate Social Responsibility and Environmental Management* 9(1), pp. 46–66.

Chonko, L. (1995) *Ethical Decision Making in Marketing*, London: Sage.

Christian Aid (2004) *Behind the Mask: The Real Face of Corporate Social Responsibility*, London: Christian Aid.

Cochran, T.C. and Miller, W. (1942) *The Age of Enterprise: A Social History of Industrial America*, New York: Macmillan.

Cockett, R. (1989) *Twilight of Truth: Chamberlain, Appeasement and the Manipulation of the Press*, London: Weidenfeld & Nicolson.

Cohen, N. (1999) 'An explosion of puffery', *New Statesman*, 29 November, pp. 14–15.

Cohen, J. and Rogers, J. (1995) *Associations and Democracy*, London: Verso.

Cohen, S. and Young, J. (eds) (1973) *The Manufacture of News*, London: Constable.

Coogan, T. (1993) *De Valera*, London: Arrow Books.

Cornelissen, J. (2004) *Corporate Communications Theory and Practice*, London: Sage.

Coyle, D. (2001) *Paradoxes of Prosperity*, London: Texere.

Crofts, W. (1989) *Coercion or Persuasion?: Propaganda in Britain after 1945*, London: Routledge.

Crossley, N. and Roberts, J. (eds) (2004) *After Habermas: New Perspectives on the Public Sphere*, Oxford: Blackwell Publishing.

Cull, J., Culbert, D. and Welch, D. (2003) *Propaganda and Persuasion*, Santa Barbara: ABC-CLIO.

Cummingham, S. (2002) *The Idea of Propaganda*, Connecticut: Praeger.

Curran, J. and Seaton, J. (1997) *Power without Responsibility: Press and broadcasting in Britain*, 5th edn, London: Routledge.

Cutlip, S. (1995) *Public Relations History: From the 17th to the 20th Century. The Antecedents*, New Jersey: Lawrence Erlbaum.

Cutlip, S., Center, A. and Broom, G. (2000) *Effective Public Relations*, 8th edn, London: Prentice Hall International.

Dahl, R. (1961) *Who Governs*, New Haven: Yale University Press.

—(1971) *Polyarchy: Participation and Opposition*, New Haven: Yale University Press.

—(1982) *Dilemmas of Pluralist Democracy*, New Haven: Yale University Press.

—(1989) *Democracy and Its Critics*, New Haven: Yale University Press.

Dartnell's Public Relations Handbook (1996) 4th edn, Chicago: Dartnell.

Davis, Aeron (2002) *Public Relations Democracy*, Manchester: Manchester University Press.

—(2003) 'Public relations and news sources', in S. Cottle (ed.) *News, Public Relations and Power*, London: Sage.

Davis, Anthony (2004) *Mastering Public Relations*, Basingstoke: Palgrave Macmillan.

Dawkins, J. (2004) 'Corporate responsibility: the communication challenge', *Journal of Communication Management* 9(2), pp. 108–19.

Dawkins, R. (1989, new edn) *The Selfish Gene*, Oxford: Oxford University Press.

Day, R. and Woodward, T. (2004) 'Disclosure of information about employees in the Directors' report of UK published financial statements: substantive or symbolic?' *Accounting Forum* 28, pp. 43–59.

Deacon, D. and Golding, P. (1994) *Taxation and Representation: The Media, Political Communication and the Poll Tax*, London: John Libbey.

Deegan, D. (2001) *Managing Activism*, London: Kogan Page.

Dilenschneider, R. (1999) 'The year ahead', *Communication World* 16(3), pp. 13–21.

Directory of British Associations (1998) Beckenham, London: CBD Research.

Doob, L. (1935) *Propaganda: Its Psychology and Technique*, New York: Henry Holt.

Doole, I. (2005) *Understanding and Managing Customers*, London: Prentice Hall.

Dorward, C. (1997) 'Managing internal communications', in R. Foster and A. Jolly (eds) *Corporate Communications Handbook*, London: Kogan Page.

Dozier, D. and Ehling, W. (1992) 'Evaluation of public relations programs', in J. Grunig (ed.) *Excellence in Public Relations and Communicative Management*, Hove: Lawrence Erlbaum.

Dozier, D., Grunig, L. and Grunig, J. (2001) 'Public Relations as Communication Campaign', in R. Rice and C. Atkin (eds) *Public Information Campaigns*, 3rd edn, London: Sage.

Draper, D. (1997) *Blair's 100 Days*, London: Faber and Faber.

Dunleavy, P. and O'Leary, B. (1987) *Theories of the State*, Basingstoke: Macmillan Education.

Edwards, M. (2004) *Civil Society*, Cambridge: Polity Press.

Elkington, J. and Hailes, J. (1998) *Manual 2000 Life Choices for the Future You Want*, London, Hodder & Stoughton.

Ellul, J. (1962) *Propaganda: The Formation of Men's Attitudes*, New York: Vintage.

Encyclopedia of the Social Sciences (1934) New York: Macmillan.

Evans. B. (ed.) (1968) *The Dictionary of Quotations*, New York: Delacorte Press.

Ewen, P. (1996) *PR! A Social History of Spin*, New York: Basic Books.

Fallows, J. (1996) *Breaking the News: How the Media Undermine American Democracy*, New York: Random House.

Fill, C. (1999) *Marketing Communications*, 2nd edn, Hemel Hempstead: Prentice Hall.

Finer, S. (1958; 1966) *Anonymous Empire: A Study of the Lobby in Great Britain*, London: Pall Mall.

Fones-Wolff, E. (1994) *The Business Assault on Labour and Liberalism 1945–60*, Urbana: University of Illinois Press.

Foreman, A. (1999) *Georgiana, Duchess of Devonshire*, London: Flamingo Harper Collins.

Frank, T. (2000) *One Market under God*, New York: Doubleday.

Franklin, B. (1994) *Packaging Politics: Political Communications in Britain's Media Democracy*, London: Edward Arnold.

—(1997) *Newszak and The News Media*, London: Edward Arnold.

—(1998) *Tough on Soundbites, Tough on the Causes of Soundbites*, London: Catalyst Trust.

—(2004) *Packaging Politics: Political Communications in Britain's Media Democracy*, 2nd edn, London: Arnold.

Freeman, R. (1984) *Strategic Management: A Stakeholder Approach*, London: Pitman.

Friedman, M. (1962) *Capitalism and Freedom*, London: Pitman.

Fuhrman, C. (1989) *Publicity Stunt!* San Francisco: Chronicle Books.

Gaber, I. (2000) 'Government by spin: an analysis of the process', *Media, Culture and Society* 22(4), pp. 507–18.

Gabriel, Y. and Lang, T. (1995) *The Unmanageable Consumer*, London: Sage.

Galbraith, J. (1983) *The Anatomy of Power*, New York: Simon Schuster.

Gandy, O. (1982) *Beyond Agenda Setting: Information Subsidies and Public Policy*, Norwood, USA: Ablex.

Gillman, F. (1978) 'Public relations in the United Kingdom prior to 1948', *Journal of the International Public Relations Association* 2(1), April, pp. 43–50.

Gillmor, D. (2004) *We the Media*, Sebastopol, California: O'Reilly.

Gladwell, M. (2000) *The Tipping Point: How Little Things Can Make a Big Difference*, London: Little Brown.

Glasgow University Media Group (1982) *Really Bad News*, London: Writers and Readers Publishing Co-operative.

Gloag, J. (1959) *Advertising in Modern Life*, London: Heinemann.

Goldenberg, E. (1975) *Making the Papers*, Massachusetts: Lexington Books.

Goldman, E. (1948) *Two-Way Street: The Emergence of the Public Relations Counsel*, Boston: Bellman.

Graham, G. (1999) *The Internet://a Philosophical Inquiry*, London: Routledge.

Grant, M. (1994) *Propaganda and the Role of the State in Inter-War Years*, Oxford: Oxford University Press.

Grant, W. (1989) *Pressure Groups, Politics and Democracy*, London: Philip Allan.

—(1995) *Pressure Groups, Politics and Democracy in Britain*, 2nd edn, Hemel Hempstead: Harvester Wheatsheaf.

—(2000) *Pressure Groups and British Politics*, Basingstoke: Macmillan.

Gray, R. and Hobsbawn, J. (1996) *Cosmopolitan Guide to Working in PR and Advertising*, London: Penguin.

Gregory, A. (1996) *Planning and Managing a Public Relations Campaign*, London: IPR/Kogan Page.

Griese, N. (2001) *Arthur W. Page: Publisher, Public Relations Pioneer, Patriot*, Atlanta: Anvil Publications.

Grunig, J. (1989) 'Presuppositions as framework for PR theory', in C. Botan and V. Hazleton (eds) *Public Relations Theory*, Hove: Lawrence Erlbaum.

—(1992a) 'Communication, public relations, and effective organisations: an overview of the book', in J. Grunig (ed.) *Excellence in Public Relations and Communications Management*, Hove: Lawrence Erlbaum, pp. 1–28.

—(ed.) (1992b) *Excellence in Public Relations and Communications Management*, Hove: Lawrence Erlbaum.

—(1992c) *Public Relations as a Two-Way Symmetrical Process*, Culemborg, Holland: Phaedon (speech to the School of Journalism and Communications, Utrecht).

—(1997) 'A situational theory of publics: conceptual history, recent challenge and new research', in D. Moss, T. Macmanus and D. Vercic (eds) *Public Relations Research: An International Perspective*, London: International Thomson Business Press, pp. 3–46.

Grunig, J. and Grunig, L. (1992) 'Models of public relations and communications', in J. Grunig (ed.) *Excellence in Public Relations and Communicative Management*, Hove: Lawrence Erlbaum.

Grunig, J. and Hunt, T. (1984) *Managing Public Relations*, New York: Holt, Rinehart & Winston.

Grunig, J. and White, J. (1992) 'The effects of worldviews on public relations', in J. Grunig (ed.) *Excellence in Public Relations and Communication Management*, Hove: Lawrence Erlbaum.

Grunig, L. (1995) 'Empowering women and culturally diverse employees', in D. Dozier, L. Grunig and J. Grunig (eds) *Manager's Guide to Excellence in Public Relations and Communication Management*, Hove: Lawrence Erlbaum.

Grunig, L., Grunig, J. and Dozier, D. (2002) *Excellent Public Relations and Effective Organisations*. London: Lawrence Erlbaum.

Habermas, J. (1989) *The Structural Transformation of the Public Sphere*, Massachusetts: MIT Press [original German edition 1962].

—(1996) *Between Facts and Norms*, trans. William Rehg, Cambridge: MIT Press.

Hagen, I. (1992) 'Democratic communications: media and social participation', in J. Wasko and V. Mosco (eds) *Democratic Communications in the Information Age*, Toronto: Garamond Press, pp. 16–27.

Halfon, R. (1998) *Corporate Irresponsibility: Is Business Appeasing Anti-business Activities?* London: Adam Smith Institute.

Hannington, T. (2004) *How to Measure and Manage Your Corporate Reputation*, Aldershot: Gower.

Harrabin, R. (2000) 'Reporting sustainable development: a broadcast journalist's view', in J. Smith (ed.) *The Daily Globe: Environmental Change, the Public and the Media*, London: Earthscan, pp. 49–63.

Harris, N. (1973) *Humbug: The Art of P.T. Barnum*, Boston: Little, Brown.

Harris, P. and Lock, A. (1996) 'Machiavellian marketing: the development of political marketing in the UK', *Journal of Marketing Management* 12(4), pp. 313–28.

Harris, P., Moss, D. and Vetter, N. (1999) 'Machiavelli's legacy to public affairs: a modern tale of servants and princes in UK organisations', *Journal of Communication Management* 3(3), pp. 201–17.

Harris, T. (1991) *The Marketer's Guide to Public Relations*, New York: John Wiley.

Harrison, S. (1994) 'Codes of practice and ethics in the UK communications industry', *Business Ethics* 3(2), pp. 109–16.

—(1995) *Public Relations: An Introduction*, London: Routledge.

—(1996) 'Teaching the truth', a paper at Public Relations Educators' Forum, St Mark and St John College, Plymouth, 24–6 March.

—(1998) 'The local government agenda: news from the town hall', in B. Franklin and D. Murphy (eds) *Making the Local News*, London: Routledge.

—(ed.) (1999) *Disasters and the Media*, Basingstoke: Macmillan Business.

Hawthorn, J. (ed.) (1987) *Propaganda, Persuasion and Polemic*, London: Edward Arnold.

Heath R. (1992) 'The wrangle in the marketplace: a rhetorical perspective of public relations', in E. Toth and R. Heath (eds) *Rhetorical and Critical Approaches to Public Relations*, New Jersey: Lawrence Erlbaum, pp. 17–36.

—(1994) *Management of Corporate Communications*, Hove: Lawrence Erlbaum.

—(ed.) (2005) *Encyclopedia of Public Relations*, London: Sage.

Heath, R. and Bryant, J. (2000) *Human Communication Theory and Research*, London: Lawrence Erlbaum.

Heath. R. and Cousino, K. (1990) 'Issues management: end of the first decade progress report, *Public Relations Review* 16(1), pp. 6–17.

Henderson, D. (2001) *Misguided Virtue: False Notions of Corporate Social Responsibility*, London: Institute of Economic Affairs.

Henwood, D. (1997) *Wall St: How It Works and for Whom*, London: Verso.

Herman, E. (1992) *Beyond Hypocrisy: Decoding the News in an Age of Propaganda*, Boston: South End Press.

Herman, E. and Chomsky, N. (1988) *Manufacturing Consent*, New York: Pantheon Books.

Heywood, R. (1990) *All about Public Relations*, 2nd edn, London: McGraw-Hill.

Hiebert, R. (1966) *Courtier to the Crowd*, Ames, IA: Iowa State University Press.

Hilton, S. and Gibbons, G. (2002) *Good Business: Your World Needs You*, London: Texere.

Hollingsworth, M. (1997) *The Ultimate Spin Doctor: The Life and Times of Tim Bell*, London: Hodder & Stoughton.

Holtz, S. (1998) *Public Relations on the Net*, New York: American Management Association.

Holub, R. (1991) *Jürgen Habermas: Critic in the Public Sphere*, London: Routledge.

Homan, M. (2003) *Promoting Community Change*, California: Brooks Cole.

Horgan, J. (2001) *Irish Media: A Critical History since 1922*, London: Routledge.

Humphrys, J. (1999) *Devil's Advocate*, London: Hutchinson.

Hutton, J. (2001) 'Defining the relationship between public relations and marketing: public relations' most important challenge', in R. Heath (ed.) *Handbook of Public Relations*, London: Sage, pp. 205–14.

Hutton, W. (1999) *The Stakeholding Society*, Cambridge: Polity Press.

Institute of Public Relations (1958) *A Guide to the Practice of Public Relations*, London: Newman Neame.

IPR (1998a) *Handbook*, London: IPR.

—(1998b) Managing Communication in a Changing World, London: IPR.

Jackall, R. (ed.) (1995) *Propaganda*, Basingstoke: Macmillan.

Jackall, R. and Hirota, J. (2000) *Image Makers: Advertising and Public Relations and the Ethos of Advocacy*, London: University of Chicago Press.

James, B. and Moloney, K. (1995) *Towards a Classification of Environmental Groups*, working paper, Bournemouth University.

Jefkins, F. (1988) *Public Relations Techniques*, London: Heinemann Professional Publishing.

Jefkins, F. and Yadin, D. (1998) *Public Relations*, 5th edn, London: Financial Times Prentice Hall.

Jenkins, H. (2004) 'A critique of conventional CSR theory: an SME perspective', *Journal of General Management* 4, summer, pp. 37–57.

Jensen, J. (1997) *Ethical Issues in the Communication Process*, New Jersey: Lawrence Erlbaum.

John, S. and Thomson, S. (eds) (2003) *New Activism and the Corporate Response*, Basingstoke: Palgrave Macmillan.

Jones, N. (1995) *Soundbites and Spindoctors*, London: Cassells.

—(1997) *How the General Election Was Won and Lost*, London: Indigo.

—(1999) *Sultans of Spin*, London: Victor Gollancz.

—(2002) *The Control Freak: How New Labour Gets Its Own Way*, London: Politico's.

Jordan, G. (ed.) (1991) *The Commercial Lobbyists*, Aberdeen: Aberdeen University Press.

—(1998) 'Towards regulation in the UK: from "general good sense" to "formalised rules"', *Parliamentary Affairs* 51(4), pp. 524–38.

Jordan, G. and Maloney, W. (1997) *The Protest Business?* Manchester: Manchester University Press.

Jowett, G. and O'Donnell, V. (1992) *Propaganda and Persuasion*, London: Sage.

Kemp, G. (1988) 'Public relations in marketing', in W. Howard (ed.) *The Practice of Public Relations*, 3rd edn, London: Heinemann, pp. 125–36.

Kisch, R. (1964) *The Private Life of Public Relations*, London: Macgibbon & Kee.

Kitchen, P. (ed.) (1997) *Public Relations: Principles and Practice*, London: International Thomson Business Press.

Kitchen, P. and Papasolomou, I. (1997) 'The emergence of marketing PR', in P. Kitchen (ed.) *Public Relations: Principles and Practice*, London: International Thomson Business Press, pp. 239–71.

Klein, N. (2000) *No Logo*, London: Flamingo Harper Collins.

Korten, D. (1995) *When Corporations Rule the World*, New York: Kunarian Press.

Kotler, P. (1997) *Marketing Management*, 9th edn, New Jersey: Prentice Hall.

Kotler, P. and Mindak, W. (1978) 'Marketing and public relations', *Journal of Marketing* 42, October, pp. 13–20.

Kruckeberg, D. (1998) 'The future of PR education: some recommendations', *Public Relations Review* 24(2), pp. 235–47.

Kruckeberg, D. and Starck, K. (1988) *Public Relations and Community*, Westport, CT: Praeger.

Kunczik, M. (1997) *Images of Nations and International Public Relations*, London: Lawrence Erlbaum Associates.

Kymlicka, W. (2002) 'Civil society and government: a liberal-egalitarian perspective', in N. Rosenblum and R. Post (eds) *Civil Society and Government*, Princeton: Princeton University Press, pp. 111–22.

Lambert, R. (1938; reprinted 1945) *Propaganda*, London: Thomas Nelson.

—(1940) *Ariel and All His Quality*, London: Victor Gollancz.

Langer, J. (1998) *Tabloid Television: Popular Journalism and the 'Other' News*, London: Routledge.

Lasswell, H. (1927) *Propaganda Technique in the World War*, New York: Knopf [republished with introduction in 1971 by the MIT Press, Massachusetts].

Lasswell, H. (1934) 'Propaganda' entry in *Encyclopedia of the Social Sciences*, vol. 12, 1st edn, London: Macmillan.

Le Bon, G. (1896) *The Crowd: A Study of the Popular Mind*, London: Macmillan.

Lee, M. (2005) *The First Presidential Communications Agency: FDR's Office of Government Reports*, Albany, NY: State University of New York Press.

L'Etang, J. (1996a) 'Public relations as diplomacy', in J. L'Etang and M. Pieczka (eds) *Critical Perspectives in Public Relations*, London: International Thomson Business Press, pp. 14–34.

—(1996b) 'Corporate responsibility and public relations ethics', in J. L'Etang and M. Pieczka (eds) *Critical Perspectives in Public Relations*, London: International Thomson Business Press, pp. 82–105.

—(1998) 'The development of British public relations in the twentieth century', for the IAMCR Conference, Glasgow. Later published as 'State propaganda and bureaucratic intelligence: the creation of public relations in the 20th century', *Public Relations Review* 24(4), winter 1998, pp. 413–41.

—(1999) 'Grierson's influence on the formation and emergent values of the public relations industry in Britain', at Breaking the Boundaries conference, Stirling University, 28–31 January.

—(2004a) 'Public relations and democracy: historical reflections and implications for practice', in S. Oliver (ed.) *Handbook of Corporate Communications and Public Relations*, London: Routledge, pp. 342–57.

—(2004b) *Public Relations in Britain*, London: Lawrence Erlbaum Associates.

L'Etang, J. and Pieczka, M. (1996) (eds) *Critical Perspectives in Public Relations*, London: International Thomson Business Press.

Levine, M. (1993) *Guerrilla PR*, New York: Harper Business.

Lieberman, T. (2000) *Slanting History: The Forces That Shape the News*, New York: The New Press.

Lindblom, C. (1997) *Politics and Markets*, New York: Basic Books.

Lindner, R. (1998) *From Workhouse with Infirmary to an NHS Hospital*, Bournemouth: Zerwas Press.

Lippmann, W. (1919) 'Liberty and news', *Atlantic Monthly*, December, pp. 779–87.

—(1922) *Public Opinion*, London: George Allen & Unwin.

Lloyd, J. (2004a) *What the Media Are Doing to Our Politics*, London: Constable.

—(2004b) 'Selling out to the market', *British Journalism Review* 15(4), pp. 7–11. Accessed on 14.2.05 at www.bjr.org.uk/data/2004/no4 _ lloyd.htm.

Lubbers, E. (ed.) (2002) *Battling Big Business*, Totnes: Green Books.

Lukes, S. (1974) *Power: A Radical View*, London: Macmillan.

McAlpine, A. (1997) *The New Machiavelli*, London: Aurum Press.

McCarthy, T. (1996) *The Critical Theory of Jurgen Habermas*, Massachusetts: The MIT Press.

McElreath, M. (1997) *Managing Systematic and Ethical Public Relations Campaigns*, 2nd edn, London: Brown & Benchmark.

McGrath, C. (2005) *Perspectives on Lobbying: Washington, London, Brussels*, Lampeter: Edward Mellen Press.

McKinnon, L., Tedesco, J. and Lauder, T. (2001) 'Political power through public relations', in R. Heath (ed.) *Handbook of Public Relations*, London: Sage, pp. 557–64.

McLellan, D. (1979) *Marxism after Marx*, London: Macmillan PaperMac.

McNair, B. (1995) *An Introduction to Political Communication*, London: Routledge.

—(1996) 'Performance in politics and the politics of performance', in J. L'Etang and M. Pieczka (1996) (eds) *Critical Perspectives in Public Relations*, London: International Thomson Business Press.

McQuail, D. (1987) *Mass Communication Theory*, London: Sage.

—(2004) 'PR Must Die: spin, anti-spin and political public relations in the UK, 1997–2004' in *Journalism Studies* 5(3), pp. 325–38.

McSmith, A. (1997) *Faces of Labour: The Inside Story*, London: Verso.

Mallinson, W. (1996) *Public Lies and Public Truths*, London: Cassell.

Manheim, J. (2001) *The Death of a Thousand Cuts*, London: Lawrence Erlbaum.

Manning, P. (1998) *Spinning for Labour: Trade Unions and the New Media Environment*, Aldershot: Ashgate.

Marchand, R. (1998) *Creating the Corporate Soul: The Rise of Public Relations and Corporate Imagery in American Big Business*, Berkeley: University of California Press.

Marquand, D. (2004) *Decline of the Public: The Hollowing-out of Citizenship*, Cambridge: Polity Press.

Marsh, C. (2001) 'Public relations ethics: contrasting models from the rhetorics of Plato, Aristotle, and Isocrates', *Journal of Mass Media Ethics* 16(2–3), pp. 78–98.

Marsh, D. and Locksley, G. (1983) 'Capital: the neglected face of power', in D. Marsh (ed.) *Pressure Politics*, London: Junction Books.

Marston, J. (1963) *The Nature of Public Relations*, New York: McGraw-Hill.

Martin, J. (1992) *Cultures in Organisations: Three Perspectives*, New York: Oxford University Press.

Mattelart, A. and Mattelart, M. (1998) *Theories of Communication*, London: Sage.

Merton, R. (1946) *Mass Persuasion: The Social Psychology of a War Bond Drive*, New York: Harper & Brothers.

Merton, R. (1995) 'Mass persuasion: a technical problem and a moral dilemma', in R. Jackall (ed.) *Propaganda*, Basingstoke: Macmillan, pp. 260–75 [first published 1946].

Michie, D. (1998) *The Invisible Persuaders*, London: Transworld Publishers.

Mickey, T. (2003) *Deconstructing Public Relations: Public Relations Criticism*, London: Lawrence Erlbaum.

Micklethwait, J. and Woolridge, A. (2003) *The Company*, London: Weidenfeld & Nicolson.

Miller, C. (1987) *Lobbying Government*, Oxford: Blackwell.

Miller, D. (1994) *Don't Mention the War: Northern Ireland, Propaganda and the Media*, London: Pluto.

—(1997) 'Public relations and journalism', in A. Briggs and P. Cobley (eds) *The Media: An Introduction*, Harlow: Addison Wesley Longman, pp. 65–80.

Miller, D. and Dinan, W. (2000) 'The rise of the PR industry in Britain, 1979–98', *European Journal of Communication* 15(1), March, pp. 5–36.

Miller, G. (1989) 'Persuasion and public relations: two "Ps" in a pod', in G. Botan and V. Hazleton (eds) *Public Relations Theory*, Hillsdale: Lawrence Erlbaum Associates, pp. 45–66.

Miller, K. (1999a) *The Voice of Business: Hill and Knowlton and Post War Public Relations*, Chapel Hill: University of North Carolina.

—(1999b) 'Public relations in film and fiction: 1930s to 1995', *Journal of Public Relations Research* 11(1), pp. 3–28.

Moloney, K. (1996) *Lobbyists for Hire*, Aldershot: Dartmouth Press.

—(1997) 'Teaching public relations in UK universities: teaching about a practice with an unpleasant odour attached', *Working Papers in Public Relations Research, no. 1*, Bournemouth University. ISBN 1-85899-026-2.

—(1998) 'It's a PR job: a question of reputation and its consequences for teaching, researching and doing PR', *Working Papers in Public Relations Research, no. 2*, Bournemouth University. ISBN 1-85899-071-8.

—(1999) 'Publicists – distribution workers in the pleasure economy of the film industry', in J. Bignell (ed.) *Writing and Cinema*, Harlow: Longman.

—(2000a) 'Nicco and Charlie: two political servants', in P. Harris, A. Lock and P. Rees (eds) *Machiavelli, Marketing and Management*, London: Routledge, pp. 164–75.

—(2000b) *Rethinking PR: The Spin and the Substance*. London: Routledge.

—(2001) 'The man who was PRO first' for the 6th International Conference on Corporate and Marketing Communications, Queen's University, Belfast, 23–4 April.

—(2004) 'Democracy and public relations', *Journal of Communication Management* 9(1), pp. 89–92.

Moloney, K. and Colmer, R. (2001) 'Does PR enhance or trivialise democracy?' *Journal of Marketing Management* 17, pp. 957–68.

Moloney, K. and Harrison, S. (2004) 'Comparing two public relations pioneers: American Ivy Lee and British John Elliot', *Public Relations Review* 30, pp. 205–15.

Moloney. K., Richards, B., Scullion, R. and Daymon, D. (2003) 'Mapping the production of political communications: a model to assist in understanding the relationships between the production and consumption of political messages', *Journal of Public Affairs* 3(2), pp. 166–75.

Moore, S. (1996) *An Introduction to Public Relations*, London: Cassell.

Morris, S. (2000) *Wired PR*, London: FT.com.

Mosca, V. (1996) *The Political Economy of Communication*, Sage: London.

Moss, D. and Warnaby, G. (1997a) 'A strategic perspective for public relations', in P. Kitchen (ed.) *Public Relations: Principles and Practice*, London: International Thomson Business Press.

Moss, D. and Warnaby, G. (1997b) 'The role of public relations in organisations', in P. Kitchen (ed.) *Public Relations: Principles and Practice,* London: International Thomson Business Press.

Nelson, J. (1992) *Sultans of Sleaze: Public Relations and the Media*, Monroe, ME: Common Courage Press.

Newman, W. (1993) 'New words for what we do', *IPR Journal*, October, pp. 12–15.

O'Shaughnessy, N. (1996) 'Social propaganda and social marketing', *European Journal of Marketing* 30(10–11), pp. 62–75.

—(1999) Paper on political marketing as a hybrid concept, for Political Marketing conference, Bournemouth University, 15–16 September.

Oborne, P. (1999) *Alastair Campbell: New Labour and the Rise of the Media Class*, London: Aurum.

Olasky, M. (1984) 'Retrospective: Bernays' doctrine of public opinion', in *Public Relations Review* 10(3), pp. 3–12.

—(1987) *Corporate Public Relations: A New Historical Perspective*, Hove: Lawrence Erlbaum.

Olins, W. (2003) *On Brand*, London: Thames & Hudson.

Oliver, S. (ed.) (2004) *Handbook of Corporate Communication and Public Relations*, London: Routledge.

Olson, M. (1982) *The Rise and Decline of Nations*, New Haven: Yale University Press.

Packard, V. (1981) *The Hidden Persuaders*, 2nd edn, London: Penguin [1st edn 1957].

Parsons, P. (2004) *Ethics in Public Relations: A Guide to Best Practice*, London: Kogan Page.

Pearson, J. and Turner, G. (1965) *The Persuasion Industry*, London: Eyre & Spottiswoode.

Pearson, R. (1989) 'Beyond ethical relativism in public relations', in J. Grunig and L. Grunig (eds) *Public Relations Research Annual*, vol. 1, Hillsdale, NJ: Lawrence Erlbaum, pp. 67–86.

—(1992) 'Perspectives on public relations history' in E. Toth and R. Heath (eds) *Rhetorical and Critical Approaches to Public Relations*, New Jersey: Lawrence Erlbaum, pp. 111–30.

Piasecki, A. (2000) 'Blowing the railroad trumpet', *Public Relations Review* 26, pp. 53–65.

Pilling, R. (1998) 'The changing role of the local journalist', in B. Franklin and D. Murphy (eds) *Making the Local News*, London: Routledge.

Pimlott, J. (1951) *Public Relations and American Democracy*, Princeton: Princeton University Press.

Posner, R. (2003) *Law, Pragmatism and Democracy*, Massachusetts: Harvard University Press.

Pratkanis, A. and Aronson, E. (1992) *Age of Propaganda*, New York: Freeman.

Price, V. (1992) *Public Opinion*, London: Sage.

Putnam, R. (2000) *Bowling Alone*, New York: Simon & Schuster.

Quinn, S. (2005) 'Convergence's fundamental question', *Journalism Studies* 6(1), pp. 29–38.

Raucher, A. (1968) *Public Relations and Business*, Baltimore: Johns Hopkins Press.

Rees, L. (1992) *Selling Politics*, London: BBC Books.

Reichenbach, H. (1932) *Phantom Fame: The Anatomy of Ballyhoo*, London: Noel Douglas.

Rein, I., Kotler, P. and Stoller, M. (1997) *High Visibility: The Making and the Marketing of Professionals into Celebrities*, Illinois: NTC Business Books.

Richards, B. (2004) 'Terrorism and public relations', *Public Relations Review* 30(2), pp. 169–76.

Richards, P. (1998) *Be Your Own Spin Doctor*, Harrogate: Take That.

Ries, A. and Ries, L. (2002) *The Fall of Advertising and the Rise of PR*, New York: HarperBusiness.

Roberts, J. (2003) 'The manufacture of corporate social responsibility: constructing corporate sensibility', *Organisation* 10(2), pp. 249–65.

Robins, K., Webster, F. and Pickering, M. (1987) 'Propaganda, information and social control', in J. Hawthorn (ed.) *Propaganda, Persuasion and Polemic*, London: Edward Arnold.

Rosenblum, N. and Post, R. (eds) (2002) *Civil Society and Government*, Oxford: Princeton University Press.

Saffir, L. (2000) *Power Public Relations*, 2nd edn, Illinois: NTC Business Books.

Salter, L. (2005) 'The communicative structures of journalism and public relations', *Journalism* 6(1), pp. 90–106.

Saul, J. (1993) *Voltaire's Bastards: The Dictatorship of Reason in the West*, New York: Vintage Books.

Scammell, M. (1995) *Designer Politics: How Elections Are Won*, London: Macmillan.

—(2000) 'Media and democracy: democracy and media', in M. Scammell and H. Semetko (eds) *The Media, Journalism and Democracy*, Aldershot: Ashgate, pp. 12–49.

Schlesinger, P. and Tumber, H. (1994) *Reporting Crime: The Media Politics of Criminal Justice*, Oxford: Clarendon Press.

Schnattschneider, E. (1975, reissued) *The Semisovereign People*, Hillsdale, IL: The Dryden Press.

Schulman, M. and Anderson, C. (2001) 'The dark side of the force', in B. Edwards, M. Foley and M. Diani (eds) *Beyond Tocqueville: Civil Society and the Social Capital Debate in Comparative Perspective*, New Hampshire: University Press of New England, pp. 112–24.

Schultz, M. (2002) *The Expressive Organisation*, Oxford: Oxford University Press.

Scott, J. (1991) *Who Rules Britain?* Cambridge: Polity Press.

Seitel, F. (1995) *The Practice of PR*, 6th edn, New Jersey: Prentice Hall.

Shanahan, J. (ed.) (2001) *Propaganda without Propagandists*, New Jersey: Hampton Press.

Sighele, S. (1898) *Psychology of Sects*, Paris: Giard and Briere [reprinted in translation 1975, New York: Arno Press].

Simmons, J. (1991) *The Victorian Railway*, London: Thames & Hudson.

Simmons, J. and Biddle, G. (1999) *The Oxford Companion to British Railway History*, Oxford: Oxford University Press.

Simmons, T. (2004) *My Sister's A Barista: How They Made Starbucks a Home from Home*, London: Cyan.

Smythe, D. (1981) *Dependency Road: Communications, Capitalism, Consciousness and Canada*, Norwood, USA: Ablex.

Snow, N. (2003) *Information War: American Propaganda, Free Speech And Opinion Control since 9–11*, New York: Severn Stories Press.

Spicer, C. (1997) *Organisational Public Relations: A Political Perspective*, London: Lawrence Erlbaum.

Sproule, J. (1997) *Propaganda and Democracy*, Cambridge: Cambridge University Press.

Sriramesh, K. and Vercic, D. (eds) (2003) *The Global Public Relations Handbook*, New Jersey: Lawrence Erlbaum Associates.

Stauber, J. and Rampton, S. (1995) *Toxic Sludge is Good for You*, Maine: Common Courage Press.

Sternberg, E. (1994) *Just Business: Business Ethics in Action*, London: Little, Brown.

Stonier, T. (1989) 'The evolving professionalism: responsibilities', *International Public Relations Review* 12(3), pp. 30–6.

Street, J. (2001) *Mass Media, Politics and Democracy*, Basingstoke: Macmillan.

Surma, A. (2005) 'Public relations and corporate social responsibility: developing a moral narrative', *Asia Pacific Public Relations Journal* 5(2), pp. 1–12.

Susskind, L. and Field, P. (1996) *Dealing with an Angry Public: The Mutual Gains Approach to Resolving Disputes*, New York: The Free Press.

Tallents, S. (1932) *The Projection of England*, London: Faber & Faber.

Tannen, D. (1998) *The Argument Culture: Changing the Way We Argue and Debate*, London: Virago.

Tarrow, S. (1994) *Power in Movement*, Cambridge: Cambridge University Press.

Taylor, P. (1999) *British Propaganda in the Twentieth Century: Selling Democracy*, Edinburgh: Edinburgh University Press.

—(2002) 'Strategic communications or democratic propaganda?' *Journalism Studies* 3(3), pp. 437–41.

TBI Yearbook (2004) London: Informa Media Group.

Tedlow, R. (1979) *Keeping the Corporate Image*, Connecticut: JAI Press.

Thorson, E. and Moore, J. (1996) *Integrated Communication: Synergy of Persuasive Voices*, New Jersey: Lawrence Erlbaum.

Toth, E. (1992) 'The case for pluralistic studies of public relations: rhetorical, critical and systems perspectives', in E. Toth and R. Heath (eds) *Rhetorical and Critical Approaches to Public Relations*, New Jersey: Lawrence Erlbaum, pp. 3–16.

Traverse-Healy, T. (1988) *Public Relations and Propaganda – Values Compared*, Gold Paper No. 6, Geneva: International Public Relations Association.

Trotter, W. (1916) *The Instincts of the Herd in Peace and War*, London: Macmillan.

Truman, D. (1951) *The Governmental Process: Political Interests and Public Opinion*, New York: Alfred A. Knopf.

Truman, M., Klemm, M. and Giroud, A. (2004) 'Can a city communicate? Bradford as a corporate brand', *Corporate Communications: An International Journal* 9(4), pp. 317–30.

Tunstall, J. (1964) 'Public relations in advertising', in *The Advertising Man in London Advertising Agencies*, London: Chapman & Hall, pp. 155–92.

Turner, G., Bonner. F. and Marshall, P. (2000) *Fame Games: The Production of Celebrity in Australia*, Cambridge: Cambridge University Press.

Tutt, B. (1999) 'Political marketing, partisan politics and the televising of the House of Commons', at political marketing conference, Bournemouth University, 15–16 September.

Tye, L. (1998) *The Father of Spin: Edward L. Bernays and the Birth of Public Relations*, New York: Crown.

Useem, M. (1984) *The Inner Circle*, New York: Oxford University Press.

Vercic, D. and Grunig, J. (2000) 'The origins of public relations theory in economics and strategic management', in D. Moss, D. Vercic and G. Warnaby (eds) *Perspectives in Public Relations Research*, London: Routledge, p. 38.

Vogel, D. (1996) *Kindred Strangers: The Uneasy Relationship between Politics and Business in America*, New Jersey: Princeton University Press.

Wallas, G. (1908) *Human Nature in Politics*, London: Constable.

Webster, F. (1995) *Theories of the Information Society*, London: Routledge.

Weidenfeld, W. (1998) 'Preface', in P. Berger (ed.) *The Limits to Social Cohesion*, Colorado: Westview Press, pp. 11–12.

Weiss, J. (2003) *Business Ethics: A Stakeholder and Issues Management Approach*. 3rd edn, Mason, OH: Thomson South-Western.

Wernick, A. (1991) *Promotional Culture*, London: Sage.

West, R. (1963) *PR: The Fifth Estate*, London: Mayflower Books.

White, J. (1991) *How to Understand and Manage Public Relations*, London: Business Books.

White, J. and Mazur, L. (1995) *Strategic Communications Management*, Wokingham: Addison-Wesley Publishing, and London: Economist Intelligence Unit.

Williams, F. (1946) *Press, Parliament and People*, London: Heinemann.

World Radio TV Handbook (2004) Oxford: WRTH Publications.

Wring, D. (1997) 'Reconciling marketing with political science', *Journal of Marketing Management* 13(7), pp. 651–63.

—(1998) 'A "spin" off the old wheel: The Machiavellian role of Morrison and Mandelson as political communicators', in Proceedings of the Machiavelli at 500 Conference, Centre for Corporate and Public Affairs, Manchester Metropolitan University, 18–19 May.

Yaverbaum, E. and Bly, R. (2001) *Public Relations for Dummies*, California: IDG Books Worldwide.

Index

226 *Index*

PR propaganda, xii, 2, 8, 10, 14, 50, 56–78, 83, 86, 88, 101, 106, 113, 115, 118, 132, 141, 151, 154, 162, 164–76, 184, 202
PR skills, 4, 162
PR Whig history of, 3
PR, media-savvy (journalism), 160
Pratkanis, A. and Aronson, E., 43, 140, 215
press agent, 3, 34, 42, 44, 48, 51–54, 132, 135, 138, 161, 167, 189, 197, 201
press agentry, PR as, 3, 44, 48, 51, 54, 138, 201
press conferences, 1, 131, 198
press releases, 6, 43, 45, 48, 134, 138, 154, 157, 162, 168, 195, 199
Price, V., 55, 215
pricing, 144, 149
PR-isation, 13, 74, 161
PR-ised, 175
private subsidy, 169
pro bono work, 170
Prof. Anne Gregory, 179, 192, 200, 201, 202
profession of the decade, PR as, xi, 7, 16, 27
promotional culture, 78, 122
promotional modes, 137
propaganda, 2, 3, 8, 10–11, 14, 23, 41–59, 61, 63–78, 93–94, 97, 101–3, 115, 117, 120, 122, 123, 125–27, 144, 151, 165–67, 170, 172, 176, 183, 185–87, 191, 193–94, 196, 199, 202, 211, 214, 216; black, 44; model, PR as, 13, 21, 50, 80, 89, 94, 155
PRWatch, 99
PRWeek, 17, 20, 22, 65, 179, 180, 186, 192, 197, 199–201
public affairs, 8, 20, 43, 57, 89, 113, 119, 127, 179, 190, 194, 197, 198, 209
public domain, 3, 6, 31, 32, 34, 65, 84, 113, 125, 132, 141, 177
public information campaigns, 59, 60, 71, 125, 171
public interest, 10, 37–38, 49, 51–52, 65, 80, 82, 88, 90, 99–100, 113, 118, 126, 155, 183, 188
public opinion, 9, 19, 21, 28, 38, 41, 43, 45, 47–49, 55, 58–59, 71–72, 89, 90, 91, 104, 113, 117, 118, 121, 129–30, 170, 184, 191, 214
Public Relations Consultants' Association, 17, 99

public relations practitioners, 6, 10–11, 16–17, 20, 24–25, 43, 59, 61, 98, 106, 109, 115, 120, 127–28, 130, 151–52, 154, 158–59, 161, 164, 168, 180–81, 213
public relations state, xi, 59, 121, 132
public sphere, 31, 44, 49–50, 90, 113, 177, 180, 182, 184
public subsidy, 12, 82–83, 87
publicity expert, PR as, 51
publics, 13, 19, 54, 74, 84, 97, 112–17, 125, 145–46, 162–63, 173–77, 193, 208
puffery, 1, 137, 206
puffs, 25
Putnam, R., 173, 215

Quinn, S., 153, 215

railways, 34, 51, 58, 151, 184, 191
Ratners, 144, 146
Raucher, A., 42, 49, 51–52, 215
Rees, L., 122, 213, 215
Reichenbach, H., 132, 215
Rein *et al*, 16, 215
representative democracy, 6, 9, 75, 79, 87, 93, 96, 128
reprobate, PR as, 176
reputation, x, xii, 1–2, 3, 6, 9, 12–13, 18–26, 36, 51, 61, 66, 71–73, 84, 91, 101, 105, 108, 117, 134–49, 152, 163, 176–77, 179, 187, 190, 197–200, 213
Research and Information Unit, 121
resistance, civic, xi, 56, 169
rhetoric, PR as, 39, 55, 209
Richard Reader, 128, 197
Richards, B., xiv, 44, 213, 215
Richards, P., 179, 215
Ries, A. and Ries, L., 23, 215
Rivals, The, 12
Roberts, J., 109, 110, 183, 206, 215
Robins *et al*, 66–67, 215
Roosevelt administration, 43
Rootes cars, 64
Rosenblum H. and Post, R., 79, 211, 215

Saffir, L., 54, 65, 215
Salt Manufacturers' Association, 75–76, 187
Salter, L., 68, 215
Salvation Army, 143
Saul, J., 215